HUMAN SECURITY REPORT 2009/2010

THE CAUSES OF PEACE AND THE SHRINKING COSTS OF WAR

PUBLISHED FOR THE

 HUMAN SECURITY REPORT PROJECT

SIMON FRASER UNIVERSITY, CANADA

NEW YORK • OXFORD

OXFORD UNIVERSITY PRESS

2011

Oxford University Press

Oxford University Press, Inc., publishes works that further Oxford University's objective of excellence in research, scholarship, and education.

Oxford New York

Auckland   Cape Town   Dar es Salaam   Hong Kong   Karachi
Kuala Lumpur   Madrid   Melbourne   Mexico City   Nairobi
New Delhi   Shanghai   Taipei   Toronto

With offices in

Argentina   Austria   Brazil   Chile   Czech Republic   France   Greece
Guatemala   Hungary   Italy   Japan   Poland   Portugal   Singapore
South Korea   Switzerland   Thailand   Turkey   Ukraine   Vietnam

Copyright © 2011 by Human Security Research Group.

Published by Oxford University Press, Inc.
198 Madison Avenue, New York, New York 10016
www.oup.com

Oxford is a registered trademark of Oxford University Press

ISSN 1557-914X

ISBN 978-0-19-986081-4

1 3 5 7 9 8 6 4 2

Printed in Canada on acid-free paper
Cover design: Susan Turner, Zuke Creative
Cover photo: Chris Kevlen / Panos Pictures. Democratic Republic of the Congo

In-House Team for the Preparation of the *Human Security Report 2009/2010*

Andrew Mack, director and editor-in-chief

Zoe Nielsen, executive director

Mai Bui, research officer

Tracey Carmichael, senior manager, e-resources

Gwen Echlin, research assistant, e-resources

Wendy Fehr, development director

Shawna Korosi, human resources manager

Sebastian Merz, research manager, data

Marko Pajalic, research officer, e-resources

Lindsey Ridgway, research assistant, e-resources

Former Members of the In-House Team: Tara Cooper, research manager, data; Josip Dasovic, research associate; Emina Dervisevic, research officer, e-resources; Kathryn Scurfield, research assistant, e-resources; Mila Shah, research assistant, data

Copy-Editing: Kirsten Craven, Craven Editorial
Proofreading: Ruth Wilson, West Coast Editorial Associates
Design and Layout: Susan Turner, Zuke Creative

ACKNOWLEDGEMENTS

This publication was made possible by the generous support given by the Department for International Development (United Kingdom); the Department of Foreign Affairs and International Trade (Canada); the Norwegian Agency for Development Cooperation; the Norwegian Royal Ministry of Foreign Affairs; the Swedish International Development Cooperation Agency; and the Swiss Federal Department of Foreign Affairs.

Special thanks to our collaborators at the Uppsala Conflict Data Program (UCDP), Sweden, and the International Peace Research Institute Oslo (PRIO), Norway, and to Michael Spagat.

We would also like to thank Luke Condra, Beth Daponte, Evelyn Depoortere, Olivier Degomme, Manuel Fröhlich, Michel Garenne, Richard Garfield, Jack Goldstone, Richard Gowan, Steve Hansch, Birger Heldt, Cullen Hendrix, Margaret Kruk, Bethany Lacina, Monty Marshall, Robert Muggah, Robin Nandy, Connie Peck, Jon Pedersen, Steven Pinker, Loretxu Pinoges, Les Roberts, Bruce Russett, Nicholas Sambanis, Paul Spiegel, Ian Smillie, Ramesh Thakur, and Teresa Whitfield for their input and valuable comments. Responsibility for the views expressed in this *Report*, however, remains solely that of the Human Security Report Project.

The new *Human Security Report* offers an encouraging message both for the United Nations and for the peoples of the developing world where most armed conflicts still take place.

While global media reporting continues to create the impression that we live in an ever-more violent world, the reality behind the headlines is quite different. The world has become much less insecure over the past 20 years.

This study provides the first comprehensive analysis of this remarkable change. It shows how international wars have declined from an average of some seven a year in the 1950s to less than one a year in the new millennium—a decline that has saved millions of lives.

And with the end of the Cold War came another radical change. Civil war numbers started to drop sharply, with the deadliest conflicts—those killing 1,000 or more people a year—declining by more than 70 percent between 1988 and 2008.

As the conflict between the US and the Soviet Union ebbed in the late 1980s, superpower support for proxy wars in the developing world dried up and many of these conflicts ground to a halt, saving countless more lives in the process.

This was not the only change. No longer paralyzed by Cold War politics, the UN—along with other international agencies, governments, and civil society organizations—led a dramatic upsurge of peacemaking initiatives aimed at ending wars via mediation rather than through force of arms.

Peacemaking in civil wars confronts many challenges, of course, and many of the new initiatives initially failed. But when the number of diplomatic interventions to end wars jumps fivefold in a decade, as it did from the 1980s to the 1990s, even a modest success rate can produce impressive results.

Peacemaking seeks to stop ongoing wars; peacekeeping aims to prevent them from starting again. Here too we have witnessed a major change. Between 1991 and 2007, the number of UN peacekeepers in the field increased by some 700 percent.

Their efforts have made a real difference. Despite the much-publicized failures, the evidence that peacekeeping missions sharply reduce the risk of conflicts from recurring is compelling.

The rise in national incomes and state capacity throughout the developing world has also helped reduce conflict numbers. I have long argued that there can be no development without security, and no security without development, and neither can be sustained without respect for human rights and the rule of law. This study presents persuasive evidence from the research community to demonstrate that this assertion is indeed the case.

Many challenges remain, but the central message of this latest *Human Security Report* is that the system of global security governance that has evolved over the past two decades really does have the potential to help new generations avoid "the scourge of war."

Kofi Annan
United Nations Secretary-General (1997–2006)
Chairman of the Kofi Annan Foundation

CONTENTS

List of Figures and Tables

PART I   The Causes of Peace

Chapter 1

Chapter 3

Chapter 4

PART II   The Shrinking Costs of War

Chapter 6

Chapter 7

Chapter 8

PART III   Trends in Human Insecurity

Chapter 10

Chapter 11

Chapter 12

Adam Dean / Panos Pictures. AFGHANISTAN.

THE CAUSES OF PEACE AND THE SHRINKING COSTS OF WAR

The *Human Security Report 2009/2010* focuses on trends in political violence around the world, the consequences of this violence, and the factors that drive it.

The *Report* describes—and explains—the major decline in the number of conflicts that have taken place since the end of the Cold War, the longer-term decline in international conflict numbers, the reduction in the deadliness of warfare since the 1950s, and the recent increase in minor armed conflicts.[1]

The *Report* is divided into three parts. Part I: The Causes of Peace examines the forces that have driven down the number of international conflicts since the 1950s, and the number of civil wars since the early 1990s.

Part II: The Shrinking Costs of War focuses on the human costs of war and examines the paradox of mortality rates that decline during wartime, as well as the challenges and controversies involved in measuring *indirect* war deaths—those caused by war-exacerbated disease and malnutrition.

Part III: Trends in Human Insecurity reviews recent trends in conflict numbers and death tolls around the world, and updates the conflict and conflict-related trend data from previous Human Security Report Project (HSRP) publications.

Part I: The Causes of Peace

In sharp contrast to the thousands of books and scholarly articles written about the causes of the Cold War, a mere handful of articles has been published about the decline in warfare that followed the end of the Cold War. As Australian historian Geoffrey Blainey once observed, "For every thousand pages published on the causes of wars there is less than one page directly on the causes of peace."[2] Blainey exaggerated—but not much.

The extent of the changes in the global security environment since the end of World War II, which were briefly outlined in the first *Human Security Report* in 2005, has been remarkable.

As we noted in that publication, the number of conflicts being waged around the world increased threefold during the Cold War years then sharply declined—a change that went largely unheralded, even at the UN (United Nations).

Why Has International War Become Increasingly Rare?

In the 1950s, there were on average just over six international conflicts being fought around the world each year—we include anticolonial conflicts in this category. In the new millennium, there has been less than one international conflict each year on average.

Moreover, there has not been a single war between the major powers for an unprecedented 60 years. This period, which historians sometimes refer to as the "Long Peace," has been described by historian Evan Luard as "a change of spectacular proportions: perhaps the single most striking discontinuity that the history of warfare has anywhere produced."[3] This did not mean that the major powers were peaceful—indeed, France, the UK, the US, and Russia/USSR top the list of countries that have been involved in the greatest number of international wars since 1946—but they fought in poor countries, not against other major powers.

International conflicts are not only fewer, they have also become far less deadly. In the 1950s, the average international conflict killed some 20,000 people a year on the battlefield. In the post-Cold War 1990s, the average annual battle-death toll was less than 6,000; in the new millennium that figure has halved.

Part I: The Causes of Peace, begins with a review of the diverse literature that seeks to explain the decline in international conflicts. It focuses on three scholarly approaches that have dominated debates on global security for decades. The ideas that underpin them also drive, and sometimes rationalize, the defense and security policies of the world's governments.

Realism: Peace through Strength—and Nuclear Weapons

So-called realist scholars believe that war results from the ineluctable struggles for power between states trapped in an "anarchic" international system that lacks any overarching authority, and thus any effective mechanisms for preventing or resolving deadly conflicts.

From this perspective, the absence of war between the major powers during the Cold War years is best explained by a stable balance of power between East and West—in particular by the deterrence provided by the mutual possession of nuclear arsenals. As Kenneth Waltz, the leading proponent of the pacifying impact of nuclear weapons, puts it, "peace has become the privilege of states having nuclear weapons, while wars are fought by those who lack them."[4]

But Waltz is wrong for two reasons. First, the four countries that have fought most international wars since the end of World War II—France, the UK, the US, and Russia/USSR—are all nuclear-armed states.

Second, possession of nuclear weapons has signally failed to prevent war on a significant number of occasions since the end of World War II. US weapons did not deter China from attacking US forces in the Korean War, nor North Vietnam from attacking South Vietnam and US forces in the 1960s and 1970s. Israeli nuclear weapons did not dissuade Egypt from attacking Israel in 1973, and the Soviet nuclear arsenal did not deter the mujahedeen from waging war against the Soviet army in Afghanistan in the 1980s—nor did it prevent a Soviet defeat.

More generally, the statistical evidence on the utility of realist "peace-through-strength" policy prescriptions is inconclusive. This is true whether we are talking about the deterrent effect of alliances and military balance, or seeking peace through military preponderance.

Liberalism: Peace through Democratization and Interdependence

Liberal scholars, who have a much less pessimistic view of human nature and agency than realists, believe that the risk of war between states has been reduced by the steady growth in the number of democracies in the international system and by growing international economic interdependence.

The best-known liberal theory is *the democratic peace*, whose central—and uncontested—finding is that fully democratic states never, or to be more precise, almost never, go to war against each other.

Democratic peace theory does not argue that democracies are generally peaceful—democracies frequently fight non-democracies—simply that democratic states generally do not fight each other.

Other liberal scholars place less stress on the conflict-reducing effect of democracy and a lot more on the security impact of the ever-growing interdependencies that are associated with today's globalized economy. Indeed, the libertarian Cato Institute argues that when measures of both democratization and economic liberalization are included in statistical analyses, "economic freedom is about 50 times more effective than democracy in diminishing violent conflict."[5]

Although the debate over the relative impact of democracy versus economic interdependence on the risk of war is both unresolved and highly technical, there is little dissent from the proposition that increasing levels of international trade and foreign direct investment are associated with a reduced risk of interstate war.

But increased interdependence is not the only economic driver of international peace. In the modern era, there are far fewer economic incentives for embarking on war than there were in the era of colonial expansion. Today it is almost always cheaper—politically as well as economically—to buy raw materials from other countries than to mount invasions to seize them. As John Mueller puts it, "free trade furnishes the economic advantages of conquest without the unpleasantness of invasion and the sticky responsibility of imperial control."[6]

Peace through Ideas: The Change in Attitudes to War

Prior to World War I, as historian Michael Howard has noted, "war was almost universally considered an acceptable, perhaps an inevitable and for many people a desirable way of settling international differences."[7] Today the traditional benefits of conquest have not only largely disappeared but resorting to war as an instrument of statecraft is legally and normatively proscribed, except in self-defense or with the authorization of the UN Security Council.

This shift in global norms is evident in the now-universal recognition of the illegitimacy of colonial conquest and the near-absence among national governments the world over of the sort of aggressive hypernationalism associated with German and Japanese Fascism prior to World War II. What the French call *bellicisme*—the glorification of warfare—is completely absent in the developed world and very rare elsewhere—though it is characteristic of some radical Islamist organizations like al-Qaeda.

International Peace is "Overdetermined"

It is difficult to determine the causes of peace between developed states with any degree of precision—not because there are too few plausible explanations, but because there are too many. Peace in Western Europe, for example, has been variously attributed to the fact that the states of the region are all democracies, that their elite and popular cultures have become war-averse, and that they have liberal capitalist economies that are bound together by high levels of economic interdependence. Most are sheltered by the US "nuclear umbrella" and the world's most powerful military alliance, and all are deeply enmeshed in other regional and international organizations.

While the diversity of possible explanations for the decline in international conflict complicates the task of analysis, the fact that the Long Peace between the major powers is supported by so many different pillars almost certainly helps account for its durability.

Explaining Civil Wars

The decline of international conflict and the end of the Cold War have led to a major shift in focus in the conflict research and policy communities. Today civil war and international terrorism, not international conflict, dominate research and policy agendas.

And it is not just the focus of research on the causes of war that has shifted but also the methodological approaches. Over the past two decades, statistical analysis of the drivers of intrastate war and peace has burgeoned and become increasingly influential—not least in policy communities.

Yet, although the new wave of research has generated some striking results, its findings are widely divergent—indeed, consensus is notable mostly by its absence. This is clearly a source of major concern, as is the fact that the current quantitative models are extremely poor at predicting the outbreak of conflict.

One of the major drivers of the quantitative revolution in conflict research has been the inherent limitation of even the most insightful qualitative case-study analysis, namely that the methodology of the latter cannot determine the universal (or near-universal) risk factors that can inform broad policies of conflict prevention.

Quantitative research has two advantages over qualitative research. At the most basic level, cross-national data on conflict numbers and battle deaths can reveal long-term global and regional trends in the incidence and deadliness of conflicts that qualitative research cannot. Such descriptive statistics are the only means of tracking changes in the global security landscape.

Statistical analysis of the drivers of intrastate war and peace has burgeoned.

Statistical models, as suggested above, take the analysis to a different level and can reveal possible causal connections between the onset of conflict and such structural factors as GDP (gross domestic product) per capita, measures of governance, "youth bulges," infant mortality rates, inequality, trade "openness," and country size/population.

The most robust finding from the quantitative conflict research is that there is a very strong association between GDP per capita and the risk of war: high incomes are associated with low risks of war. But there is much less consensus on why this should be the case.

Some of the findings that have been generated by statistical research on the causes of war have been striking and have had a major impact on the policy community. The World Bank's 2011 *World Development Report*, for example, relies heavily on quantitative research findings in its analysis of the security implications of state fragility. However, despite real progress in many areas, research in this field continues to confront major methodological and data challenges that raise serious questions about the policy usefulness of the many contested findings.

Quantitative researchers are well aware of these challenges, of course, and a number of promising initiatives are underway that seek to address them. But some of the limitations are inherent in the nature of the data and models that quantitative researchers have to work with.

Here we simply note a few of the more critical methodological problems:

- Quantitative datasets do not include direct measures of fear, hatred, grievance, humiliation, or feelings of identity and solidarity, despite the fact that case-study research indicates these variables can play a critical role in catalyzing political violence. Quantitative researchers are well aware of this limitation, of course, but there are simply no sources of usable data on attitudes and beliefs for the vast majority of country-years in the conflict datasets. The use of indirect proxy measures for psychological variables like grievance has been widely criticized.

- Quantitative models struggle in trying to deal with the issue of agency—the capacity of individuals, particularly political leaders, to make choices and act on them. Agency can obviously play a critical role in transitions from peace to war—and war to peace. Researchers using conflict models have little choice but to ignore agency—there is simply no way to collect cross-national data on 100-plus countries over 50 or more years on what decisions were made and why.

- The structural data—GDP per capita, infant mortality rates, etc.—that conflict models rely on are slow-changing and are thus rarely able to account for large short-term shifts in global or regional conflict trends. As noted previously, the most robust finding in the quantitative literature is that the risk of conflict shrinks as incomes rise. But this finding cannot explain the rapid decline in conflict numbers in the post-Cold War period.

- The standard unit of analysis in most conflict models is the country-year, and here researchers make two assumptions that are unrealistic. First, it is assumed that observations in successive country-years are independent of each other—clearly, in many cases they are not. Second, the models assume that increases or decreases in the risk of war can be explained solely in terms of socio-economic and other changes within countries. This assumption is often unrealistic because the conflict dynamics of civil war do not stop at national boundaries—the interconnections between political violence in Afghanistan and Pakistan being an obvious case in point.

- Statistics for poor countries—where most wars take place—are mostly inadequate and frequently terrible. This in part explains why the number of countries included in different conflict datasets varies so widely. The different composition of the datasets in turn explains some of the variance in findings.

The limitations of contemporary conflict models and datasets go a long way towards explaining why researchers have produced such widely divergent findings about the causal impacts of ethnicity, inequality, grievances, repression, democracy, economic growth, and dependence on primary commodities.

This lack of consensus, coupled with the fact that civil war models—to quote one recent study—"have performed notoriously poorly at prediction,"[8] suggests that only the most robust results should be used to inform policy decisions.

Quantitative models struggle to deal with the issue of agency.

Finally, there is growing interest in the quantitative research community in so-called mixed-methods approaches that combine both quantitative and qualitative methods. As Paul Collier, one of the most influential figures in the quantitative revolution, has recently argued, quantitative analysis "should be seen as complementing qualitative in-country research rather than supplanting it."[9]

The embrace of mixed methods is predicated on the belief that the two approaches are complementary and that drawing on the insights of each will provide a richer and more policy-relevant understanding of both the drivers of war and the determinants of peace in the twenty-first century.

The East Asian Peace

Between the two extremes of single-country case studies that are typical of qualitative analysis and cross-national statistical analysis at the global level lies the "middle-range" of regional security analysis.

In the years since the end of World War II, East Asia, the region made up of Northeast and Southeast Asia, has undergone two major security transformations. From the late 1940s to the late 1970s, the number of conflicts nearly doubled. Since then, they have more than halved. Battle-death trends changed even more dramatically. Between 1946 and 2008, more people were killed in East Asia's conflicts than in all other regions of the world combined—but the overwhelming majority of these deaths occurred before 1980. Since the end of the Vietnam War and China's invasion of Vietnam in 1979, battle-death tolls have plummeted.

In explaining this transformation, we focus first on the major political changes that took place in the region in the late 1970s—changes that quantitative conflict models cannot easily explain—and second, on the security implications of the long-term increase in levels of economic development across the region.

Changes in the incidence and intensity of wars in the first three decades following the end of World War II were driven primarily by politics. The growing rejection of colonialism in the developing world drove the upsurge of anticolonial conflicts in Southeast Asia that started in the 1940s, but by the late-1950s wars of liberation were essentially over. Conflict numbers continued to increase, however, in part because anticolonial conflicts had been replaced by violent struggles for control over the post-colonial state, and in part as a consequence of Cold War rivalries in the region.

The deadliest wars in this period—the Chinese Civil War (1946–1949), the anticolonial struggles in French Indochina (1946–1954), the Korean War (1950–1953), and the Vietnam War (1965–1975)—were all driven in part by the geopolitics of the Cold War, and each was characterized by a high level of foreign military intervention.

The importation of large numbers of major conventional weapons drove death tolls sharply upwards.

China, the Soviet Union, the US, and sometimes its allies, provided either combat forces or massive military and economic assistance—or both—to warring parties. In each case, the importation of large numbers of major conventional weapons into the war zones drove the death tolls sharply upwards.

The End of the Era of Intervention

With the end of both the Vietnam War in 1975 and China's invasion of Vietnam in 1979, major power interventions in the region effectively stopped. As a consequence, battle-death numbers dropped dramatically. In 1972, at the height of the Vietnam War, there were almost 300,000 battle deaths in East Asia; in 1980 the toll had fallen to some 20,000. By 2008 it was less than 1,000.

While the ending of major power intervention in East Asia provides the most compelling explanation for the dramatic decline in battle-death tolls across the region, it is much less compelling as an explanation for the 60 percent decline in the number of armed conflicts from 1978 to the mid-1990s.

While foreign military interventions drove up the costs of conflicts in the region, they were rarely the original cause of those conflicts.

There is always a multiplicity of reasons why wars start and finish, but in East Asia the evidence suggests that the security impact of increasing levels of economic development has been of critical importance.

East Asia's post-Vietnam history appears to support claims that rising incomes lead to fewer wars.

Several reasons have been advanced to explain why high incomes should be associated with reduced risks of civil war. The most plausible is that as national incomes rise, state capacity increases, which in turn provides governments with the political and economic resources to prevent rebellions and to crush militarily those that cannot be stopped via negotiation, the buying off of grievances, or political co-optation.

Rebel groups, often living in the rural periphery, are generally excluded from the benefits of rising levels of development, so the balance of resources relevant to preventing wars—and winning those that cannot be prevented—tilts progressively in favour of governments as incomes rise.

East Asia's post-Vietnam history appears to support claims that rising incomes lead to fewer wars. From the late 1970s to the mid-1990s, average income per capita almost doubled in East Asia, while conflict numbers more than halved.

But rising national income—and hence state capacity—has another less obvious effect. Greater state capacity does not simply increase the probability that governments will co-opt or defeat their adversaries; it also reduces the risk of wars starting in the first place. Development, in other words, is an important long-term form of conflict prevention. We can see this effect clearly in Southeast Asia. From 1951 to 1979, 12 new conflicts started; from 1980 to 2008, there were just three—a 75 percent reduction.

Explaining the Global Decline in Civil Wars

The final chapter of Part I examines the dramatic and unexpected decline in the number of civil conflicts that started in the early 1990s after three decades of steady increase. Our analysis again stresses the role of politics in driving system-wide change. In this case, however, the catalyst was the end of the Cold War.

After an initial increase during the years that immediately followed the end of the Cold War, civil—or intrastate—conflict numbers dropped by almost 50 percent between 1992 and 2003. Then things changed. From 2003 to 2008, the number of civil conflicts increased again, reducing the overall decline (from 1992 to 2008) to some 30 percent. High-intensity civil conflicts, however, have remained at a low level, resulting in a 77 percent net decrease since 1988.

This extraordinary change went largely unnoticed in the policy community, the media, and by many in the research community. In the 1990s this was perhaps not surprising. As United States Institute of Peace (USIP) President Richard Solomon noted in 2005, the 1990s—the decade of Somalia, Rwanda, and Bosnia—seemed to be characterized by "an unending series of ethnic or religiously fuelled conflagrations."[10]

The end of the Cold War liberated the UN from the political stasis of four decades of East-West rivalry.

Central to our analysis is the impact of the end of the Cold War itself. This momentous—though largely unpredicted—event directly caused, or indirectly catalyzed, a series of changes that have had a major impact on the global security landscape.

First, the deep ideological division that had driven conflicts both between and within states in the international system for more than 40 years simply disappeared. The security significance of this change was profound. According to one recent study, Cold War ideological struggles had "lengthened at least thirty of the civil wars fought since 1945 and in several cases prevented their resolution."[11]

Second, the flow of resources from the US and the Soviet Union and their allies to warring parties in various proxy wars in the developing world simply shrivelled up. This, Ann Hironaka has pointed out, was one of the factors leading "to the end of nearly all the large-scale communist insurgencies in the world."[12]

Third, the UN, liberated from the political stasis imposed upon it by more than four decades of East-West rivalry, spearheaded an extraordinary upsurge of international initiatives directed at preventing wars, stopping those that could not be prevented, and seeking to prevent those that had stopped from starting again.

Most notable among these initiatives were *peacemaking* (UN-speak for negotiations to end wars) and post-conflict *peacebuilding* (whose security function is to prevent wars that have ended from starting again).

The UN did not act alone, of course.

The World Bank, other international agencies, regional security organizations, donor governments, and huge numbers of international NGOs (nongovernmental organizations) were also actively involved, as were national governments and national NGOs in war-affected countries.

The Upsurge in International Activism and Other Changes

The increase in international activism directed at preventing wars, and negotiating the end to those that could not be prevented, that followed the end of the Cold War has been extraordinary.

The changes include:

- A fivefold increase in the number of international mediation efforts from the 1980s to the 1990s.
- A tenfold increase from 1991 to 2007 in the number of Friends of the Secretary-General, Contact Groups, and other political arrangements that support peacemaking and post-conflict peacebuilding initiatives.
- A threefold increase in UN and non-UN peace operations from 1988 to 2008. There are currently more than 30 such operations underway around the world.
- An increase in the number of countries contributing troops to peace operations from 51 in 1988 to some 200 in 2008.
- A thirteenfold increase in the number of multilateral-sanctions regimes between 1991 and 2008.
- A ninefold increase in the number of ongoing disarmament, demobilization, and reintegration operations from 1989 to 2008.

In addition to noting the increase in international policy initiatives, we discuss the likely security impact of three remarkable shifts in global norms that have taken place since the end of the Cold War:

- A steep increase in the number of democracies in the international system. This is relevant because inclusive democracies not only rarely go to war against each other but are also less prone to civil war.
- An increase in national and international prosecutions of human rights crimes that has been associated with a decline in human rights abuses worldwide.
- A substantial decline in governmental political discrimination against minority groups worldwide that has been associated with a decline in the number of wars of self-determination.

And since the end of the Cold War, average income per capita in the developing world has increased by nearly 50 percent, boosting the capacity of governments to resolve conflicts, buy off political opposition, and defeat insurgencies that cannot be prevented.

Does International Activism Really Make a Difference?

Determining the extent to which international activism has contributed to the decline in conflict numbers is difficult. The answer depends very much on what criteria for success are employed—a somewhat contentious issue. How, for example, do we determine the success of peacebuilding? For some critics, the bar is set very high, while for others success simply means that a country does not fall back into war within five or 10 years.

Many critics have claimed that peacemaking and peace-keeping missions are ineffective—which raises an obvious question. How can it then be argued that these initiatives constitute a plausible explanation for the 77 percent decline in the number of high-intensity civil conflicts since the end of the Cold War?

There are several possible answers:

- Prior to the end of the Cold War, the international community did extraordinarily little to help end civil wars, or to prevent those that had ended from restarting. And while it is true that UN peacemaking and peacebuilding missions of the early 1990s had relatively low success rates, in the pre-Cold War years virtually nothing was being attempted. Even a low success rate is a huge improvement on zero.

- Despite the low success rates, the absolute number of successes will increase over time as the number of peace-making, peacebuilding, and other conflict-reducing activities being implemented by the international community increases.

- It is likely that the success rate of many international initiatives has improved over time. "Lessons learned" and "best practices" exercises have increasingly informed policies in this area, increasing their effectiveness. In other words, looking at average success rates over a particular period may obscure the fact that peacemaking and peacebuilding have become progressively more effective within that period.

No one, of course, is suggesting that international activism is the sole explanation for the decline in conflict numbers. The direct impacts of the end of the Cold War, which included stopping the flow of resources to proxy wars, for example, have also had an effect, as have changes in global norms and rising national incomes.

In making the case that peacemaking and peacebuilding make a difference, we review these additional potential causes of the post-Cold War decline in conflict numbers. We conclude that while these explanations complement our main thesis, none contradicts it.

We also briefly review the policy implications of our analysis. We point out that the end of the Cold War, while important at the time, does not directly impact today's security situation and thus has no current policy relevance. On the other hand, the indirect effect of the ending of East-West hostilities—namely the liberation of the UN from the paralyzing rivalries of the Cold War—continues to have an impact. Indeed the policy relevance of this change has never been more important.

Part II: The Shrinking Costs of War

Challenging a number of widely held assumptions about global trends in wartime violence, Part II reveals that nation-wide mortality rates actually fall during most wars. This is a deeply counterintuitive finding; however, the evidence for it is compelling.

The prepublication version of Part II, released early in 2010, contained a review of trends in under-five mortality rates (U5MRs) in conflict-affected countries in sub-Saharan Africa from 1970 to 2008. It found that in 78 percent of cases, national mortality rates were lower at the end of the conflict than they were at the beginning. However, some commentators argued that focusing on Africa meant that many high-intensity and long-duration conflicts elsewhere in the world were being ignored, and that our sample of African countries contained too many low-intensity conflicts.

Nationwide mortality rates actually fall during most wars.

To address these concerns, we expanded the scope of our investigation and undertook a review of all countries that had experienced periods of war between 1970 and 2008—considering only those countries that had suffered 1,000 or more battle deaths in a given year. Somewhat surprisingly, given the higher death threshold, our original findings were strengthened. Between 1970 and 2008, the U5MR declined in some 90 percent of country-years in war. Of the 52 countries that experienced war in the period from 1970 to 2008, only eight countries (or 15 percent) experienced any increase in the U5MR during wartime.

A major World Bank study published in 2008 found that these trends are not limited to U5MRs. The data in the Bank's study indicated that the median adult mortality rate for war-affected countries around the world also declined during periods of warfare, as did infant mortality rates.

This is not to suggest, of course, that war causes mortality rates to decline. The reality is simply that today's armed conflicts rarely generate enough fatalities to reverse the long-term downward trend in peacetime mortality that has become the norm for most of the developing world.

Why Wars Have Become Less Deadly

Three interrelated developments account for the long-term decline in the deadliness of warfare.

First, today's wars generate far fewer battle deaths on average than they did in the past, and there is a clear, though not consistent, association between battle deaths and indirect deaths from war-exacerbated disease and malnutrition. So, if battle deaths decline, we would expect overall war mortality to decline as well. (Total—or *excess*—war deaths are made up of battle deaths and indirect deaths.)

The deadliest year for war deaths since World War II was 1950, mostly because of the huge death toll in the Korean War. The average conflict that year resulted in some 33,000 battle deaths; in 2008 the average toll was less than 1,000.

If we look at the average number of people killed per conflict per year by decade, the decline in the deadliness of warfare is still remarkable. The average conflict in the new millennium kills 90 percent less people each year than did the average conflict in the 1950s.

This dramatic decline is due in large part to the changing nature of warfare. Compared with the Cold War years, relatively few of today's conflicts involve interventions by major powers, or prolonged engagements between huge armies equipped with heavy conventional weapons.

These wars are also generally highly localized, which again tends to reduce their human cost. This is in part because today's armies are a lot smaller on average than those of the Cold War years, but also because rebel organizations in civil wars rarely have the capacity to project military power over long distances.

The second factor contributing to the decline in the deadliness of war is the decades-long international campaign to promote public health in developing countries that has led to a steady reduction in mortality rates worldwide.

Increased immunization coverage has been a key factor driving the overall reduction in child mortality in recent decades. And it is important to note that immunization in peacetime reduces child mortality in wartime. Children who have not been immunized are highly vulnerable to disease when conflict breaks out.

Since children under five typically have a wartime mortality rate that is double that of adults, any reduction in child mortality in conflict zones will clearly have a considerable impact on the overall excess death toll.

The third factor contributing to the decline in wartime mortality has been the remarkable increase in the level and scope of humanitarian assistance since the end of the Cold War. Aid per displaced person in war-affected countries has more than tripled over the past two decades. It has also become more cost-effective, benefitting in many cases from peacetime improvements in public health programs.

> Rebel organizations in civil wars rarely have the capacity to project military power over long distances.

A major focus of humanitarian assistance has been the four disease clusters—acute respiratory infections, diarrheal diseases, malaria, and measles—that are the major killers in wartime. Although highly contagious, all are preventable and/or treatable at very low cost.

In addition to preventing and treating disease, a significant share of humanitarian aid budgets is devoted to treating severe malnutrition, a condition that increases the vulnerability of individuals to disease and is a cause of death in its own right.

The impact of humanitarian assistance is very evident when conflict-displaced people have access to basic health services, adequate nutrition, shelter, and clean water and sanitation. Under these conditions, mortality rates decline rapidly, often falling to the pre-war rate or even lower within four to six months.

The Controversy over Death Tolls in the Democratic Republic of the Congo

While the evidence for the counterintuitive finding that mortality rates usually decline during periods of warfare is compelling, it stands in sharp contrast to the findings of the most ambitious and comprehensive survey-based research project ever undertaken to estimate excess war deaths.

Data from a series of five surveys undertaken by the International Rescue Committee (IRC) in the Democratic Republic of the Congo (DRC) over a period of some eight years indicate that the mortality rate in the east of the country jumped dramatically after the war started in 1998 and has remained elevated ever since, despite declining significantly in late 2001 and more gradually thereafter.

By 2007, according to the IRC, some 5.4 million people had died who would have lived had there been no war. More than 90 percent of these excess deaths were the result of disease and malnutrition, not war-related injuries. But a close investigation of the IRC's methodology suggests that the 5.4 million figure is far too high.

To estimate the excess death toll, the IRC's researchers used epidemiological survey methodology to determine the overall mortality rate during the periods surveyed. They took the average mortality rate for sub-Saharan Africa as their measure of the baseline mortality rate.

We argue that the IRC's choice of the baseline mortality rate for the DRC was too low—a fact also noted by a number of experts who have reviewed the IRC's findings. Far from being an average sub-Saharan African country, the DRC languishes at the bottom of most development measures for the region.

The effect of changing the IRC's baseline estimate to a more realistic figure is remarkable—the excess death toll drops dramatically.

The baseline data issue is not the only problem.

In the case of the first two surveys, which cover the period of August 1998 to March 2001, the IRC's researchers did not select the areas to be surveyed in a way that ensured they were representative of the region as a whole. This failure to follow standard survey practice means no confidence can be placed in any excess mortality estimates from the period—although no one doubts the death tolls in parts of the region were very high.

The excess death estimates for the final three surveys, the only ones to cover the entire country, were not affected by the methodological errors evident in the first two surveys. Here the major problem, as noted above, lay with the inappropriately low baseline mortality rate. The impact of changing this rate to a more realistic one for the period covered by the last three surveys is dramatic. The estimated excess death toll dropped from 2.8 million to less than 900,000. This is still a huge toll, but it is less than one-third of the IRC's original estimate for the period.

There is one final reason for questioning the IRC's extraordinarily high excess death toll estimates: the accuracy of the overall mortality rate revealed by its surveys is also suspect.

In 2007 the well-regarded Democratic and Health Surveys (DHS) organization carried out an independent nationwide population health survey in the DRC that covered much the same period as the IRC's surveys. It reported a U5MR that was approximately half that recorded by the IRC for the same period. Both estimates cannot be correct.

When Part II was released, there was no way of knowing whether the IRC's mortality estimate was too high or the DHS estimate too low. But as this *Report* was going to press, we were made aware of a new UNICEF (United Nations Children's Fund) Multiple Indicator Cluster Survey undertaken in the DRC in 2010. The preliminary results of this survey indicate a U5MR in the DRC in 2004 that is very close to that of the DHS.[13]

With major surveys by the DHS and UNICEF producing very similar estimates of the U5MR in the DRC, the likelihood that the IRC estimate is correct shrinks dramatically.

Given that child mortality rates are a reasonable proxy measure for overall mortality rates, and given that the latter are used to estimate excess deaths, it follows that the IRC's excess death total is almost certainly far too high—and this is true regardless of which baseline mortality rate is used.

There is a more general problem with using retrospective mortality surveys to estimate excess death tolls, namely that it is almost never possible to obtain reliable data on pre-war mortality trends in poor countries. But access to this information is critical if researchers hope to determine accurately the number of *excess deaths*—i.e., those that would not have occurred had there been no war.

If the mortality rate in a country was declining before a war, which is generally the case, and there is no reason to assume that it would not have continued to decline had there been no war, then the declining trend—the counterfactual—must be taken into account when estimating the excess death toll.

The IRC's choice of baseline mortality rate for the DRC is too low.

In practice, this is rarely done. Researchers usually take a single point estimate of the mortality rate immediately before the war and assume that, had there been no war, it would have remained constant.

Failing to take into account pre-war mortality trends can lead to serious errors. Excess death tolls will be underestimated if mortality rates had been declining before the war, and overestimated if they had been increasing. The resulting errors can be very large—and they increase over time.

In practice, the use of population surveys to generate estimates of nationwide excess war death tolls raises data and methodological issues so challenging that they can very rarely be overcome. But, as we point out, there are more appropriate—and less error-prone—means of estimating the impact of warfare on population health.

The 25 percent increase in conflict numbers between 2003 and 2008 is primarily due to a rise in minor conflicts.

The final chapter of Part II examines the World Health Organization-affiliated Health as a Bridge for Peace (HBP) initiative. HBP proponents believe that the role of health professionals should encompass not simply caring for the sick and injured in wartime but also enhancing conflict prevention via education, seeking to stop ongoing wars via mediation, and building state legitimacy through contributions to public health policy in post-conflict environments. The impact of HBP initiatives has at best been mixed.

Part III: Trends in Human Insecurity

Part III reviews trends in political violence around the world up until 2008 and examines a number of recent developments that suggest that the improvements in global security noted in this and earlier HSRP publications may be under threat.

From 1992 until 2003, the number of *state-based armed conflicts*—those involving a government as one of the warring parties—dropped by some 40 percent. Since 2003, however, the global incidence of armed conflicts has increased by 25 percent. Meanwhile, *non-state conflicts*—violent confrontations between communal groups, rebels, or warlords that do not involve a state as a warring party—increased by a startling 119 percent from 2007 to 2008. And a quarter of the conflicts that started or reignited between 2003 and 2008 were associated with Islamist political violence and the so-called War on Terror.

Several other developments have raised concerns about current and future security trends:

- A particular source of disquiet for security planners in the West has been the fact that in 2008 four of the five most deadly conflicts in the world—Iraq, Afghanistan, Pakistan, and Somalia—pitted Islamist insurgents against national

governments and their US and other supporters. In 2010 these four countries remained mired in conflict with few signs of progress being made towards resolving the issues that have driven the violence.

- In 2008 US officials were warning that the world economic crisis—which subsequently deepened—would push tens of millions of people below the poverty line in the developing world, heightening communal tensions, stirring social unrest, and potentially causing new conflicts.[14]

- In 2005 a major USIP report had warned that progress towards reducing conflict numbers is being threatened by the intractability of the conflicts that remain—i.e., that today's conflicts are more difficult to bring to an end than those of previous decades. If correct, this would mean that the successful negotiation of peace settlements will become far more challenging in the future than it has been in the past.

These developments are an obvious cause for concern. It is not just that the positive trend from 1992 to 2003 was reversed from 2004 to 2008 (the most recent year for which data were available at the time of writing). The real worry is that we may again be witnessing a long-term trend of steadily rising political violence around the world reminiscent of the Cold War years when conflict numbers tripled over some four decades.

A Different Take on the Evidence

A close examination of both conflict trends and the other concerns noted above reveals a less alarming picture, however. The conflict data do indeed reveal some worrying trends, not least the deadliness of some of the conflicts associated with the struggle between Islamist radicals and the US and its allies—in Iraq, Afghanistan, and Pakistan. But our analysis suggests that these do not necessarily presage a repeat of the long-term increase in conflict numbers that characterized the Cold War period. We also point to some long-term trends underway for 20 or more years that are more encouraging.

The 25 Percent Increase in Conflict Numbers between 2003 and 2008

It is important to note that the 25 percent increase in conflict numbers between 2003 and 2008, while real enough and clearly a source of concern, is primarily due to a rise in the number of minor conflicts, which, as their name suggests, do not kill many people.

Although the number of minor conflicts has increased, high-intensity conflicts, those that produce 1,000 or more battle deaths per year, have dropped since 1988. In that year, there were 23 wars being waged around the world; in 2008 there were just five—a 78 percent decrease.

Battle-death tolls from all conflicts have only seen a modest upturn over the last few years. Much of this increase was due to the conflict in Iraq.

The increase in battle deaths since 2003 needs to be seen in the context of the dramatic, though very uneven, decline in estimated war-death tolls since 1946. In 1950 (the first year of the Korean War) there were some 600,000 battle deaths worldwide; in 1972 (the deadliest year of the Vietnam War) the toll was more than 300,000; in 1982 (the height of the Iran-Iraq War) it was 270,000; in 1999 (when wars were being fought between Ethiopia/Eritrea and in East Africa's Great Lakes region) it was 130,000. In 2008 the battle-death toll was 27,000.

The accuracy of any individual estimate can certainly be challenged—estimating war death numbers is far from being an exact science. The overall trend, however, is not in doubt— and it is not really affected by the small increase in battle-death tolls over the last few years.

Is the Economic Crisis Increasing the Risk of Conflict in the Developing World?

As noted earlier, a number of analysts—and high-level officials—have argued that the global economic crisis that started in 2008, and is still reverberating around the world, may catalyze new wars. In 2008 the concern was that rising food and energy prices, reduced investment and aid flows, declining commodity prices, and sharp decreases in remittances[15] would trigger economic shocks in poor countries, and that these would in turn increase political instability and hence the probability of war. This was a reasonable concern because there is some statistical evidence that indicates that economic shocks increase the risk of war.

There is no doubt that the impact of the crisis was severe in many parts of the developing world in 2009, pushing tens of millions of people deeper into poverty. But these impacts did not lead to any increase in conflict numbers for that year.

Moreover, according to the World Bank's *Global Economic Prospects*, projected GDP per capita growth rates for 2010 in developing-country regions were surprisingly high given the interconnectedness of the international economic system and the gravity of the continuing crisis in the developed world. In East Asia and the Pacific, the predicted growth rate for 2010 was 8.7 percent; in Latin America, 4.5 percent; in the Middle East and North Africa, 4.0 percent; in South Asia, 7.5 percent; and in sub-Saharan Africa, 4.5 percent.[16]

While concerns about the security risks of the economic crisis were wholly understandable in 2008 and 2009, by 2010 it seemed clear that much of the developing world had coped with the crisis far better than had been expected.

There is, in other words, no compelling reason to believe that the security-enhancing impact of rising levels of development will decrease in the foreseeable future.

The Explosion of Non-State Conflict Numbers between 2007 and 2008

As we noted earlier, non-state conflict numbers jumped by an unprecedented 119 percent between 2007 and 2008. This is a real source of concern, but again it needs to be seen in context. The increase in 2008 was largely associated with fighting in just two countries: Kenya and Pakistan. What is more, non-state conflicts tend to be short-lived, they pose no direct threat to the security of governments, few last more than a year, and their battle-death tolls are very small—in 2008 they constituted only 11 percent of the state-based toll.

> The impact of the economic crisis was severe in 2009 but it did not lead to any increase in conflict numbers in that year.

And although the non-state battle-death toll in 2008 was higher than in the previous three years, it was still less than half of that recorded in 2002, the first year for which non-state data were available at the time of writing.

Deaths from One-Sided Violence in 2008: The Lowest on Record

One-sided violence refers to the use of lethal force, by governments or non-state armed groups, against civilians that causes 25 or more deaths in a calendar year. One-sided-violence deaths are not considered battle deaths, even when they occur in the context of armed conflicts. Defenseless civilians cannot fight back and killing them does not therefore constitute conflict.

While some advocacy groups and researchers have argued that violence directed against civilians is very common, and has been growing, the evidence suggests that both claims are unfounded. First, one-sided-violence death tolls have tended to be very small compared with those of state-based conflicts. In 2008, for example, the estimated death toll from one-sided violence was just 12 percent of that from state-based conflict.

Second, the evidence suggests that the incidence of one-sided violence is declining. In fact, in 2008 the one-sided-violence death toll was the lowest since 1989—the first year for which there are data.

There is one unexpected finding that emerges from the one-sided-violence data—namely the change in the identity of the majority of perpetrators of violence against civilians. In 1989 governments were responsible for an estimated 75 percent of one-sided-violence deaths; in 2008 their share had shrunk to less than 20 percent. By 2008, 80 percent of civilians being killed were victims of insurgent groups, not governments.

Are Wars Really Becoming More Intractable?

In 2005 a study published by USIP stressed that many of the remaining armed conflicts were intractable—meaning they were both persistent and highly resistant to efforts to bring about political settlements.

The fact that conflicts active today show an increasing average duration, and have become more likely to reignite after they have stopped, might appear to suggest that wars are becoming more intractable.

In each decade since the 1970s the percentage of conflicts that lasted 10 years or more has declined.

There is some reason for skepticism, however. Although measuring intractability is far more difficult than it might at first appear, we are able to track the percentage of conflicts that started in each decade and lasted for 10 or more years. Given that the majority of conflicts last less than three years, a 10-year conflict duration seemed to be a reasonable measure of intractability.

If conflicts were becoming more intractable over time, we would expect that in each passing decade the percentage of conflicts lasting 10 years or more would increase. But this is not what has happened. In fact, in the 1980s and 1990s the percentage of conflicts that lasted for 10 years or more declined. In the 1970s, some 30 percent of conflicts lasted for 10 or more years; in the 1990s less than 10 percent did so. This indicates that, on balance, conflicts are becoming less intractable over time.

There can be no doubt that a significant proportion of today's conflicts have lasted for decades and resisted attempts to resolve them. But this does not necessarily mean they will

continue into the future. As the USIP study notes, some of the cases on its list of 18 intractable conflicts had already ended by 2005. By 2008 some 40 percent of these conflicts were no longer active. They were not so intractable after all.

Is Islamist Violence a Growing Threat?

Between 2004 and 2008, nine out of the 34 conflicts that started or restarted around the world were associated with Islamist political violence. The most deadly of these conflicts—Iraq, Afghanistan, Pakistan, and Somalia—are also associated with foreign military intervention by the US and other countries. Large-scale foreign military intervention in armed conflicts, as we noted earlier, tends to be associated with elevated battle-death tolls.

There is obvious cause for concern here. If four out of five of the world's deadliest conflicts are associated with Islamist political violence, and the number of Islamist conflicts is growing, the prognosis for global security is not good. However, there is no compelling evidence to support claims that Islamist violence has been increasing worldwide—though it has clearly increased in Afghanistan, Pakistan, and Somalia. (In Iraq there was a major decline in death tolls in 2007, but Islamist violence has been increasing again more recently.)

Prospects for the Islamist radicals are not encouraging. Support for al-Qaeda across the Muslim world has been declining for more than five years. This has not been a result of the US-led War on Terror, which is widely perceived in the Muslim world as a war against Islam. The shift arises because Muslim communities around the world have become increasingly alienated by the Islamists' extremist ideology, their harshly repressive policies, and by the fact that—in the name of Islam—they mostly kill their coreligionists.

The strategic challenge that Islamist radicals confront in their quest for power is that they lack the conventional military forces needed to defeat the armies of the states they seek to overthrow, while their violent tactics and repressive policies have alienated popular Muslim support to such an extent that waging a successful revolutionary struggle from a mobilized popular base is not an option either.

Which Countries Have Fought Most Wars?

As noted earlier, the 60-plus years since the end of World War II constitute the longest period of peace between the major powers for hundreds of years. But while the major powers did not fight each other during this period, they were far from peaceful. Indeed, the countries that fought most of the international wars (we include armed interventions in civil wars under this heading) in the period from 1946 to 2008 were all major powers. France and the UK were first and second on the list, followed by the US, Russia/USSR, the Netherlands, Portugal, Spain, and Australia.

In fact, the majority of international conflicts that have occurred since the end of World War II have been waged by rich countries against the governments or peoples of poor countries.

If we turn to countries that have experienced the greatest number of intrastate wars, a very different picture emerges. India tops the list, followed by Russia/USSR (the only industrialized country present), Burma, Ethiopia, Indonesia, and the DRC.

If we take yet another measure and rank countries in terms of the number of conflict years they have experienced, we find that Burma comes out on top, having experienced an extraordinary 246 conflict years between 1946 and 2008. This amounts to an average of four conflicts in each calendar year since 1946. India, Ethiopia, the Philippines, and the UK make up the remainder of the top five.

Finally, when we compare which countries have been involved in the most wars of all types, France, the UK, the US, Russia/USSR, and India make up the top five.

Conclusion

Debates about the causes of war and peace are unlikely to be resolved any time soon for reasons detailed in this *Report*. As we also point out, attempts by quantitative researchers to predict future conflicts do not have a very good track record.

For these reasons and more, it is not possible to claim with any confidence that we will see fewer conflicts in the future—or indeed more. But much has been learned over the past few decades and today we can point with some confidence to long-term trends that decrease the risk of war.

Take the case of international conflicts. We have argued that the demise of colonialism and the Cold War removed two important causes of war from the international system, and that the impact of growing levels of economic interdependence, the fourfold increase in the number of democracies, and an emerging norm of war-averseness have reduced the risks of war still further.

None of these factors is less important today—on the contrary. The Cold War remains over, and no system-wide polarized conflict has replaced it or appears likely to for the foreseeable future. The number of democratic states has continued to rise, as has membership of international organizations. Global economic interdependence continues to deepen, and the war-averseness norm continues to

proscribe resorting to war, except in self-defense or with the authorization of the UN Security Council.

A similar argument applies to civil wars. The peacemaking and peacebuilding policies that we have identified as being an important part of the explanation for the decline in conflict numbers in the 1990s have been strengthened in the new millennium. And there is no sign that the normative changes we identified are likely to be reversed.

Moreover, national incomes continue to increase across all regions in the developing world. This, we have argued, means that governments have more resources to prevent wars and to prevail in those that cannot be prevented or stopped by non-violent means. Insurgents do not benefit from rising national incomes to the same degree as governments, which means that over time the balance of resources—and hence power—will favour the latter over the former.

The trend to smaller wars, which has meant fewer battle deaths per conflict, shows few signs of being reversed. And improvements in population health throughout most of the developing world in peacetime mean that individuals will be less susceptible to conflict-exacerbated disease and malnutrition in wartime. Moreover, the level of humanitarian assistance has continued to rise in the new millennium, notwithstanding the fact that the number of conflicts is down.

We have, in other words, identified trends that reduce both the risks and the costs of international and civil wars. This has interesting implications. While the future remains impossible to predict, and will surely deliver some unpleasant surprises as it has in the past, there are no obvious countervailing system-level forces that appear powerful enough to reverse the positive effects of the trends we have identified.

Of course, the fact that something is not obviously fore-seeable does not mean it cannot happen. Recent events, from the banking crises in the developed world to the popular uprisings against repressive regimes in the Middle East and North Africa, remind us how frequently major changes come as a complete surprise—and to the expert community as well as laypersons. "Prediction," as the Danish physicist Niels Bohr once noted, "is very difficult, especially about the future."[17]

The policy initiatives we have described are part of an emerging, though still inchoate, architecture of global security governance, one focused primarily on the prevention of civil wars. This mode of governance remains inefficient and prone to serious failures. But notwithstanding these and other challenges, it has, since its emergence some 20 years ago, been quite effective in reducing the level of political violence around the world. This is no mean achievement.

ENDNOTES

1. References for all statistics in the Overview are found in the main body of the *Report* unless otherwise noted.

2. Geoffrey Blainey, *The Causes of War*, 3rd ed. (New York: The Free Press, 1973), 3.

3. Evan Luard, *War in International Society: A Study in International Sociology* (New Haven: Yale University Press, 1987).

4. Kenneth Waltz, "Peace, Stability, and Nuclear Weapons," Institute on Global Conflict and Cooperation, Policy Paper No. 15, University of California, Berkeley, August 1995, 11.

5. James Gwartney, Robert Lawson, with Erik Gartzke, *Economic Freedom of the World: 2005 Annual Report* (Washington, DC: The Cato Institute, 2005), 4.

6. John Mueller, *Capitalism, Democracy, and Ralph's Pretty Good Grocery* (Princeton: Princeton University Press, 1999), 245.

7. Michael Howard, *The Causes of War and Other Essays*, 2nd ed. (Cambridge: Harvard University Press, 1983), 9.

8. Cullen S. Hendrix and Sarah M. Glaser, "Trends and Triggers: Climate Change and Civil Conflict in Sub-Saharan Africa" (paper presented at the international workshop on Human Security and Climate Change, Asker, Norway, June 2005), 4, http://www.gechs.org/downloads/holmen/Hendrix_Glaser.pdf (accessed 2 September 2010).

9. Paul Collier, Anke Hoeffler, and Dominic Rohner, "Beyond Greed and Grievance: Feasibility and Civil War," *Oxford Economic Papers* 61, no. 1 (August 2009): 3.

10. Richard H. Solomon, "Foreword," in *Leashing the Dogs of War*, ed. Chester A. Crocker, Fen Osler Hampson, and Pamela Aall (Washington, DC: USIP Press, 2007), iv.

11. Ann Hironaka, *Neverending Wars: The International Community, Weak States, and the Perpetuation of Civil War* (Cambridge: Harvard University Press, 2005), 106.

12. Ibid., 124.

13. UNICEF, "Democratic Republic of the Congo: Multiple Indicator Cluster Survey, MICS–2010," preliminary findings, Figure 1, September 2010, 10, http://www.childinfo.org/files/MICS-RDC_2010_Preliminary_Results_final_EN_imprime.pdf (accessed 11 April 2011).

14. Paul Richter, "Economic Crisis Brings Security Risks," *Los Angeles Times*, 27 October 2008, http://articles.latimes.com/2008/oct/27/world/fg-crisis27 (accessed 15 November 2010).

15. These challenges are spelled out in detail in the World Bank's "Swimming against the Tide: How Developing Countries Are Coping with the Global Crisis" (background paper prepared for the G20 Finance Ministers and Central Bank Governors Meeting, Horsham, UK, March 2009), http://siteresources.worldbank.org/NEWS/Resources/swimmingagainstthetide-march2009.pdf (accessed 15 November 2010).

16. The World Bank, *Global Economic Prospects*, June 2010, http://web.worldbank.org/WBSITE/EXTERNAL/EXTDEC/EXTDECPROSPECTS/EXTGBLPROSPECTSAPRIL/0,,menuPK:659178~pagePK:64218926~piPK:64218953~theSitePK:659149,00.html (accessed 15 November 2010).

17. The original source of this quotation, which is often attributed to US baseball star Yogi Berra, is unknown. See *The Economist*, "The Perils of Prediction," 2 June 2007, http://www.economist.com/blogs/theinbox/2007/07/the_perils_of_prediction_june (accessed 15 November 2010).

Fethi Belaid / AFP / Getty Images. TUNISIA.

THE CAUSES OF PEACE

Part I describes and analyzes the remarkable, but little understood, decline in international conflicts since the 1950s and intrastate conflicts in the post-Cold War era. It also examines the very uneven decline in battle deaths over the same period.

THE CAUSES OF PEACE

Introduction

Scholars have developed a number of theories to explain the decline in the number and deadliness of international conflicts. All have their strengths and weaknesses; none is compelling on its own.

Both quantitative and qualitative researchers examining the causes of war and peace confront major methodological and data challenges. Some two decades of research have, however, uncovered a number of robust findings.

East Asia has gone from being one of the most war-wracked regions of the world to one of the most peaceful. The remarkable reduction in political violence in the region is due in part to the end of major power military interventions, and in part to rising levels of economic development—and hence state capacity.

The end of the Cold War and the huge increase in international initiatives directed towards ending ongoing wars, and preventing those that have stopped from starting again, provide the most compelling explanation for the remarkable decline in the number of intrastate conflicts over the past two decades.

INTRODUCTION

Since the Cold War ended some 20 years ago, there has been a major decline in the number of armed conflicts being waged around the world, with high-intensity conflicts dropping by almost 80 percent. Despite the obvious importance of this change, it has been largely ignored by the research community.

The Causes of Peace, Part I of this *Report*, offers a comprehensive explanation of the drivers of war and peace in the post-World War II world.

Chapter 1 examines the decline in international conflicts—a category that includes anticolonial conflicts as well as wars fought between states. International conflicts thus defined have been declining since the late 1960s. From 1946 to 1967, there were on average between six and seven international conflicts being fought around the world each year; in the new millennium there was less than one conflict per year on average.

Some researchers see the absence of war between the major powers during the Cold War as resulting from a stable East-West "balance of power"—one underpinned by the deterrent effect of the mutual possession of nuclear weapons. But while nuclear weapons may have helped deter wars between the major powers, they did not deter less powerful actors from attacking the states that possessed them. And far from being peaceful, four of the five nuclear weapons states—France,

the United Kingdom, the US, and Russia/USSR—have been involved in more international wars than any other country.

Among liberal peace theorists, proponents of the *democratic peace thesis* point to the fact that democracies very rarely fight each other. Insofar as this theory is correct, then given that the number of democracies around the world has risen dramatically over the past 40 years, there will have been fewer and fewer countries in the international system likely to fight each other.

Advocates of the *capitalist peace thesis*, on the other hand, maintain that increased economic interdependence between states—most importantly increased international trade and cross-investment—creates powerful economic interests in avoiding war, while conquest becomes less and less profitable.

Finally, *constructivists* argue that a major shift in popular and elite attitudes to war helps explain the decline in international conflicts. Since the end of World War II, war has been normatively proscribed except in self-defense or with the authorization of the UN (United Nations) Security Council. Like all norms, this one is sometimes breached—as was the case with the US-led invasion of Iraq in 2003—but this does not mean that it is ineffective.

With the Cold War over and international wars becoming increasingly rare, conflict researchers have shifted focus to explaining the causes of civil wars that make up the overwhelming majority of today's conflicts. The resulting research has yielded a number of important findings that have resonated in the policy community.

Chapter 2 examines some of these findings and reviews the pros and cons of qualitative and quantitative research on the causes of intrastate conflicts. While quantitative conflict research has become increasingly influential in the policy community, it is plagued with divergent findings and its models have a poor track record at prediction. Chapter 2 examines the methodological and data challenges that this emerging field continues to confront, and discusses the efforts taken to address them.

But despite the widespread lack of consensus over the causes of civil war, very few quantitative researchers would disagree that there is a robust association between high levels of national income and a lower risk of war. Other things being equal, high national incomes translate into greater state capacity and more resources for governments to buy off grievances and defeat insurgents in those wars that cannot be prevented.

The conflict trends in East Asia over the past 30 years, which are the focus of Chapter 3, provide an instructive example of the association between rising levels of economic development and the incidence of armed conflict. As national incomes in the region have steadily risen since the late 1970s, state capacity and performance legitimacy have also increased—and conflict numbers have declined by some 60 percent. Indeed, insurgents—who have been largely excluded from the benefits of economic growth in the region—have not achieved a single military victory since the 1970s.

However, the state capacity thesis does not explain the dramatic decline in the deadliness of warfare in East Asia after the mid-1970s. Here the answer is found with the effective ending of Cold War-driven major power interventions in the region. The bloodiest wars in East Asia, and indeed the world, from 1946 to 1979 were the Chinese Civil War, the Korean War, the French war in Indochina, and the US war in Vietnam.

Each of these wars was marked by massive foreign intervention—either direct with troops, or indirect via the provision of finance and military hardware. The combination of huge armies and the external supply of heavy conventional weapons and sometimes huge numbers of troops assured very high death tolls. But with the end of the Vietnam War in 1975 and China's short-lived border war with Vietnam in 1979, major-power military interventions essentially stopped.

Chapter 4, the final chapter in Part I, includes an analysis of the extraordinary transformation of the global security landscape that followed the end of the Cold War.

The end of East-West hostilities not only removed a major source of conflict from the international system and helped end the various superpower proxy wars, it also liberated the UN to lead a raft of initiatives designed to stop ongoing wars and prevent those that had stopped from starting again.

The UN did not act alone of course. Other international agencies, donor governments, and huge numbers of NGOs (nongovernmental organizations) were also active players in what was in essence an embryonic mode of global security governance focused primarily on stopping ongoing civil wars (*peacemaking*) and on preventing them from starting again (*post-conflict peacebuilding*).

Other drivers of peace, including the impact of three major shifts in security-related global norms and rising incomes and state capacity, also played a role, though we believe a relatively minor one. We conclude by arguing that these latter factors complement rather than contradict the international activism thesis.

The still-evolving post-Cold War system of global security governance associated with the above changes is messy, inefficient, and prone to failure. But it has also been the primary driver of the remarkable decline in political violence around the world over the past two decades.

CHAPTER 1

Why International Wars Have Become Increasingly Rare

The changes in the international security landscape over the past 60 years have been remarkable. In the 1950s there were on average between six and seven international conflicts being fought around the world each year; in the new millennium the average has been less than one. The decline in international conflicts precedes, and has been greater than, the decline in civil wars. The latter did not start to decline worldwide until after the end of the Cold War. International conflict numbers—which here include wars of colonial liberation—have been dropping since the late 1960s.

International conflicts are not only fewer, they have also become less and less deadly. In the 1950s, a decade whose battle-death toll was driven by the hugely destructive Korean War, the average international conflict killed more than 21,000 people a year. In the 1990s the average annual battle-death toll was approximately 5,000. In the new millennium it was less than 3,000.

Researchers rely on two broad, but contrasting, approaches in seeking to explain the causes of international war and peace. In this chapter we examine the evidence for each and ask if it provides a compelling explanation for the decline in the frequency and deadliness of international conflict since the end of World War II. In the scholarly community the two approaches are usually labelled *realism* and *liberalism*. The conceptions of global politics and human nature that inform them are sharply divergent—although there is some overlap in practice.

Realism and liberalism are not simply academic theories. The ideas that underpin them also drive—or sometimes rationalize—the international security policies of governments. *Realists* tend to be pessimistic about human nature, seeing individuals and governments as motivated primarily by self-interest and inescapable competition. They believe that the causes of war have their origins in power struggles between states in an international system that lacks effective mechanisms to prevent deadly conflicts. This leads them to advocate policies of *peace through strength* and alliance-building as the surest means of guaranteeing national security. This does not mean, however, that realism should be equated with war-mongering—many of the most trenchant critics of the US decision to invade Iraq were realists who argued that no American interests would be served by the invasion.

Liberals are less pessimistic about human nature, and the prospects for peace between states, and believe that the surest path to avoiding deadly international conflict lies with increasing economic interdependence between states, their growing enmeshment in international institutions, and the spread of democracy.

Liberals do not eschew the use of force—and indeed have been the major supporters of using military force to prevent gross violations of human rights. But when it comes to reducing the risks of war, they have a clear preference for nonmilitary means—from quiet diplomacy to economic sanctions.

In addition to reviewing the core claims of liberalism and realism, we also include discussion of a third approach, whose proponents are sometimes described as *constructivists*. Here the focus is on neither military power, economic interdependence, international institutions, nor governance per se, but rather on the role of ideas in changing popular and elite beliefs about the legitimacy of war as an instrument of statecraft.

Changing Patterns of International Conflict

Before discussing realist and liberal theories in detail, we will look briefly at the trends in international conflict in the post-World War II era. *International conflicts* are conventionally defined as violent contests between the military forces of two or more states. In the case of the Uppsala Conflict Data Program's (UCDP) datasets, a conflict is deemed to have occurred if the fighting results in at least 25 battle deaths in a given year.

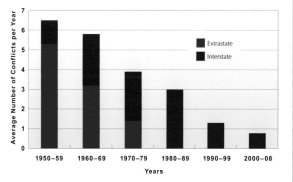

Figure 1.1 Average Number of International Conflicts per Year, 1950–2008

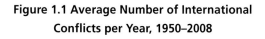

Data Source: UCDP/PRIO.[1]

There has been a steady decline in the number of international conflicts—defined here to include interstate and extrastate conflicts—around the world. Extrastate, or anticolonial conflicts, ended in the 1970s.

The issue of whether to include wars of colonial liberation as "international" conflicts is contested. Some scholars count them as civil wars *within* a colonial power. Others, including UCDP, believe they are *sui generis* and should be treated as separate from both interstate and intrastate conflicts. UCDP uses the term "extrastate" to describe anticolonial conflicts.

For the purpose of this chapter, the arguments for including wars of liberation from colonial rule under the rubric of "international" conflicts are compelling. While national

liberation struggles are clearly not inter*state* conflicts, they are conflicts between very different nations—i.e., they are, literally, international. And like international wars more conventionally defined, they involve the projection of power by one of the warring parties across national boundaries. Moreover, the consequence of liberation struggles after 1946 was almost invariably the creation of a new state led by the victorious nationalists.

Part of the purpose of this chapter is to examine the utility of different approaches to preventing and ending wars. Anticolonial struggles are particularly interesting from this perspective. In almost all of these conflicts, the party that was weaker in conventional military terms prevailed—an outcome that is very much at odds with the assumption of realist scholars that material power is a critical factor both in deterring wars and prevailing when the opponent cannot be deterred. Both the initiation and consequent outcome of anticolonial conflicts are inexplicable without reference to global norms as drivers of change—an explanation that is again at odds with realist assumptions.

Figure 1.1 shows the changing trends in international conflict since the end of World War II. Two things are apparent. First, until the end of the 1960s, most international conflicts were anticolonial struggles. Second, there has been a decline in the average number of international conflicts of all types over the past six decades. International conflicts, although relatively rare, remain important because for most of the post-World War II period they have been far more destructive and deadly than civil wars.

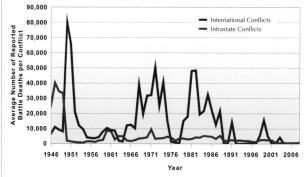

Figure 1.2 Reported Battle Deaths per State-Based Armed Conflict: International Conflicts versus Intrastate Conflicts, 1946–2008

Data Sources: PRIO; UCDP/HSRP Dataset.[2]

With very few exceptions, international conflicts have been far more deadly than intrastate conflicts.

Figure 1.2 shows the average number of battle deaths per year from international and intrastate conflict. The data illustrate two things very clearly. First, they show just how much more deadly the average international conflict has been compared with the average conflict waged within states. And second, they show that the deadliness of international conflicts has declined sharply, though very unevenly, over time.

"Peace through Strength"—the Realist Prescription

All realists are pessimists, but they are pessimistic for different reasons. For *classical* realists like Hans Morgenthau, the "will to power" is innate in human nature and it is this drive that determines the national security policies of states.[3] It follows that each state will seek to aggrandize power at the expense of other states. The resulting power struggles will sometimes culminate in war.

The deadliness of international conflicts has declined sharply over time.

Neo-realists like Kenneth Waltz and John Mearsheimer focus not on human nature, nor the political make-up of individual states, but on the anarchic nature of the international system.[4] By anarchy neo-realists do not mean chaos but rather the absence of any form of global government. Without effective international governance, the argument goes, there are no institutions that can authoritatively resolve disputes and provide security to individual states the way that national governments can provide security for individual citizens. Neo-realists are profoundly skeptical that the UN (United Nations) might ever play such a role.

In realist theory, fear and suspicion are omnipresent features of international anarchy because states, particularly the major powers, have the capacity to attack each other, because there are unavoidable uncertainties about their future intentions, and because there is no superordinate authority to impose or maintain the peace. In such a system it follows that states have no choice but to resort to "self-help"—i.e., they must provide for their own security. Hence, the strategic maxim, "If you want peace, prepare for war."

But when it comes to the most effective strategies for achieving peace, realist scholars disagree quite profoundly. Some realists, like Waltz and Mearsheimer, argue that a "balance of power" between adversaries is the best guarantee of

peace. Others, notably A. F. K. Organski and Jacek Kugler,[5] hold that preponderance of power is the best way to avoid war.

Peace and the "Balance of Power"

The claim that a balance of military power has the effect of reducing the risk of war between states is not implausible. The argument goes something like this: where there is rough parity in the military forces between two states, neither can be sure of victory, war will likely be protracted, and winning is likely to be highly costly. It follows that the payoff of avoiding war will be greater than the payoff of fighting. And since states are assumed to be rational actors, they will be dissuaded from going to war by the anticipated costs and peace will be preserved.[6] Some proponents of balancing take the argument further, pointing to the military rule of thumb that attacking forces need to be three times more powerful than defending forces to be assured of victory. Insofar as this is true, and insofar as there is rough parity in the balance of forces, then neither side has the military advantage needed to wage an offensive war successfully. Both understand this and each is thus deterred from attacking the other.

Security Dilemmas and Arms-Racing

At the heart of balance of power theory lurks the stability-eroding threat of the *security dilemma*.[7] Security dilemmas arise because, under conditions of anarchy, states that harbour no aggressive intentions towards one another may nevertheless find themselves embroiled in wars they never intended.

The logic of the security dilemma is simple enough. Consider a hypothetical situation in which a state, convinced of the virtues of balancing the military power of potential adversaries in a world of strategic uncertainty, embarks on a prudential defense buildup. Its purpose is wholly defensive, but its arms buildup may nevertheless be perceived by other states as indicating aggressive intent. If other states—equally prudential and equally defensive—respond by building up their military capabilities, their actions may be misperceived by the first state as an indication of hostile intent, prompting it to build up its forces still further.

The risk here is that escalating mutual suspicion will generate a conflict spiral and arms race that culminates in a war that neither side originally intended. The outbreak of World War I is often cited as a case in point.

The war-provoking risks of arms-racing have been a major source of concern for students of the dynamics of security dilemmas. But the extent of the risk is far from clear from the statistical evidence. A much-cited 1979 study by Michael

Wallace found that in 28 cases where serious disputes between great powers were preceded by an arms race, war occurred 23 times—i.e., 82 percent of the time. But where such disputes were not preceded by an arms race, they escalated into war in only three out of 71 times (4.2 percent).[8]

Wallace's methodology was subject to sharp criticism, however, and the findings of some subsequent research suggested that less than 30 percent of all arms races culminated in war. Some types of arms competition were associated with a considerably greater probability of subsequent conflict. Those that were associated with a high defense burden—i.e., high levels of defense expenditure—and a territorial dispute, for example, culminated in war 59 percent of the time.[9]

Even if 100 percent of arms races culminated in war, it still could not be assumed that the former necessarily caused the latter. In reality both the arms race and the war are likely being driven by the dispute itself—i.e., each may be the effect of the same cause.

Much of the research on the strategic outcomes of power-balancing has involved statistical analyses of the risk of war between pairs of states, but states can also balance power by creating, or joining, military coalitions with other states. Such alliances, argue Morgenthau and Waltz, can deter aggression.[10] Critics, however, claim that "alliance commitments can serve to provoke and to expand war,"[11] and note that entangling alliance commitments can drag coalition members into conflicts they never sought and could have avoided had they not joined the alliance in the first place.

The statistical evidence on the security benefits of joining or forming alliances, like that on arms-racing, is inconclusive. Some studies show that nations in alliance relationships are more war-prone than nations that are not alliance members, while others show they are less war-prone.[12]

But here too, we need to be careful not to jump to conclusions about causal relationships. Even where alliance formation has been followed by war, which has often been the case in the twentieth century, this does not necessarily mean that the creation of the alliance caused the war. It is perfectly possible, indeed quite likely, that the creation of the alliance was an effect of the anticipation of war, not the cause of its subsequent outbreak.

Brett Ashley Leeds argues that different types of alliances are associated with very different risks of war, but that these relationships may be hidden by the very statistical models used to detect them.[13]

While it is clear that we should be skeptical about claims that "peace through balancing" strategies are reliable means of preventing war, we should not assume that rejecting balance-of-power strategies in order to avoid the risks associated with security dilemmas will necessarily avoid war. Security dilemma dynamics are only one possible cause of war—some states actively pursue aggression, and where this is the case, joining alliances and other "peace through strength" strategies make perfect sense. Scholars who worry about the dangers of security dilemmas often urge policies of reassuring adversaries. But attempting to "reassure" states bent on aggression amounts to little more than appeasement—a strategy that may be, quite literally, self-defeating.

Aggressor states can only be deterred—or defeated if deterrence fails—but this may be a decreasingly important challenge since the evidence indicates that cross-border aggression has become increasingly rare.

Peace through Military Preponderance

Some of the strongest critics of balance-of-power approaches to preventing war are other realists who believe that military preponderance, or hegemony, is the most stable form of power distribution in the international system (at least in the medium term) and thus more conducive to peace.[14] Here the argument is that militarily dominant powers have no need to fight, while other states are deterred from attacking them by the high probability that they will lose. A benign hegemon may also use its suasion over the states in its sphere of influence to help create stability-enhancing "rules of the game" that prevent disputes from escalating into war.

The statistical evidence on the security benefits of joining or forming alliances, like that on arms-racing, is inconclusive.

The statistical evidence tends to support the "peace through preponderance" thesis. In a study published in 1988, William Moul examined the escalation of serious disputes among the great powers between 1815 and 1939. His statistical analysis suggested that where power was balanced—i.e., where there was rough parity between the great powers—there was a much greater probability that disputes would escalate into war than when the disputes were between unequals.[15]

But this finding was not just applicable to great-power relationships. In a much-cited 1993 analysis, Stuart Bremer examined factors associated with militarized disputes between pairs of states from 1816 to 1965. Controlling for a range of intervening factors, he found that a marked disparity of power between two states reduced the probability of war while parity increased it.[16]

In an article published in 2008, Håvard Hegre confirmed the earlier findings that the greater the inequality of power between any two states, the lower the risk of war.[17] But the policy prescriptions that flow from this finding are far from clear since Hegre also found that attempts to achieve preponderance led "unambiguously" to a higher risk of conflict onsets. In other words, while preponderance itself may reduce the risk of war, the process of trying to attain it increases the risk.[18]

Preponderance Theories Challenged

As with other realist claims, there are reasons for skepticism about the peace through preponderance thesis. First, if it were true, we might expect that the most powerful states would experience the least warfare. However, since the end of World War II, the opposite has in fact been the case. Between 1946 and 2008, the four countries that had been involved in the greatest number of international conflicts were France, the UK, the US, and Russia/USSR.[19] Yet, these were four of the most powerful conventional military powers in the world—and they all had nuclear weapons.

The fact that major powers tend to be more involved in international conflicts than minor powers is not surprising. Fighting international wars requires the capacity to project substantial military power across national frontiers and often over very long distances. Few countries have this capacity; major powers have it by definition.

But there is a more serious challenge to the preponderance thesis. From the end of World War II until the early 1970s, nationalist struggles against colonial powers were the most frequent form of international conflict. The failure of the far more powerful colonial powers to prevail in these conflicts poses a serious challenge to the core assumptions of preponderance theories—and marked a remarkable historical change.

During most of the history of colonial expansion and rule there had been little effective resistance from the inhabitants of the territories that were being colonized. Indeed, as one analyst of the wars of colonial conquest noted, "by and large, it would seem true that what made the machinery of European troops so successful was that native troops saw fit to die, with glory, with honor, en masse, and in vain."[20]

The ease of colonial conquest, the subsequent crushing military defeats imposed on the Axis powers by the superior military industrial might of the Allies in World War II, and the previous failure of the UN's predecessor, the League of Nations, to stop Fascist aggression all served to reinforce the idea that preponderance—superiority in military capability—was the key both to peace through deterrence and victory in war.

But in the post-World War II world, new strategic realities raised serious questions about assumptions regarding the effectiveness of conventional military superiority. In particular, the outcomes of the wars of colonial liberation, the US defeat in Vietnam, and the Soviet defeat in Afghanistan demonstrated that in some types of conflict, military preponderance could neither deter nationalist forces nor be used to defeat them. The outcomes of these conflicts posed a major challenge for preponderance theories.

> While preponderance itself may reduce the risk of war, the process of trying to attain it increases the risk.

Not only did the vastly superior military capabilities of the colonial powers fail to deter the nationalist rebels from going to war but in every case it was the nationalist forces that prevailed. The colonial powers withdrew and the colonies gained independence. Military preponderance was strategically irrelevant.

Writing about US strategy in Vietnam six years before the end of the war, Henry Kissinger noted:

> We fought a military war; our opponents fought a political one. We sought physical attrition; our opponents aimed for our psychological exhaustion. In the process, we lost sight of one of the cardinal maxims of guerrilla warfare: the guerrilla wins if he does not lose. The conventional army loses if it does not win.[21]

For the nationalist forces, military engagements were never intended to defeat the external power militarily—that was impossible. The strategy was rather to seek the progressive attrition of the metropole's political capability to wage war— "will" in the language of classical strategy.[22] In such conflicts, if the human, economic, and reputational costs to the external power increase with little prospect of victory, support for the war in the metropole will steadily erode and the pressure to withdraw will inexorably increase.

But asymmetric political/military strategies were not the only reason that relatively weak nationalist forces prevailed over militarily preponderant colonial powers in the post-World

War II era. In the aftermath of World War II, there had been a major shift in global norms with respect to the legitimacy of colonial rule—a shift that made crushing nationalist rebellions politically more difficult for the colonial powers.

In 1942 Winston Churchill had defiantly declared that "I have not become the King's First Minister in order to preside over the liquidation of the British Empire."[23] Less than 20 years later, another British prime minister, Harold MacMillan, sounded a very different note: "The wind of change is blowing through this [African] continent and, whether we like it or not, this growth of national consciousness is a political fact. We must all accept it as a fact, and our national policies must take account of it."[24]

The "wind of change" made crushing anticolonial uprisings fought in the name of self-determination politically difficult for the colonial powers who were after all signatories to the UN Charter that had strongly proclaimed the right to self-determination.

Understanding this shift in global norms helps explain the failure of the colonial powers to prevail in the wars of colonial liberation.

The anticolonial nationalists had history on their side, plus international political, and sometimes material, support from the US, from European countries that were not colonial powers, and, of course, from the Soviet Union. In many cases power was transferred to nationalist movements without any violence—fighting was often more about the timing of independence than its principle.

Traditional realist "peace through strength" theories, with their focus on the importance of material capability in deterring war, and winning if deterrence fails, and their deep skepticism about the importance of ideas as drivers of change in the international system, have never been able to provide compelling explanations for the strategic successes of militarily weak insurgents in national liberation wars.

The Nuclear Peace

Finally, we turn to what for many is the most compelling realist argument of all—namely that peace has reigned between the major powers for more than 60 years because of the existence of nuclear weapons.

Waltz noted in 1995 that "never in modern history, conventionally dated from 1648, have the great and major powers of the world enjoyed such a long period of peace."[25] Many scholars and practitioners believe that this remarkable war-free period is attributable in large part to the nuclear "balance of terror."

The logic of the "nuclear peace" is simple. Where nuclear adversaries both possess so-called mutual assured destruction capabilities, each can respond with a devastating nuclear counterstrike if the other attacks it with nuclear weapons. In such a world, war between nuclear powers becomes completely irrational. Peace is assured because no conceivable political or strategic gains can make the mutual slaughter and destruction of nuclear war worth contemplating. As former US President Ronald Reagan put it, "A nuclear war cannot be won and must never be fought."[26]

Since resort to nuclear weapons was thought most likely to occur in a conventional war that one side was losing, nuclear weapons states also have a strong incentive to avoid conventional wars.

The "nuclear peace" extends to the non-nuclear allies of the nuclear powers who benefit from so-called extended deterrence. Thus, Germany, Japan, South Korea, and Australia do not need their own nuclear deterrent because their security from external attack has been guaranteed by the "nuclear umbrella" provided by their US ally.

For supporters of nuclear deterrence, it is precisely the unparalleled destructiveness of atomic arsenals that has made war "unthinkable" and has rendered aggression between the major powers obsolete. Even proponents of nuclear disarmament concede that nuclear deterrence may have been effective. As the 2009 *Report of the International Commission on Nuclear Non-Proliferation and Disarmament* noted:

> It is hard to contest the almost universally held view that the absence of great power conflict since 1945 must be at least in part attributed to the fear of nuclear war. On the face of it, nuclear weapons on the other side will always provide a formidable argument for caution, and it does seem that they generated a degree of mutual respect and careful handling between the U.S. and USSR during the Cold War.[27]

Waltz, the leading proponent of the security-enhancing role of nuclear weapons—and of the benefits of nuclear proliferation—makes a stronger case:

> Nuclear weapons helped to maintain stability during the Cold War and to preserve peace throughout the instability that came in its wake. Except for interventions by major powers in conflicts that for them are minor, peace has become the privilege of states having nuclear weapons, while wars are fought by those who lack them.[28]

The Dubious Utility of Nuclear Weapons

Waltz's suggestion that the nuclear weapons states enjoy peace because they are nuclear armed is simply untrue. As mentioned previously, the four countries that have fought the most international conflicts since the end of World War II—France, the UK, the US, and Russia/USSR—are all nuclear-armed states.

And some of the "minor interventions" Waltz refers to are not so minor. They include the major international conflicts fought by the major powers since the end of World War II—including the Korean and Vietnam wars.

Claims that nuclear weapons provide a reliable and consistent deterrent against conventional war, while plausible in theory, are far from being universally true. From 1945 until the first Soviet nuclear test in 1949, America's nuclear monopoly proved powerless to prevent the consolidation of Soviet control over Eastern Europe—the greatest expansion of the Soviet empire during the entire Cold War period.

The case for the "nuclear peace" is far from being compelling.

US nuclear weapons did not deter China from attacking US forces during the Korean War, nor did they prevent the North Vietnamese from engaging militarily with the US during the Vietnam War. Israeli nuclear weapons did not deter Egypt from attacking Israel in 1973, Britain's independent nuclear deterrent failed to deter Argentina from invading the Falkland Islands in 1982, and Soviet nuclear weapons did not dissuade the mujahedeen from waging war against the occupying Soviet army in Afghanistan—nor did they prevent a Soviet defeat.

Part of the reason for the non-use of nuclear weapons in these conflicts is that in no case did the nuclear weapons state in question perceive the strategic issue at stake to be sufficiently important to warrant the huge carnage, the international opprobrium, and the likely political backlash that the use of nuclear weapons would have caused.

Abhorrence of, and political resistance to, the actual use of nuclear weapons derives in part from what Nina Tannenwald has called the "nuclear taboo"—the widespread popular and elite revulsion against using weapons that would cause the annihilation of possibly tens of millions of innocent civilians.[29]

It is true that neither the US nor the Soviet Union, nor any of their Cold War allies, has suffered a major conventional attack on its homeland and it is quite possible that nuclear deterrence was one of the factors that prevented such attacks. But the deterrent effect of nuclear weapons is by no means the only plausible explanation for the absence of major power war in this period. As John Mueller has argued: "world war in the post-1945 era has been prevented not so much by visions of nuclear horror as by the generally-accepted belief that conflict can easily escalate to a level, nuclear or not, that the essentially satisfied major powers would find intolerably costly."[30]

The point here is that if the claimed efficacy of nuclear deterrence derives from the fact that the horrific costs of nuclear war outweigh any conceivable benefits, then much the same argument can be made for the deterrent effect of major conventional warfare in the aftermath of World War II. According to Mueller's argument, the costs of World War II, where the death toll likely exceeded 50 million, were horrifying enough on their own to make the Cold War adversaries determined to avoid future world wars.

Moreover, the claim that it was nuclear deterrence that had kept the peace during the Cold War is both speculative and unprovable. While both sides in the Cold War—prudentially—had contingency plans for war, there is no compelling evidence that either side wanted war and was deterred from waging it solely by the existence of nuclear weapons. The claimed "success" of nuclear deterrence, in other words, is necessarily speculative; the deterrence failures—some noted above—are not.

In the post-Cold War era the strategic relevance of nuclear weapons in the security planning of the major powers is much reduced. Civil wars and terrorism are the major focus of security for these states in the new millennium, and nuclear weapons have no conceivable strategic role in either case.

Today nuclear weapons are no longer seen as an indispensable guarantor of peace between the major powers, but rather as a source of instability rising from their attempted acquisition by minor powers and terrorists.

The case for the "nuclear peace" is not implausible, but it is far from being compelling either.

The Liberal Peace

Liberal peace theorists tend to be more optimistic about human nature than realists and less convinced of the virtues of military solutions to security problems. Like realists, they disagree over some issues. Liberal peace theories make the case that both the incidence and the threat of international war have been reduced since the end of World War II by changes in the international system. First, the number of democracies has increased dramatically over the past 30 years and democratic states very rarely fight each other. Second, there has been a dramatic increase in international economic interdependence. In addition, nation-states have become increasingly enmeshed in transnational and international institutions.

Democracy and Peace

The "democratic peace" thesis is the best known of the three elements of the liberal peace. It has been described by Jack Levy as being "close as anything we have to an empirical law in international relations."[31] It rests on the finding, which has been replicated in many studies, that liberal democracies almost never fight each other, and on the claim that this forbearance derives primarily from their democratic nature.

It follows from democratic peace theory that, since the share of democratic governments has almost doubled since the end of the Cold War, as Figure 1.3 shows, the net risk of war between states in the international system should have declined.

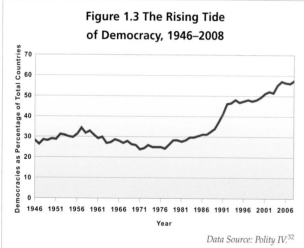

Figure 1.3 The Rising Tide of Democracy, 1946–2008

Data Source: Polity IV.[32]

In 1946, 28 percent of the world's governments were democratic. By 2008 that share had more than doubled.

Yale University's Bruce Russett, one of the leading theorists of the democratic peace thesis, spells out the case for the democratic peace in nontechnical language in the text box, The Democratic Peace.

The Realist Response

As Russett points out, the democratic peace thesis does not claim that democracies are always peaceful—they frequently fight nondemocracies. Indeed, as noted earlier, three democracies—France, Britain, and the US—are ranked first,

second, and third in the league table of countries that have been involved in the highest number of international conflicts between 1946 and 2008.

Moreover, leading realist scholars Edward Mansfield and Jack Snyder have argued that even if democratic states almost never fight each other, the process of becoming a democracy increases the risk of conflict. Looking at the history of wars from 1811 to 1992, they found that states experiencing a democratic transition have been about 40 percent more likely to become involved in hostilities than states experiencing no regime change.[33] This, the authors argue, should raise questions about the "policy of promoting peace by promoting democratization."[34]

> The democratic peace thesis does not claim that democracies are always peaceful—they do fight nondemocracies.

However, while the percentage increase in risk is substantial, the absolute level of risk is extremely small. For states whose governments were becoming more democratic over a period of five years, the risk of being embroiled in an interstate war over the following five years was just over 4 percent; for the states that experienced no such change, the risk was just under 3 percent.[35] This small increase in a relatively tiny risk hardly seems to warrant abandoning efforts to assist countries to democratize, or the security benefits that increasing the number of inclusive democracies seemingly bestows. Moreover, Mansfield and Synder's basic thesis that transitions towards democracy increase the risk of interstate war has been strongly challenged on methodological and empirical grounds by Vipin Narang and Rebecca Nelson.[36]

Like most claims about the causes of peace and war, the democratic peace thesis is contested. The finding itself—that democracies very rarely go to war against each other—is not in doubt, but critics argue it is not the democratic nature of democratic states that accounts for the absence of war between them but other factors. Realists, for example, argue that it was the common interest in maintaining a united front against a mutual—Soviet—enemy, plus nuclear weapons, that prevented war between the Western democracies during the Cold War, not the nature of their political institutions.[37]

In 1990, as the Cold War had ended and the presumed war-inhibiting effect of a common enemy had disappeared with it, noted neo-realist Mearsheimer offered this gloomy view of Europe's future: "The prospect of major crises, even wars, in Europe is likely to increase dramatically now that the Cold War is receding into history. The next forty-five years in Europe… are likely to be substantially more violent than the past forty-five years."[38]

It is now two decades since Mearsheimer wrote his much-cited article, yet the threat of war between Western European states seems even more remote than it was in the Cold War years.

The Capitalist Peace

There is widespread agreement among scholars of the liberal peace that economic interdependence between national economies is, on balance, a positive force for peace. Most scholars working in this field see such interdependence as complementing the effect of democratic institutions in promoting peace between liberal democracies. Erik Gartzke, however, argues that what he calls the "capitalist peace" supplants the democratic peace.[39]

The executive summary of the 2005 Cato Institute report, in which a much-publicized article by Gartzke appeared, noted,"When measures of both economic freedom and democracy are included in a statistical study, economic freedom is about 50 times more effective than democracy in diminishing violent conflict."[40]

The overriding national objective of almost all modern states is wealth maximization, not so much for its own sake but because national wealth is a necessary condition for meeting the huge number of demands that citizens have imposed on modern states, particularly liberal states.

In previous eras, invading other countries to seize control of their land or raw materials had a certain economic logic— land and raw materials were seen to be central to creating wealth and were valued for their own sake as well. But today there are far fewer economic incentives for invading other countries than there were in previous eras. Ownership of land and raw materials is not a necessary condition for creating wealth in the modern world—if it were, Singapore and Luxembourg would be poverty-stricken, and Angola and the Democratic Republic of the Congo would be rich.

Moreover, in today's global marketplace it is almost always cheaper in both financial and political terms to buy raw materials from other countries than to endure the international odium of mounting an invasion in order to seize them. As Mueller puts it, "free trade furnishes the economic advantages of conquest without the unpleasantness of invasion and the sticky responsibility of imperial control."[41]

Trade is the element of international economic interdependence that has received the most attention from democratic peace theorists, but it is not necessarily the most important. Cross-investment is also critical.

As the economies of countries become more and more enmeshed with each other as a result of wealth-enhancing cross-investment, the costs of fighting a war will outweigh any conceivable economic benefit that might follow from starting one. Indeed, if one state goes to war against another under such circumstances, it is effectively attacking itself.

Solomon Polachek, Carlos Seiglie, and Jun Xiang found that both trade and foreign direct investment (FDI) were associated with a reduced risk of conflict between pairs of states in the 1990s.[42] In particular, they noted that a 10 percent increase in FDI was associated with an average 3 percent decrease in net conflict. They found that trade had a comparable impact.

Insofar as this thesis is correct, if international trade and FDI levels continue to grow, as seems highly probable, the risk of interstate conflict should decline still further.[43]

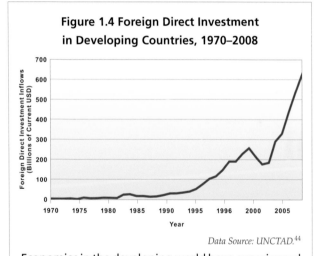

Figure 1.4 Foreign Direct Investment in Developing Countries, 1970–2008

Data Source: UNCTAD.[44]

Economies in the developing world have experienced a dramatic acceleration of foreign direct investment over the last two decades.

Figure 1.4 shows the dramatic increase in FDI in the developing world. The increase in trade levels between rich and poor countries follows a similar trajectory.[45]

Not surprisingly, democratic peace theorists, while agreeing that economic interdependence helps reduce conflict between states, reject Gartzke's wholesale dismissal of the impact of democracy on the prospects for international peace. The debate between Gartzke and his critics, which has focused

THE DEMOCRATIC PEACE   *By Bruce Russett*

The democratic peace is an empirical observation, a fact. Since the beginning of the twentieth century, when real democracy started to take hold in many countries, violent conflicts between democracies have been rare, and full-scale wars between democracies have been virtually nonexistent.

A more precise statement of the democratic peace thesis is that the more democratic any two countries are, the less likely they are to get into disputes that kill people, and the less violent any conflicts that do arise between them are likely to be. These facts have important implications for global security, since the number of democratic governments in the world has doubled since 1990 and the number of dictatorships has halved, while the number of armed conflicts has declined substantially. By democracy I mean a country with free and competitive elections that the government really can lose, and in which nearly everyone can vote and a broad range of people might achieve high office.

The association between different types of government and the risk of war is striking. Two highly democratic countries are some 80 percent less likely to get into a violent dispute with each other than are two countries—otherwise similar—that are ruled by strong dictatorships. In medical research such a reduction in risk would be a very big deal.

The democratic peace is a strong generalization, a probabilistic statement that allows some exceptions. My colleagues and I have spent much of the last 15 years analyzing the evidence for the democratic peace. We have found that it stands up with different definitions of democracy and different measures of international violence and war. But it is *not* an iron law—there are no iron laws about social and political phenomena. Individual leaders can make bad decisions. Democracy is dependent on a separation of powers, on checks and balances that work better in some countries than in others, and in particular countries better at some times than others.

The democratic peace is a thesis about pairs of democratic countries. It does *not* mean that democracies are necessarily peaceful in their relations with nondemocracies, although there is some evidence that democracies are less likely to get into violent international conflicts in general, and when they do it is usually the dictators who start, or escalate, the violence. But here the evidence is not nearly as strong as for the propositions about peace between pairs of countries. Great powers, whether democracies or dictatorships, get into a lot of conflicts. This is not surprising, since great powers have widespread interests, and the military capabilities to attack distant countries—attributes that weaker powers lack.

Several influences help explain the democratic peace phenomenon. Both policy-makers and publics in democracies, for example, may share the belief that it is unnecessary, and therefore unwise, to get into violent conflicts with countries whose governments and peoples are accustomed to resolving conflicts nonviolently and might be expected to follow that practice in dealing with international conflicts.

However, probably the most important contribution to keeping the peace between democracies is the fact that democratic states have institutions for replacing their leaders peacefully. Democratic leaders must address the concerns of a majority of their populations in order to stay in office. Some wars may be popular at first, but long wars, costly in money and blood, are rarely popular, as their costs are mostly born by the general populace. Democratic leaders know that if they fight unpopular wars, they risk being thrown out of office in the next election.

Democracies win well over half of the wars they are involved in, and 90 percent of those they start. The fact that democracies are formidable opponents provides an incentive for other countries, including other democracies, to try and avoid waging war against them. Dictators, by contrast, do not have to satisfy a broad electorate and, even if they start and lose a war, they often can stay in power afterwards by paying off a small circle of cronies and the security forces they need to repress opposition.

While democratic governance contributes to international peace, it is *not* a panacea. And democratic peace rhetoric can be misused—notably to legitimate the resort to war in the name of establishing democracy. Even putting domestic and international legal considerations aside, the historical record demonstrates that efforts to establish democracy in other countries by force usually fail. The experiences of Germany and Japan after World War II were rare exceptions. Few other defeated dictatorships have had such favourable political, social, and economic conditions for starting or reviving democracy. In the case of the two defeated Axis powers, these included an advanced capitalist economy with a highly skilled labour force, previous experience of democracy, an ethnically homogenous population, occupiers who were resolutely committed to reinstating democratic institutions, no oil curse, and most of Germany's neighbours being democratic. Some US government officials may have thought Iraq looked like Germany. They were wrong.

The democratic peace complements other security-enhancing influences. A new democracy is safest in a neighbourhood mostly populated by other democracies, for example. International commerce, meaning trade and finance, is also a force for peace. Pairs of countries whose mutual trade accounts for a high percentage of their national income are nearly as likely as a pairs of democracies to stay free of warfare. Trade produces politically powerful interest groups that have a big stake in avoiding costly military conflict. In turn, peace promotes more trade. There is also an indirect contribution to peace in that democracies trade more heavily with other democracies where rule of law and respect for property rights prevail. And trade promotes economic growth, which itself enhances democracy.

International governmental organizations (IGOs) are another force for peace—particularly the strongly institutionalized IGOs that are composed mostly of democracies. Those organizations promote and help stabilize the democratic institutions of their new members. Many of them make democracy a condition for membership. Pairs of countries sharing membership in many such organizations have about a 30 percent lower risk of violent conflict than do countries sharing few or no such memberships. That is less than the contribution of democracy and trade, but still substantial. Strong ties

of trade and IGO membership make a contribution to peace even with countries that are not democratic—grounds for peace between the United States and China.

Countries that rank near the top of the measures for all three of these security-promoting influences—democracy, trade, and shared IGO memberships—are over 90 percent less likely to fight each other than are countries ranked near the bottom of all three.

Together, these three influences create a self-reinforcing cycle that constitutes key elements of what I call the Kantian system—the reference being to Immanuel Kant's prescient insights into the role of democracy and commerce in promoting international peace. They are also key elements of what we call globalization, and their contribution to peace is part of the good news about globalization.

The democratic peace has been most evident in Europe since the end of World War II: a region that has been bound together in peace for an unprecedented 60-plus years after centuries of bloody warfare. But it is *not* limited to Europe. The three influences also operate, if less strongly, in much of the rest of the world, including among poorer countries. One example is Mercosur, an IGO that promotes free trade in South America and that was established by newly democratic countries when they got rid of their dictators. Democracy is a condition for membership in Mercosur. It has become a mutual protection society for democratic leaders who use it to promote commerce and economic growth and reduce old antagonisms that had led to wars and threats of war in the past.

Democratization often follows when governments and their peoples observe that democracy works in other countries, especially neighbouring countries, by bringing human rights and steady, if not spectacular, increases in standards of living. They begin to see the value of being able to hold elected officials accountable at the polls. No democracy with an income equal to that of Argentina in the 1980s has ever reverted to dictatorship.

The democratic peace counsels patience. Over time these powerful mutually reinforcing influences work to create expanding zones of war-free democratic states. While nothing is guaranteed in this world, this is the best prospect for international peace.

on research design, is complex, highly technical, and unlikely to be resolved any time soon.[46]

The sharp divergence of views and findings evident in this debate is typical of much of the quantitative conflict research literature, which is characterized both by a marked lack of consensus over findings and by many methodological disputes. Some of the latter are explored in the next chapter.

Peace is "overdetermined," and determining the impact of one causal factor vis-à-vis another is challenging.

The controversy over the capitalist peace—like many others in this field—points to a more general problem within the literature on the causes of peace between democracies, particularly between the long-established democracies. It is true that OECD (Organisation for Economic Co-operation and Development) democracies do not fight each other, but these same democracies also have liberal capitalist economies and high levels of economic interdependence; they are members of long-established alliance systems; they possess nuclear weapons, or shelter under the "nuclear umbrella"; and they are deeply "enmeshed" in regional and international organizations. Each of these factors has been identified as reducing the probability of war.

Peace, in other words, is "overdetermined," and determining the impact of one causal factor vis-à-vis others at the onset (or termination) of warfare can be extremely challenging. In principle, isolating and determining the impact of different causal factors is possible using multi-variate statistical analysis. In practice, as the very large number of divergent findings indicate, this is very difficult. In addition, it is likely that some of these factors interact with others in complex and nonobvious ways, a fact that makes the statistical and causal modelling of these phenomena even more challenging.

Peace through Ideas: The Constructivist Contribution

Ohio University's John Mueller has posed a radical challenge to both realist and liberal theories that seek to explain the causes of international peace. He suggests that the primary driver of the decline in both the number and deadliness of international conflicts since the end of World War II has been changing public and elite attitudes towards the legitimacy of war as an instrument of statecraft. This growing norm of "war aversion,"

he argues, presents a dramatic change from past ideas about the legitimacy of the use of force in international politics.

Noting that developed states have fought zero (or near-zero) wars against each other in the past 60-plus years, Mueller suggests this is because they have "substantially abandoned war as a method for dealing with their disagreements."[47] Post-World War II attitudes towards war as an instrument of statecraft are strikingly different from those in previous eras when warfare was "almost universally considered to be an acceptable, perhaps an inevitable, and for many people a desirable, way of settling international differences."[48]

The extent of the change in global norms over the past 60-plus years is evident in the universal recognition of the illegitimacy of colonial rule noted previously; in the proscription on war except in self-defense, or with the sanction of the UN Security Council; and in the near-complete absence in foreign and defense establishments in the developed world of the type of extreme hypernationalism that underpinned German and Japanese aggression leading up to World War II. What the French call *bellicisme*—the glorification of warfare—is rarely found in governments today, though it is characteristic of some radical terrorist organizations like al-Qaeda.

It has been suggested that the decline in international conflicts is the result of changing attitudes to war.

The relatively recent changes in public and elite attitudes to war are part of what Steven Pinker and others see as a broader long-term normative trend away from the use of violence and coercion in social life. Referring to a centuries-long pattern of normative change, Pinker notes:

> Cruelty as entertainment, human sacrifice to indulge superstition, slavery as a labor-saving device, conquest as the mission statement of government, genocide as a means of acquiring real estate, torture and mutilation as routine punishment, the death penalty for misdemeanors and differences of opinion, assassination as the mechanism of political succession, rape as the spoils of war, pogroms as outlets for frustration, homicide as the major form of conflict resolution—all were unexceptionable features of life for most of human history. But today, they are rare to nonexistent in the West, far less

common elsewhere than they used to be, concealed when they do occur, and widely condemned when they are brought to light.[49]

Norms are shared understandings that create obligations to behave, or refrain from behaving, in certain ways. They determine what is, and what is not, legitimate. Sometimes they are codified in law; often they are not. Like all norms, the norms against the use of force are sometimes transgressed—the US-led invasion of Iraq without UN Security Council authorization is a case in point. But occasional transgressions do not mean that the norm is ineffective.

Realists see war-averseness as an effect of power-balancing, alliance membership, and nuclear deterrence.

It is, however, difficult to determine the impact of normative changes. Unlike democracy, international trade, FDI, and military capacity, norms of war-averseness are very difficult to measure. Neither their provenance nor their causal impact are amenable to the sort of quantitative studies that have been used to determine the impact of democratic institutions, interdependence, and military power balances on the risk of war.

Both realists and liberals have tended to treat war-averseness as epiphenomenal. Realists see it as an effect of power-balancing, alliance membership, and nuclear deterrence. For liberals, war-averseness is an outcome of growing economic interdependence and the democratic peace. Neither sees the war-averse norm as a cause of peace in its own right. Mueller argues this may be a mistake. With respect to claims about the contribution of capitalism to peace, for example, he argues:

> It is not so much that free-market capitalism and the economic development it spawns cause peace, but rather that peace causes—or perhaps better, facilitates—capitalism and its attendant economic development. It is peace, not capitalism, that is the determining factor in the relationship.[50]

Mueller's normative theory has not been tested in any of the statistical models for the reasons noted above, but other notable strategic thinkers have made similar arguments about the independent effects of changing attitudes to war on the prospects for peace.[51]

Conclusion

For most of the Cold War period, realist assumptions prevailed in security communities in both the West and the Communist world, but these assumptions appear to be decreasingly relevant in the post-Cold War era. Realists believed that it was the common interest in uniting against the Soviet threat that kept the peace between Western democracies during the Cold War. But as noted earlier, the Cold War has been over for 20 years and the prospect of war between the OECD democracies seems more remote than ever.

It is quite unclear how traditional realist security policies—creating or joining alliances, balancing military power, or seeking military preponderance—are supposed to contribute to peace between the advanced industrialized countries today. Most OECD countries feel secure from attack, not because of the mutually deterring effect of their military forces but because they do not believe that other states wish to attack them. Among the countries of Western Europe, the idea that disputes might be settled by war has become simply unthinkable.

Realists believe that such sentiments are naive because international anarchy—the absence of any supranational security authority—means that world politics is condemned to be a constant struggle for power. But as constructivist scholar Alexander Wendt famously noted nearly 20 years ago, "Anarchy is what states make of it."[52] In their dealings with each other, today's Western democracies do not find that the absence of any supranational authority is a major source of security concern.

The Cold War has been over for 20 years and the prospect of war between the OECD democracies seems very remote.

Whether or not liberal or realist security prescriptions are useful guides for policy-makers depends very much on context. "Peace through strength" and alliance-building strategies made sense when confronting Fascist Germany and Japan—states that were bent on imperial aggression. Liberal security policies—more democracy and greater international trade and economic interdependence—would have been completely irrelevant responses to the Fascist threat. And in the 1930s, the promotion of war-aversion norms, which were quite common among the upper classes in pre-World War II Britain, amounted to little more than appeasement.

Although today's world might appear very different, for neo-realists like Waltz, nothing has really changed. Writing a decade after the end of the Cold War, Waltz argued, "Every time peace breaks out, people pop up and proclaim that realism is dead. This is another way of saying that international politics has been transformed. The world, however, has not been transformed."[53]

But there are, as we have argued, reasons to believe that, contrary to Waltz, the international system may indeed have been transformed since the end of World War II, and in ways that have dramatically reduced the risk of international war. This does not mean an end to conflict—far from it—simply that the form that international conflict takes today is likely to be less violent than in the past. There is ample evidence, for example, that national trade policies and cross-investment by multinational corporations generate many often rancorous disputes. But the evidence also suggests the resulting interdependencies have created powerful incentives to prevent the disputes from escalating into cross-border warfare.

In the next chapter we examine the current academic debates about the causes of intrastate war and peace. There have been some striking findings but there is even less consensus among quantitative researchers than is the case with respect to international conflicts.

Jacques Demarthon / AFP / Getty Images. FRANCE.

CHAPTER 2

Peace, War, and Numbers: A Non-technical Guide to Recent Research on the Causes of War and Peace

Over the past 20 years, there has been a dramatic increase in the amount of statistical research being undertaken on the causes of war and peace. This chapter examines the often-striking findings produced by researchers in what has become an increasingly influential field, one whose impact is felt well beyond the research community. Quantitative conflict research findings are now regularly cited by governments, international agencies, think-tanks and NGOs (nongovernmental organizations), and in the media.

The previous chapter examined some of the findings of quantitative research on the causes of international conflict and peace. Here we examine the intrastate (or civil) wars that make up the overwhelming majority of today's armed conflicts.

Our central focus is the burgeoning literature that relies on cross-national datasets to determine the causes of civil war.[54] In particular, we examine two major challenges that sharply reduce the practical utility of quantitative research findings for policy-makers. First is the remarkable lack of consensus in the research findings on the causes of war and peace. Second is the inability of conflict models to predict the outbreak of conflicts. We also examine some innovative recent attempts to address these problems.

We start, however, with a brief introduction to the key differences between quantitative and qualitative methodologies.

Quantitative versus Qualitative Methodologies

Macro-quantitative studies of civil wars use statistical models to determine what in general increases the risks of war and the prospects for peace. Qualitative conflict analysis, by contrast, seeks to gain an understanding of the dynamics of particular conflicts and does not use statistical models.[55] Each of the two approaches serves a different, but complementary, analytic purpose. In subsequent chapters we draw on both qualitative and quantitative methods to demonstrate the explanatory utility of combining the two approaches. Such so-called mixed-methods analyses are attracting growing interest in the research community.

Qualitative Research: The Case-Study Approach

Qualitative conflict research, which has been around for far longer than quantitative research, remains highly influential in policy communities.

Rather than undertaking statistical analyses of conflict risk in large numbers of countries over many years, qualitative researchers focus on detailed and historically and culturally contextualized analyses of causal pathways to war onsets in one or a few countries. Such research is typical of much of the "current intelligence" analysis produced in foreign and defense ministries and intelligence agencies, as well as the work of think-tank analysts and country and area experts in the scholarly community.

Policy-makers are comfortable with qualitative analysis—it is the approach they mostly rely on in analyzing conflict risks in particular countries, and in formulating strategies for conflict prevention, *peacemaking* (stopping ongoing wars), and *post-conflict peacebuilding* (preventing wars that have stopped from starting again.) And it has the additional virtue of being readily comprehensible to those unfamiliar with the technical complexities of regression analysis.

The 1990s saw a dramatic increase in the number of civil war onsets.

But individual case studies, however insightful, cannot, by their very nature, reveal global and regional trends in the number or deadliness of armed conflicts—or detect the common causes that may drive them. For example, only macro-statistical analysis reveals that the most pervasive common factor shared by countries embroiled in civil conflict is low GDP (gross domestic product) per capita. And only quantitative trend data could have shown that there had been a 70 percent-plus decline in high-intensity conflicts around the world in the two decades following the end of the Cold War.[56] This remarkable decline, which remained largely unrecognized in the UN (United Nations) until the new millennium, provides supportive evidence for the effectiveness of the upsurge of international initiatives that started in the early 1990s and that was directed towards reducing the number and deadliness of armed conflicts around the world. This latter change, which is examined in depth in the final chapter of Part I, was also revealed by global trend data.

Quantitative Research: Using Statistics to Understand the Causes of War and Peace

One of the major factors driving the quantitative revolution in conflict research has been the inherent limitation of qualitative case-study analysis. Individual case studies can provide deep insights into the causes of particular conflicts and can suggest reasons why such causes might apply more broadly. But as noted above, they cannot be used to determine whether what is true for one or a few cases is true more generally. The inherent limitation of case-study analysis is summed up in the methodological imperative: "Don't generalize from the particular."

To make valid generalizations about the conditions under which the risks of war increase or decrease, a much wider evidence base is needed than qualitative studies can provide. What have come to be known as large-N datasets,

which include statistics on most countries in the world over long periods of time, were developed to meet this need. These datasets typically go back to 1945 or 1946, but some start as early as 1816. The unit of analysis is usually the country-year—so a dataset that covered 150 countries over a period of 40 years would contain 6,000 separate country-years of data.

In seeking to understand what increases and decreases the risk of a war breaking out, quantitative researchers typically rely on *multiple regression analysis*—a statistical technique that is used to determine the degree of association between different factors and the risk of conflict.[57] *Independent variables* are the factors that analysts believe may be causally related to the *dependent variable*—which in conflict research is usually the onset of war.[58] As James Fearon and David Laitin put it:

> To ascertain whether some interesting pattern, or relationship between variables, obtains, the best approach is normally to identify the largest feasible sample of cases relevant to the hypothesis or research question, then to code cases on the variables of interest, and then to assess whether and what sort of patterns or associations appear in the data.[59]

The statistics that are fed into the models that researchers deploy to reveal associations between war onsets and a range of independent variables are typically derived from socio-economic, environmental, and demographic datasets collated by the World Bank, the UN, other international agencies—and sometimes from the research community. Information on *when* wars start and end comes from datasets produced by the research community, like those created by the Correlates of War (COW) project, Uppsala Conflict Data Program (UCDP), and the International Peace Research Institute, Oslo (PRIO).

Civil War and the Quantitative Revolution

The end of the Cold War was associated with a considerable upsurge in interest in civil wars in both the research and policy communities, with much of the most innovative research coming from the quantitative research community.

The increased focus on civil wars arose partly because the security issue that had engaged Western security communities for more than four decades had simply evaporated as the Cold War ended, and partly because the 1990s had seen a dramatic increase in the number of civil war onsets around the world.

The average number of new wars starting each year in the 1990s was double that of the 1980s, with many of them attracting massive media coverage. The decade still witnessed a *net* decline in conflict numbers because there were more terminations than onsets. But the decline went largely unnoticed because the mostly undramatic endings of these wars attracted much less attention than their violent beginnings.

The increased interest in civil wars was paralleled by a growing reliance on quantitative methods, not just in the conflict research community but in political science more generally. This change had in turn been facilitated by increased access to low-cost desktop computing power, new conflict datasets, and more sophisticated conflict models.

In North America quantitative conflict research is not merely mainstream—it now dominates the field of scholarly enquiry into the causes of war.

The Growing Impact of Quantitative Conflict Research

The World Bank's project, the Economics of Civil War, Crime and Violence, led by Paul Collier, the director of the World Bank's Research Development Department from 1999 to 2003, was highly influential in raising the visibility of quantitative conflict research in policy communities. The increased demand from international agencies and donor governments that policy be "evidence-based" has generated further interest in quantitative research.

A landmark in the evolution of this increasingly influential research field was the seminal paper written by Collier and his collaborator Anke Hoeffler, entitled "Greed and Grievance in Civil War." First published on the World Bank's website in 2000, the article has had a major impact on policy communities in donor states and international agencies, as well as among researchers.[60]

There are profound disagreements between quantitative scholars about the factors that drive war and peace.

The article, which went through several iterations before being published in *Oxford Economic Papers* in 2004, has been the subject of an extraordinary number of citations and commentaries. Its statistical findings have subsequently been evaluated against a large number of country case studies.[61]

"Greed and Grievance" argued that low and falling incomes, dependence on primary commodities, and a recent history of warfare were associated with increased risk of violent conflict but that neither political nor economic grievances, inequality, or ethnic diversity made countries more war-prone.

The claim that grievances have no impact on the risk of war, which was by far the most controversial finding in the Collier/ Hoeffler paper, is subjected to a critical examination in "Why Grievances Matter" that appears in Chapter 4.

In 2007, Collier's best-selling book, *The Bottom Billion*, brought many of the key findings of the World Bank's project and subsequent work to a far wider public.[62]

The policy impact of quantitative conflict research has become even more evident with the publication of the World Bank's 2011 *World Development Report*, which focuses on security in fragile states, and which draws heavily on the work of leading quantitative scholars in the US, Europe, and elsewhere.

The Major Challenges Confronting Quantitative Conflict Research

Despite the vast amount of research and real progress in many areas, the early promise of quantitative research on civil wars has yet to be realized and the field continues to confront major methodological and data challenges. These challenges raise serious questions about the current utility of much of the work being done for the policy community.

As noted earlier, for governments and international agencies, quantitative research at the present stage of its development confronts two major limitations that reduce its value for informing policy. First, very few findings about the causes of armed conflict command widespread assent among quantitative researchers themselves, and second, conflict models are very poor at offering predictions.

Lack of Consensus About the Causes of War and Peace

Although rarely discussed in quantitative research literature, there are profound disagreements between quantitative scholars about the factors that drive war and peace. As one review put it: "Despite immense data collections, prestigious journals, and sophisticated analyses … Many statistical results change from article to article and specification to specification. Accurate forecasts are nonexistent."[63]

This bleak assessment by three leading methodologists in the US was directed at quantitative studies of international conflicts 10 years ago, but it is equally applicable, and largely for the same reasons, to quantitative studies of civil wars today.

This was made evident in a recent survey of key findings in the quantitative conflict research literature on civil war by Håvard Hegre and Nicolas Sambanis, which reported that the literature was rife with divergent findings.[64] Their research—

and that of other scholars[65]—points out that various quantitative studies have found that:

- Ethnic diversity has no impact on the risk of armed conflict—and it does.
- Dependence on primary commodities makes war more likely—and it does not.
- Increases in levels of democracy reduce the risk of war—and have no impact.
- Inequality increases the risk of war—and has no effect.
- Grievances increase the risk of war—and they do not.
- Countries whose neighbours experience civil war face increased risks of war themselves—and they do not.
- Economic growth decreases the risk of war—and it has no significant effect.
- Mountainous terrain increases the risk of war—and it does not.

Surprisingly, despite these and many other divergent findings, there have been very few attempts by researchers to resolve their differences.

A Small Number of Robust Findings

Hegre and Sambanis suggest that just three findings command widespread consensus:

- The lower a country's average income, the higher the risk of war.
- War is more likely if a country has already experienced a war—the more recent the war, the greater the risk.
- The risk of war increases as a country's size increases.

Other studies have found a somewhat greater number of consensual findings, but no one doubts that research in this field is characterized by an extraordinary amount of disagreement.[66]

The first two consensual findings identified by Hegre and Sambanis are not only robust, but they also have clear policy relevance. The first suggests that economic development is a form of long-term conflict prevention; the second suggests that peacebuilding policies in post-conflict environments should focus particular attention on trying to ensure that conflicts that have stopped do not reignite. The third finding does not have much policy relevance, however. Shrinking the size of a country's population or territory in order to reduce its risk of succumbing to war is hardly a realistic security policy—though secessionists might disagree.

The lack of agreement within the research community matters because inconclusive, divergent, and sometimes outright contradictory statistical findings are of little value to policy-makers who have neither the time, nor usually the technical expertise, to determine which, if any, of the findings is valid.

To be fair, however, we note that disagreement over the causes of war is in no sense unique to quantitative research—historians still cannot agree on the causes of World War I, notwithstanding nearly 100 years of intensive research and the production of thousands of books and scholarly articles.

Conflict Models Are Poor at Prediction

A second area of concern for policy-makers is the inability of quantitative models to predict the onset of armed conflicts. As one recent study noted, "global models of civil conflict have performed notoriously poorly at prediction."[67]

In the Collier/Hoeffler "Greed and Grievance" study, the associations between a range of variables and civil war onsets that the authors tested were "statistically significant," suggesting that each of these factors affect the probability of war onsets. But as a recent study by Michael Ward, Brian Greenhill, and Kristin Bakke points out, the Collier/Hoeffler model only predicted 7 percent—three out of 46—of the wars that actually broke out in the period examined.[68] But it also predicted five wars that did not occur—so-called false positives.

Ward and his co-authors also tested the predictive power of the model that Fearon and Laitin used in their powerfully argued and highly influential, "Ethnicity, Insurgency and Civil War" study.[69] The Fearon/Laitin model fared even worse than the Collier/Hoeffler model, predicting not one of the 107 wars that started within the period they studied.[70]

But as Fearon and Laitin point out, the low predictive power of the models is not surprising: "Predicting civil war onset in a given country year from factors that can be coded across a large sample of countries and years is a bit like trying to find a needle in a haystack."[71]

Collier agrees that the Collier/Hoeffler model is of little use for prediction, but suggests that this is not its intended purpose:

> Our analysis is not well suited to prediction…
> To predict a civil war, it is surely more useful to focus
> on near-term indicators such as political incidents and
> rising violence. Rather our model is useful in pointing
> to the typical structural risks and so provides some
> guidance on longer-term policies for prevention.[72]

One research project, the CIA-funded Political Instability Task Force (PITF), claims a far superior prediction rate than the models recently reviewed by Ward, Greenhill, and Bakke. Indeed, rather than the 7 percent rate achieved by the Collier/

Hoeffler model, the PITF model claims an extraordinary 80 to 81.5 percent success rate in predicting civil war onsets.[73]

The PITF model's level of predictive success, which is described in a recent article in the *American Journal of Political Science*, is extraordinarily high compared with any other study—and thus of great potential interest to policy-makers.[74] But PITF researchers define prediction quite differently from the more conventional definition used by Ward and his co-authors, and the two sets of findings are in no sense comparable.

Defined more conventionally, PITF's prediction rate is similar to the Collier/Hoeffler rate—but greater than that of the Fearon/Laitin model.[75] In some ways this is a remarkable achievement since PITF's result is achieved with just four independent variables—far fewer than the Collier/Hoeffler model.

But while conflict models perform badly in predicting whether or not a conflict will break out in a particular country in a particular year, they do much better in determining the risk of conflict onsets over a longer period—say, five or 10 years. This suggests that their policy value lies primarily in informing long-term conflict prevention policies, rather than warning policy-makers of the imminence of war in a particular country.

Methodological Challenges

Why should there be so many divergent findings in this field and such poor rates of prediction? Part of the reason is that many reported results are not robust—that is, they can change quite substantially in response to minor alterations in the specifications of the statistical models being used.[76]

As Chris Blattman and Edward Miguel have noted:

[The quantitative civil war literature] has been enormously provocative but has faced equally important limitations: convincing causal identification of key relationships is rare; robustness to alternative specifications or assumptions is seldom explored; country-years are often assumed to be independent units in time and space; measurement error is rarely addressed; an absence of evidence about particular effects has often been interpreted as evidence of absence; and theories of individual or armed group behavior are tested at the country level despite obvious aggregation difficulties. It would be easy to conclude that the cross-country literature has been exhausted, but that would go too far.[77]

These conclusions reflect widespread concern among a number of leading quantitative scholars about the state of the field.[78] Below we examine briefly some of the issues that have occasioned concern.

Correlation and Causation

The statistical models typically used by conflict researchers are designed to uncover associations—usually referred to as correlations. *Correlation* simply means that when the value of independent variables in a model changes, so too does the value of the dependent variable.

In the literature it is often assumed that when values of what have been identified as an independent and a dependent variable—i.e., a presumed cause and its presumed effect, respectively—vary together it is because the former causes the latter. But the correlation between the two could be spurious—i.e., the changes in both could be driven by a third unmeasured causal factor. This problem is widely recognized and researchers can attempt to reduce it by introducing control variables, but this is not always sufficient.

It is also possible that cause and effect will be confused—that the "causal arrow" will actually run in the opposite direction to that which has been assumed—or in both directions. This is the so-called endogeneity problem.[79] To give one obvious example, in the quantitative literature it is typically assumed that low income per capita is a factor that increases the risk of war—as incomes go down, the risk of war goes up, with the former driving the latter. But clearly the causal relationship between income and war can also work in the opposite direction—i.e., the low incomes may be a consequence, rather than a cause, of war. This assertion hardly needs demonstrating—it is fairly obvious that warfare can ravage national economies and drive down average incomes.

> The policy value of conflict models lies primarily in informing long-term conflict prevention policies.

Researchers can attempt to ensure they are detecting the impact of declining incomes on the risk of wars by measuring income levels two or more years prior to the onset of wars. But while this approach reduces the endogeneity problem substantially, it does not eliminate it completely. Wars rarely erupt without some warning and it is possible that the anticipation of war will drive incomes down before the fighting starts if business confidence erodes and investment slows. However, this possibility does not invalidate the finding that when incomes *rise* the risk of war falls. It is possible to argue—and demonstrate—that war causes incomes to fall; it makes little sense to argue that the absence of war causes incomes to rise.

Finally, there is the problem that even when there is a strong correlation between an independent variable and conflict onsets, there may be several different causal paths from the former to the latter.

Take the much-discussed association between mineral wealth and the risk of war. A major study by Michael Ross published in 2006 found there was a statistically significant association between mineral wealth and conflict onsets but noted that scholars have posited a diverse range of possible causal mechanisms that could lead to the latter from the former.[80] It has been argued, for example, that mineral wealth could foster conflict by:

- Providing funding via predation or extortion for rebel groups.
- Creating the perverse effect of weakening state institutions.
- Making the state that receives the resource rents an attractive target for rebel takeover.
- Generating "economic shocks" if there are sharp market-driven declines in the export values of the minerals in question.
- Making separatism a financially attractive proposition for potential secessionists in resource-rich regions.

Policy-makers need to understand the causal mechanisms that increase the risk of conflict onsets if they are to devise effective prevention policies. But in cases where there are a number of very different possible causal paths from dependence on mineral wealth to the outbreak of war, conflict models have little policy utility. They can identify correlations and measure their degree of statistical significance but cannot determine which of the possible causal mechanisms is determinate in a particular case.[81]

Statistical versus Substantive Significance

Uncovering statistically significant correlations between dependent and independent variables—i.e., those that are unlikely to occur by chance—is the goal of most statistical studies of civil war.

But statistical significance, while it may indeed point to causal relationships, is not necessarily the same as substantive significance—the type of finding most likely to be useful for policy-makers. Consider a case where researchers find that a change in the value of a particular independent variable is associated with a statistically significant increase in the risk of war of, say, 40 percent. This sounds impressive. But the probability of a civil war starting in a country-year chosen at random from a typical global dataset is normally extremely low. So, a 40 percent increase in what is a *very* low risk remains a very low risk—and thus of limited interest to policy-makers.

Statistical significance is not necessarily the same as substantive significance.

In the Fearon and Laitin dataset, for example, there are just 127 war onsets in the nearly 7,000 country-years of observations. This means that the probability of a civil war starting in any country-year chosen at random is just 1.8 percent.[82] Increasing this by 40 percent would mean that the risk of war would rise to just 2.4 percent. For policy-makers interested in knowing if—and when—a particular country is likely to succumb to civil war, this sort of finding is of little practical utility. Qualitative research is more useful here.

Quantitative Models Ignore Fear, Hatred, and Humiliation as Potential Drivers of Conflict

Case-study analyses of armed conflicts find that fear, hatred, humiliation, resentment, concern for legitimacy and honour, nationalism, and feelings of solidarity are all sentiments that can be central to understanding the causes of war. But they are almost completely ignored in mainstream quantitative conflict research, where researchers rely primarily on slow-changing structural variables like GDP per capita, infant mortality rates, ethnicity, or economic inequality that are readily available in World Bank, UN, and other datasets.

It is not that quantitative scholars believe that emotions, attitudes, and beliefs are unimportant, of course, but rather that their research methodologies normally require access to data for 100-plus countries over many decades. However, opinion survey and other data on people's emotions, attitudes, and beliefs for most countries, and over such long periods of time, simply do not exist.

"The quantitative data that exist," notes Stanford political scientist Jeremy Weinstein, "have limited the questions scholars have been able to ask about civil war."[83]

In principle, the challenge that missing data on attitudes presents can be addressed by the use of proxy variables—i.e., factors for which there are available data that can "stand-in" for the missing variable. Income inequality, for example, is often used as a proxy for "grievance." But the use of proxy measures in this field is often controversial.

Accounting for Agency

Agency—the capacity for human beings to make choices and act on them—obviously plays a critical role in transitions from peace to war, and war to peace. At some stage in the causal path to war, a decision has to be made by one of the parties to initiate hostilities. Agency factors, though rarely included in conflict models, always matter.

With respect to war initiation, agency encompasses far more than the decisions of individual political leaders to commit to combat. It also embraces a wide range of human actions that may push high-risk situations across the threshold from peace into war. Individual decision-makers can obviously play a critical role in moving a country towards war, but so too can small groups and mass movements.

> Agency factors, though rarely included in conflict models, always matter.

Notwithstanding the obvious importance of human agency, most quantitative models, as we have pointed out, rely on structural variables, i.e., on things that are—like country size or GDP per capita—rather than things that happen. The latter, which are often referred to as events data, include a wide variety of agency-driven phenomena—antiregime demonstrations, strikes and boycotts, the ousting of political leaders, or rigged elections, etc. These are often identified as potential trigger or precipitator factors that can push a crisis situation across the threshold into open warfare.[84]

Access to events data is problematic, however. Unlike the structural data on which most conflict models rely, no national or international agency collects global statistics on political events that might be useful in testing conflict models.

In the research community, a considerable effort was put into collecting socio-political events data from the 1940s to the late 1970s, with the findings being published in the *World Handbook of Political and Social Indicators* series in 1964, 1972, and 1983. But human coding of events data is expensive, time-consuming, and prone to error, and the *World Handbook* series is no longer being published. As a study published in the *Journal of Conflict Resolution* in 2003 pointed out, "this type of cross-national event research has virtually disappeared from the literature."[85]

There have nevertheless been some studies that have sought to use events data in an effort to improve the ability of quantitative models to predict conflict onsets, but thus far without a great deal of success.[86] As the Genocide Prevention Task Force report noted: "While scholars have had some success in identifying long-term risk factors, it has proven much more difficult to find generalizable near-term indicators, 'accelerators,' or triggers."[87]

There appear to be a number of reasons for this lack of success. First, many of the events that would appear to be prime trigger candidates are extremely common but turn out to be only rarely associated with conflict onsets.[88] Second, some events that appear to have been triggers in particular cases are so rare that their association with conflict onsets would not be statistically significant in regression analyses. Third, to repeat a point made earlier, finding an association is not the same as determining a cause. To determine whether or not putative triggers actually cause the onset of war requires the sort of painstaking "process tracing" methodology that only qualitative researchers employ.[89]

Should We Assume That the Future Will Be Like the Past?

A central assumption in most large-N studies of civil war is that the causes of war are both universal and time-independent. With respect to the causes of war and peace, in other words, it is assumed that the future will be like the past. It logically follows that if statistical models can explain the past, they should also provide a reliable guide to the future. But this takes for granted what really needs to be demonstrated, namely that the impact of independent variables will not change over time.

This particular challenge has received little attention in the quantitative literature, but as Graham Brown and Arnim Langer have argued:

> The prospect that even some of our strongest findings of conflict may not hold as valid now as they did in the past, or vice versa, should be tantalizing rather than a matter of concern. This means taking the passage of absolute time much more seriously.[90]

Brown and Langer demonstrate that the impact of independent variables can indeed change over time by taking the well-known Fearon and Laitin model and rerunning it for successive 20-year periods. They found that, while the association between income per capita and conflict remained robust from period to period, other associations did not.[91]

In other words, the assumption that the impacts of presumed causal factors do not change over time was not supported.

Data Challenges

Accessing reliable quantitative data is particularly challenging for conflict researchers. Statistics for poor countries—where most wars take place—are rarely adequate and often terrible, and researchers have to make difficult choices about what to include in their datasets and what to leave out.

But access to reliable data is by no means the only problem. Reviewing 12 datasets covering the period from 1960 to 1993, Nicholas Sambanis found that the number of armed conflict onsets that each contained varied sharply.[92] The differences were largely a consequence of methodological choices researchers made with respect to:

- The types of political violence that are included under the rubric of "civil war."
- The combat fatality thresholds. If the thresholds are high (typically 1,000 battle deaths a year), there will clearly be fewer conflict onsets than if they are much lower (say, 25 battle deaths a year).
- The criteria used to determine when wars start and when they end.

> Today serious political violence rarely affects more than a small fraction of a nation's territory.

The following example illustrates how increasing or decreasing the number of country-years included in a dataset can make a major difference to substantive findings. Indeed correlations can simply disappear.

One of the most widely publicized findings from the Collier/Hoeffler "Greed and Grievance" article was that there is a strong association between the risk of war and a country's dependence on primary commodities. But missing data, together with the decision to study five-year intervals instead of individual country-years, meant that the authors had to exclude one-third (27 of 79) of the countries in which civil war onsets occurred between 1960 and 1999.[93]

When Fearon reran the statistical tests with a sample that included 16 of the 27 excluded cases, he found that the much-publicized correlation between commodity dependence and the onset of war simply disappeared.[94] The Collier/Hoeffler finding was not robust.[95]

As mentioned previously, if associations are truly robust, like that between income per capita and the risk of war, then minor changes in either datasets or model specifications should make little difference to the findings.

Reliance on Country-Year Data Can Be Problematic

A number of problems arise with reliance on country-year data. The first, which has been noted by many conflict researchers, is the assumption that the observations in each country-year in the dataset are independent of each other. Clearly, in many cases they are not.

Second, the "footprint" of most of today's wars is relatively small, with serious political violence rarely affecting more than a small fraction of a nation's territory.[96] This fact has implications for the overwhelming majority of quantitative studies to date that use the country-year as the unit of analysis. The problem with this practice is that aggregated national data tell us about national averages, but data aggregation at the national level can hide important differences at the subnational level.

This matters because nonaverage conditions at the subnational level—deep poverty among geographically concentrated ethnic minorities, for example—could be associated with an increased risk of war onset. But such subnational differences may well be invisible in nationally aggregated data. In other words, causal relationships may be hidden by the very methodology used to uncover them.

Meeting the Challenges

This review has pointed to a number of important challenges that continue to confront quantitative conflict research and that go some of the way towards explaining the many inconsistent findings produced by conflict models—as well as their weak predictive capability.

Quantitative researchers are of course aware of these challenges and a number of promising new methodological and data initiatives are being developed to address them. Below we note just a few of them. But it is important to remember—as pointed out earlier and demonstrated in the next chapter—that some of the most important findings in this field are in fact both robust and highly policy-relevant.

Understanding Local Conflicts Requires Local Data

We highlighted some of the problems that result from the near-universal reliance on the country-year as the unit of analysis in macro-quantitative conflict research. Today's wars tend to be geographically concentrated and may be driven more by particular socio-economic conditions in the locale of the fighting than by average conditions across the entire country. But until recently, testing this claim with quantitative models was difficult because conflicts were not geo-referenced within countries and it was difficult to access local/regional—as against national—data.

Initiatives in the research community are now addressing these challenges and a number of new datasets have been—or are being—developed to address the knowledge gaps. They include the Armed Conflict Location and Events Dataset (ACLED) that maps the location of a number of conflict-related events,[97] and a new UCDP project that is adding geo-references for conflict locations to existing datasets.[98]

Some of the most innovative quantitative research currently being produced has drawn on household and other survey data generated at the local level, sometimes in conjunction with geo-referenced conflict location data. Notable examples of this so-called micro-quantitative research include studies by Ana Arjona and Stathis Kalyvas on Colombia; Chris Blattman on Uganda; Macartan Humphreys and Jeremy Weinstein on Sierra Leone; and Philip Verwimp on Uganda.[99] Two consortia of researchers are particularly active in this area, namely the Households in Conflict Network and MicroCon.[100]

However, while these studies are providing interesting new insights into particular conflicts, the data on which they rely are available for only a relatively small number of conflicts. This means there is no way of testing whether the findings apply universally.

Addressing the International Dimensions of Intrastate Wars

Most civil war models are based on the assumption that the risk of war can be explained purely in terms of factors and events that are located within individual countries. As Kristian Gleditsch and his colleagues from the Centre for the Study of Civil War (CSCW) at PRIO point out, conflict models rarely take into account transnational factors that may play an important role both in the initial outbreak of civil wars and in their subsequent evolution.[101] The somewhat inconvenient reality is that the conflict dynamics of civil war rarely stop at national boundaries.

Armed conflicts are not distributed evenly around the world; they tend to cluster together geographically. Clustering can arise from spillovers from one country to neighbouring countries—where government forces pursue rebels across borders, for example, or when rebels attack government forces from bases in cross-border sanctuaries.

Gleditsch and his CSCW colleagues have undertaken a number of studies that demonstrate the importance of taking into account the role of transnational actors and neighbourhood effects.[102] The fact that earlier studies tended to ignore transnational actors and neighbourhood effects may help explain some of the divergent findings in the literature.

The internationalization of some intrastate wars is clearly evident in the UCDP/PRIO conflict datasets that count the number of internationalized intrastate conflicts and their battle-death tolls. An intrastate armed conflict becomes an *internationalized intrastate armed conflict* when the government, or an armed group opposing it, receives support, in the form of troops, from one or more foreign states. These conflicts are perhaps the most obvious manifestation of the important role transnational actors can play in wars that are ostensibly intrastate. International intervention in civil wars, as we point out in the next chapter, is associated with elevated battle-death tolls.

Broadening the Scope of Conflict Datasets

In the research literature, armed conflict has traditionally been defined as a violent contestation between a state and another state (interstate war), or a state and a rebel group (civil war). But this very narrow definition left many forms of organized violence uncounted, including armed violence between non-state groups—rebel organizations, community groups, militias, and warlords, for example. The traditional definition also excludes organized violence against civilians—on the grounds that such "one-sided violence" is not armed conflict but rather the slaughter of defenseless individuals. To address these knowledge gaps, HSRP commissioned UCDP to collect data on these two previously uncounted forms of violence. The resulting "non-state armed conflict" and "one-sided violence" datasets are discussed in Part III: Trends in Human Insecurity.

Other researchers are also examining different manifestations of conflict. A new dataset on social conflict in Africa has been compiled by researchers at the University of North Texas. It records a broader spectrum of conflict-related events data than other datasets and includes peaceful protests, riots, communal conflicts, and military coups.[103]

As noted earlier, creating events data datasets is expensive, time-consuming, and error-prone. One way around some of these problems is to create software that automatically codes and records relevant political events. A considerable amount of research has gone into automatic coding with some encouraging results. But to the best of our knowledge, the events data produced by these automated systems have yet to be used in any macro-quantitative conflict models that seek to explain the causes of war.[104]

Building Bridges

Cross-national quantitative research and qualitative analyses of the causes of war and peace are complementary, not contradictory. Neither is sufficient on its own. Case-study material can be particularly valuable in suggesting causal mechanisms whose broad applicability can be tested by quantitative models. Conversely, findings from quantitative research can suggest fruitful lines of enquiry for the analysis of individual conflicts.

In the past there has been relatively little interaction between qualitative and quantitative researchers in this field. Indeed, the two research approaches embody what in many ways are two quite different cultures. As James Mahoney and Gary Goertz put it: "Each has its own values, beliefs, and norms. Each is sometimes privately suspicious or skeptical of the other though usually more publicly polite. Communication across traditions tends to be difficult and marked by misunderstanding."[105]

Mutual skepticism and lack of communication are still common in some quarters, but interest is growing in so-called mixed or multi-methods analyses that seek to marry the strengths of both approaches.[106]

One example of a mixed-methods approach is the two-volume World Bank study edited by Paul Collier and Nicholas Sambanis that tested the findings of the Collier/Hoeffler quantitative model using country case studies.[107] There was some support for the model's findings, but many case-study authors argued that grievances—which the Collier/Hoeffler and Fearon/Laitin models reject as explanatory variables—are important drivers of conflict. This exercise raised questions that have yet to be resolved.

In a study published in 2008, Fearon and Laitin adopted a somewhat different mixed-methods approach. They created narrative case histories of randomly chosen cases of conflict onsets from their dataset and compared the case-study findings with the findings generated by their conflict model. Their study stressed the importance of contingency and human agency factors that are so difficult to include in conflict models:

> The random narratives reinforced our prior belief that a great deal of essentially random historical contingency is involved in determining whether and

exactly when a country will "get" a civil war. Bad luck, idiosyncratic choices by leaders, complicated and ex ante unpredictable political and social interactions may all factor into explaining why a particular civil war started at a particular time, or even at all, in a particular country. It is a historian's project, and an admirable project at that, to try to understand such particularities and idiosyncrasies for particular cases. Our social science project, implausible though it may be, is to try to identify some factors and mechanisms that do "travel" across countries and years, raising the risk of civil war onset in a consistent and appreciable manner.[108]

There are, the authors argue, clear advantages in a creative mix of methods: "Done well, multi-method research combines the strength of large-N designs for identifying empirical regularities and patterns, and the strength of case studies for revealing the causal mechanisms that give rise to political outcomes of interest."[109]

Finally, we note that the micro-quantitative studies discussed earlier are using quantitative methods in what has traditionally been the domain of qualitative research on the causes of war, namely case studies of conflict dynamics in a single country. Here the prospects for collaboration and cross-fertilization of ideas are promising since both quantitative and qualitative researchers are studying essentially the same phenomena.

Conclusion

In this review we have suggested that quantitative conflict research continues to confront major methodological and data challenges that raise questions about the utility of many—but not all—of its research findings for policy-makers. We have also noted that some of the most innovative work in the field is being devoted to addressing these challenges.

In this context, it is interesting to note this thought-provoking cautionary note issued by Paul Collier, Anke Hoeffler, and Dominic Rohner, writing in *Oxford Economic Papers* in 2009. Quantitative analysis, they argue, "should be seen as complementing qualitative in-country research rather than supplanting it."[110]

In Chapter 3 we investigate further the association between income levels, state capacity, and peace. In Chapter 4 we examine one of the most controversial assertions to emerge from quantitative conflict research, namely that grievances have no causal impact on the risk of armed conflict.

CHAPTER 3

The East Asian Peace

Over the past three decades, East Asia has undergone an extraordinary transformation.[111] From 1946 to the end of the 1970s, it was the most war-wracked region in the world. Today it is enjoying "the most broadly peaceful era in its history."[112] It has been free of international conflict for almost two decades and is now one of the least violent regions in the international system.

This chapter seeks to explain this transformation. It examines the decline in the number of armed conflicts in the region and the drivers of the far more dramatic, though uneven, decline in battle deaths since the late 1970s.

The analysis starts with a description of the changing trends in the number and deadliness of armed conflicts in the region before examining the major policy shifts by the US, the Soviet Union, and China during the 1970s that sharply reduced the level of external intervention in the region. This in turn led to the steep and rapid decline in war death tolls.

By the 1980s, Northeast Asia was free of major armed conflict.[113] The remaining conflicts in Southeast Asia started to decline in 1979, a process that would see their number almost halve by the mid-1990s.

In explaining the reduction in the number of civil conflicts in Southeast Asia, we cite both the ending of Chinese support for the communist insurgencies in the subregion and the security implications of the unparalleled period of economic growth the region has experienced since the 1950s.

As noted in Chapter 2, the single-most robust finding in the cross-national statistical literature on civil wars is that increased levels of economic development are associated with a declining risk of intrastate conflict. As national economies grow, state capacities—political, economic, and administrative, as well as military—grow with them. Because rebels are largely excluded from the benefits of increased economic growth, the balance of resources relevant to winning civil wars will, over time, tend to favour governments.

There is one more rather remarkable feature of East Asia's recent strategic history, one that is directly related to the growth in the capacity of regional governments that is worth noting. Insurgent armies have not scored a single military victory in the region since the end of the Vietnam War and the Khmer Rouge's rise and fall in Cambodia in the 1970s—nor is there any prospect of them doing so in the foreseeable future.[114] This finding not only has important implications for the region's security future but, as we point out later, it stands in sharp contrast to two major studies that have argued that incumbent governments around the world are increasingly on the losing side in their struggles against violent insurgencies.

The increased levels of development in the region have been matched since the mid-1970s by a dramatic, though not universal, increase in democratization within its states. Democratization, like development, has important security implications since inclusive democracies rarely go to war against each other and are associated with a relatively low risk of civil war.

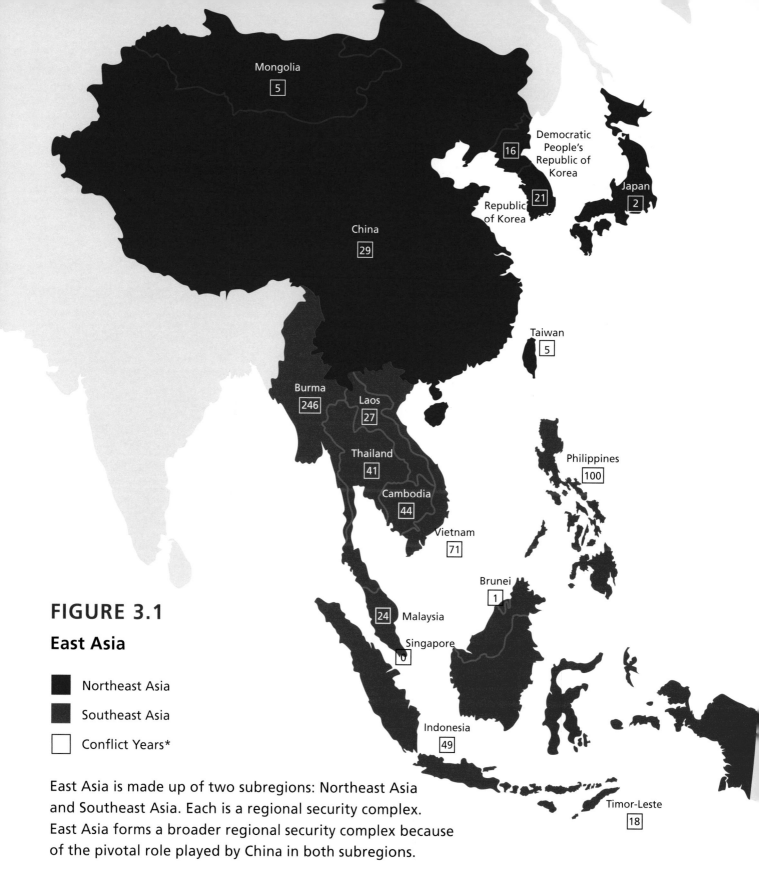

FIGURE 3.1

East Asia

- ⬛ Northeast Asia
- ⬛ Southeast Asia
- ☐ Conflict Years*

East Asia is made up of two subregions: Northeast Asia and Southeast Asia. Each is a regional security complex. East Asia forms a broader regional security complex because of the pivotal role played by China in both subregions.

Conflict years indicate the war-proneness of a particular country.

Conflict years are calculated by counting the number of state-based armed conflicts that a country experienced between 1946 and 2008, and then summing the number of years each conflict was active. For example, if a country experienced one conflict that lasted 20 years, and another that lasted one year, the country would have experienced 21 conflict years. The result is the same regardless of whether the conflicts occurred in the same or different years.

Data Source: UCDP/PRIO.[115]

The Case for Analyzing Conflict Dynamics at the Regional Level

This chapter has a broader purpose than simply determining the causes of peace in East Asia. We also seek to demonstrate the analytic value of taking the region as the "level of analysis" when attempting to understand the drivers of political violence in the post-World War II world.

In the previous chapter, we argued that case studies of individual countries can provide deep insights into the causes of particular conflicts but cannot—by definition—tell us about the factors that in general increase the probablity of a country succumbing to war.

Statistical analyses of cross-national country-year data taken over several decades, on the other hand, can tell us about general risk factors, but they rarely provide a useful guide to understanding particular conflicts.

Between the two extremes of single-country case studies and cross-national statistical analysis at the global level lies the "middle-range" of regional security analysis. Taking a regional approach to understanding the causes of war and peace can be fruitful for several reasons.

The trend in the number of armed conflicts in East Asia is quite different from the global trend.

First, regional states tend to share important commonalities in history, interaction, culture, and levels of development. They tend to have more in common than states in the more heterogeneous international system. It is not surprising, therefore, that rich, democratic, and economically interdependent countries in Western Europe should have a very different conflict risk profile from those in mostly poor sub-Saharan Africa.

Second, as we noted in the previous chapter, most of the big cross-national statistical studies of the risk of war assume that the causes of civil war are internal to individual states. But the Northeast and Southeast Asian subregions, shown in Figure 3.1, form what Barry Buzan and Ole Wæver call *regional security complexes*, by which they mean collectivities of states or other actors whose security concerns are so interlinked that they "cannot reasonably be analyzed or resolved apart from one another."[116]

East Asia as a whole also constitutes a regional security complex because of the pivotal security role China plays in

both Northeast and Southeast Asia. Cross-national statistical studies that ignore these linkages—as most do—are unlikely to provide compelling explanations of changing patterns of regional conflict.

Third, as Figure 3.2 reveals, the trend in the number of armed conflicts in East Asia is quite different from the global trend. From the early 1950s to the beginning of the 1990s, conflict numbers in the rest of the world increased eightfold but then dropped sharply. However, as Figure 3.2 shows, in East Asia conflict numbers started to drop in the late 1970s, more than a decade before the global decline.

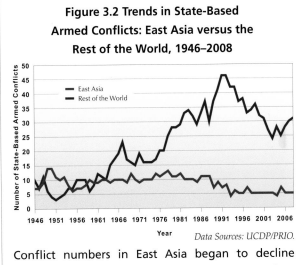

Figure 3.2 Trends in State-Based Armed Conflicts: East Asia versus the Rest of the World, 1946–2008

Data Sources: UCDP/PRIO.

Conflict numbers in East Asia began to decline in 1979; in the rest of the world they more than doubled between 1977 and 1991.

In the next chapter, we argue that changes set in motion by the ending of the Cold War provide the most compelling explanation for the global decline in conflict numbers that started in the 1990s. But they clearly do not explain the earlier decline in East Asia. Understanding this requires an analysis of regional security dynamics.

The three different levels of analysis—global, regional, and individual country—offer complementary, though sometimes quite different, insights into the drivers of war and peace. In post-World War II East Asia, armed conflict trends were driven in part by political and economic forces from outside the region—from decolonization and the geopolitics of the Cold War, to the dramatic increase in international trade and foreign direct investment (FDI) that accelerated the pace of economic development. However, trends in conflict numbers were also deeply affected by the interrelated security policies and interests of regional states.

Why Focus on East Asia?

There are several reasons to focus on East Asia:

- Security developments in East Asia are intrinsically important to an understanding of global security. More people were killed by warfare in this region from 1946 to 2008 than in all the other regions of the world combined over the same period. And as Figure 3.3 clearly shows, while most battle deaths around the world in the first three decades of the post-World War II period occurred in East Asia, since then the battle-death toll in the region has constituted a small-to-negligible share of the global total.

- The dramatic decline in conflict numbers, and the even greater decline in war deaths, in the region since the mid-1970s has received curiously little attention in the scholarly community.[117]

- East Asia's post-World War II history provides a striking illustration of the enormous impact that external intervention—and stopping it—can have on battle-death tolls.

- East Asia provides a compelling illustration of the thesis that economic development is a critically important form of long-term conflict prevention. The number of completely new civil war onsets in the region was substantially lower between 1980 and 2008 than during the previous 30-odd years, while the number of ongoing conflicts dropped by more than half between the late 1970s and the mid-1990s.

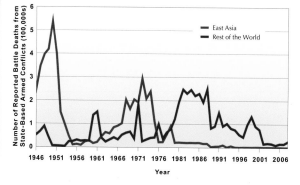

Figure 3.3 Trends in Reported Battle Deaths from State-Based Armed Conflicts: East Asia versus the Rest of the World, 1946–2008

Data Sources: PRIO; UCDP/HSRP Dataset.[118]

East Asia accounts for the majority of the global battle-death toll for the period 1946 to 2008. However, for the last 30 years, East Asia has been much more peaceful.

Trends in Political Violence in Northeast and Southeast Asia, 1946–1979

Over the past 60 years, there has been a series of remarkable changes in the East Asian security landscape. From 1946 until the late-1970s, the number of conflicts in East Asia nearly doubled; over the next three decades they more than halved. There have also been significant changes in the predominant forms of conflict and the associated battle-death tolls as illustrated in Figure 3.4.

Figure 3.4 shows that the deadliest conflicts were concentrated in two periods. Between 1946 and 1954, the conflicts with the largest death tolls were the Chinese Civil War (1946–1949), the anticolonial struggles in French Indochina (1946–1954),[119] and the Korean War (1950–1953).

Since the 1950s, there has been no more civil war in China, while the two Koreas, although remaining in a state of mutual hostility, have avoided further warfare. By the late 1950s, the wars associated with the ending of colonial rule—all of which were in Southeast Asia—were over. The anticolonial nationalists had prevailed, the colonial powers had largely withdrawn, and an important source of conflict and instability in the region had ceased to exist.[120]

The next period of high-fatality warfare was from the mid-1960s to the mid-1970s. Here most of the killing took place in Vietnam, where the US and its allies, including South Vietnam, were engaged in a bloody, but ultimately futile, war against North Vietnam and the revolutionary forces of the southern-based National Liberation Front, both of which were supported by Moscow and Beijing. More people were killed in this war than in any other during the entire post-World War II period.

The last major upsurge of fighting during this period was in 1979, the first year of a series of border clashes between China and Vietnam that lasted for most of the 1980s. Chinese forces had invaded Vietnam in response to the Vietnamese invasion of Cambodia and overthrow of the Khmer Rouge regime, which was a Chinese client state.

Each of the high-fatality conflicts in the region—the Chinese Civil War, the Korean War, the war in French Indochina, and the Vietnam War—was characterized by a high level of foreign involvement, driven by the geopolitics of the Cold War. The Chinese, the Soviets, and the US (and sometimes its allies) committed either combat forces or massive military and economic assistance—or both. In each case the importation of large numbers of major conventional weapons—aircraft, tanks, long-range artillery, and sometimes combat forces—to the battlefield drove the death tolls up.

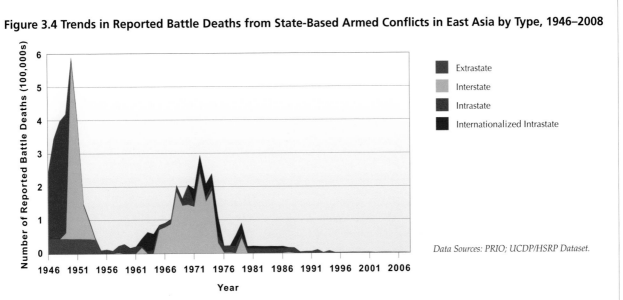

Figure 3.4 Trends in Reported Battle Deaths from State-Based Armed Conflicts in East Asia by Type, 1946–2008

Legend:
- Extrastate
- Interstate
- Intrastate
- Internationalized Intrastate

Data Sources: PRIO; UCDP/HSRP Dataset.

Intrastate—or civil—conflicts have been the most numerous, and with the notable exception of the Chinese Civil war, the least deadly form of conflict in East Asia. Interstate conflicts have been the least frequent but the most deadly form of conflict. The Vietnamese struggle against the French was the most deadly anti-colonial conflict, the other extrastate conflicts in the region had many fewer causalities. Internationalized intrastate conflicts—civil conflicts in which armed forces of other states support one or more of the warring parties—have, like interstate and extrastate conflicts, disappeared from East Asia. They were at their deadliest in the 1960s and 1970s.

Note: Figure 3.4 is a "stacked graph," meaning that the number of battle deaths in each category is indicated by the depth of the band of colour. The top line shows the total number of battle deaths of all types in each year.

Ending Major Power Interventionism in East Asia

America's defeat in Vietnam had a deep impact on US security policy. The US military had won most of the battles it fought in Vietnam but lost the war because its political capability to continue fighting had been eroded by rising popular and elite opposition to the war at home. Unable politically to continue to wage war, America's vast military power became strategically irrelevant.

Vietnam demonstrated to Washington just how difficult it was to sustain public support for costly wars against distant enemies that posed no direct threat to the US. Even before the war was over, the Nixon Doctrine had signalled that the US would no longer provide combat forces for Vietnam-type conflicts.[121] In Richard Nixon's words, there would be "no more Vietnams."[122] Since 1975 the US has not intervened militarily with major conventional forces anywhere in East Asia.[123]

The Nixon Doctrine was not the only radical policy shift by a major power in the region. Although the Soviet Union had given military aid to North Vietnam during the Vietnam

War, its influence in East Asia, which was already weak, dwindled still further after the war ended. From the 1980s onwards, active conflicts in the region were concentrated in Southeast Asia where Moscow's influence was minimal.

The shift in China's regional policy was equally far-reaching—but more complicated. With the death of Mao Tse-tung, and under the leadership of the pragmatic Deng Xiaoping, Beijing had decisively downgraded, or completely ended, its remaining support to communist rebel groups in Southeast Asia.

There were several reasons for this major shift in policy.

First, China's policy of supporting revolutionary movements in the region was already failing. The rebel groups in Southeast Asia that Beijing had been assisting were weak and on the defensive, and Chinese enthusiasm for supporting them was waning in part for this reason. None had any realistic chance of prevailing.

And the domino theory propounded by US conservatives, which had predicted that victory for the communists in "Indochina" would lead other Southeast Asian countries to succumb to communist-led rebellions, turned out to be hopelessly wrong.

Second, with the US defeat in Vietnam, China had much less reason to be concerned about US interventionism in its border regions.

Third, and most important, was the major shift in Chinese economic policy associated with the Four Modernizations program and driven by the pragmatic new leadership in Beijing that had taken power after Mao Tse-tung's death. Economic modernization required increased access to Western markets, investment, and technology, which in turn required good relations with both the West and other states in the region. The need to improve relations with the Association of Southeast Asian Nations (ASEAN) states provided further incentives for China to stop its support for rebel movements in Southeast Asia, a policy that had understandably angered governments in the subregion.[124]

Whatever weight is accorded to these different explanations, the results are not in doubt. By the early 1980s, China's policy of military interventionism had come to an end, with the exception of some relatively minor border clashes with Vietnam. In the last three decades, China has not launched a major military operation outside its borders, and Beijing

has ceased to provide material support to rebel movements in the region, with the exception of its support for the Khmer Rouge in Cambodia that continued into the 1980s. Today China's economic power, and its willingness to use it for political ends, is a far more powerful source of leverage than its military power.

With the US defeat in Vietnam, China had less reason to be concerned about US interventionism in its border region.

The ending of major-power military interventionism in East Asia led to a steep reduction in the level of political violence in the region.

As Figure 3.4 clearly shows, the battle-death toll dropped sharply following the ending of the Vietnam War in 1975, and again after the 1979 border war between China and Vietnam. The change over a very short period of time was remarkable. There were close to 300,000 battle deaths in East Asia in the peak year of the Vietnam War in 1972. In 1980 there were some 20,000 battle deaths.

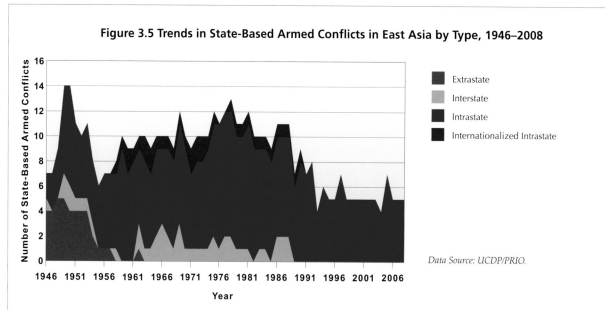

Figure 3.5 Trends in State-Based Armed Conflicts in East Asia by Type, 1946–2008

Legend:
- Extrastate
- Interstate
- Intrastate
- Internationalized Intrastate

Data Source: UCDP/PRIO.

In East Asia, the wars of colonial independence were over by the early 1960s. The last two—comparatively minor—interstate conflicts ended in the 1980s. Internationalized intrastate conflicts came to an end in the early 1990s. For the last 18 years, all conflicts in the region have been intrastate conflicts, and all have taken place in Southeast Asia.

Note: Figure 3.5 is a "stacked graph," meaning that the number of conflicts in each category is indicated by the depth of the band of colour. The top line shows the total number of conflicts of all types in each year.

In 1978 there were 13 conflicts being waged in the region; by the mid-1990s, there were just five. The ending of the modest level of Chinese support for communist insurgencies in Southeast Asia played a minor role in this decline.[125]

A recent study by David Cunningham of civil wars between 1945 and 2004 found that conflicts in which there was external intervention lasted twice as long on average as those in which there was none.[126] Where rebel groups have relied on external support, and that support has been withdrawn, then—other things being equal—the military balance will shift in favour of the government forces and the rebels are likely to lose.

However, as we argue, the ending of external support for the communist insurgencies in Southeast Asia is not a sufficient explanation for the decline in armed conflict numbers in the subregion. With the exception of Vietnam and Cambodia, Chinese aid to fraternal parties in the 1970s had always been extremely modest. Furthermore, the communist insurgencies in Burma, Indonesia, and Thailand were facing major challenges prior to China's decision to cease support.

Conflict in East Asia in the Post-Vietnam Era

With the exception of the brief engagements between China and Vietnam along Vietnam's northern border, all the conflicts that have been fought since the early 1980s have been in Southeast Asia. In 1980 there were nine intrastate conflicts in the subregion and one interstate conflict. The former included five conflicts in Burma, two in the Philippines, and one each in Thailand and Indonesia.

Figure 3.5 shows a few episodes of interstate armed conflict in the region continuing into the 1980s. Border clashes between China and Vietnam continued throughout the decade and there was a very brief low-level conflict between Thailand and Laos. The death tolls from these conflicts were so small compared with earlier wars that they are not even visible in Figure 3.4.

One internationalized intrastate conflict continued into the 1980s—that in Cambodia, where Vietnamese troops had maintained a considerable military presence since the late 1970s.

In 2008 there were just five ongoing conflicts in the region—less than half as many as in 1980. All were in Southeast Asia. Two were in Burma, still the poorest country in the subregion, two were located in impoverished rural areas of the Philippines, and there was one Muslim separatist conflict in southern Thailand. Islamist terrorism in Indonesia generated a great deal of media coverage but by early 2011 appears to have been largely contained.[127]

Explaining the Decline in Conflict Numbers

The end of major power interventions in East Asia provides the most compelling explanation for the dramatic drop in battle deaths in the region that started as the Vietnam War ended. As noted above, however, the end of intervention does not provide a compelling explanation for the decline in conflict numbers—the level of external Chinese support for the Southeast Asian insurgencies was simply too low.

What else might account for the 60 percent decline in conflict numbers from 1978 to the mid-1990s in Southeast Asia[128]—and for the absence of civil war in Northeast Asia during this period and subsequently?

An important part of the answer is to be found in the decades-long increase in economic development in most countries in the region.

As we noted earlier, the most robust finding in the statistical literature on the causes of war is that there is a close association between levels of economic development and the risk of armed conflict. As national per capita incomes rise, the risk of war declines. "Per capita income," James Fearon has noted, "is the single best predictor of a country's odds of civil war outbreak, empirically dominating other factors."[129]

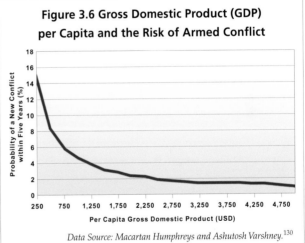

Figure 3.6 Gross Domestic Product (GDP) per Capita and the Risk of Armed Conflict

Data Source: Macartan Humphreys and Ashutosh Varshney.[130]

There is a strong association between levels of economic development and the risk of armed conflict: the poorer the country, the greater the risk.

The association between income and conflict risk is evident in Figure 3.6. Here we can see that the probability of succumbing to conflict within five years for countries with a per capita income of USD 250 is approximately 15 percent. For countries with a per capita income of some USD 5,000, the five-year risk is around 1 percent—a huge reduction. These are average risks, of course. Individual countries will have different risk profiles.

The evidence from East Asia in the post-Vietnam War era appears to confirm this association. From the late 1970s to the mid-1990s, average incomes in East Asia almost doubled, while conflict numbers more than halved, as Figure 3.7 indicates.

The claim that factors associated with rising incomes have caused conflict numbers to fall in East Asia confronts one obvious objection, however. Figure 3.7 clearly shows that from the 1950s to the end of the 1970s, average incomes in the region had increased just as steadily as they had in the 1980s and beyond. Yet, conflict numbers did not decrease between the mid-1950s and the late 1970s, they doubled. If the peace-through-development thesis was correct, then we would expect conflict numbers to have declined in the earlier period as well as the latter.

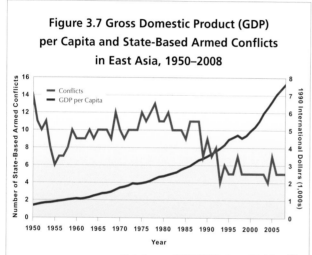

Figure 3.7 Gross Domestic Product (GDP) per Capita and State-Based Armed Conflicts in East Asia, 1950–2008

Data Sources: UCDP/PRIO; Angus Maddison.[131]

Although incomes have been increasing in East Asia since the 1950s, conflict numbers did not start to decline until 1979. Prior to this, the security dynamics of the Cold War overwhelmed the conflict-reducing effects of rising incomes.

This is a valid point. It is in fact very difficult to determine the independent effect of development versus other factors in reducing the number and deadliness of conflicts in the region and—perhaps more importantly—in preventing completely new conflicts from starting.

The increase in conflict numbers in the earlier period was driven in part by the interventionist policies of the major powers and in part by the struggles for control over the post-colonial state in Southeast Asia. The conflict-reducing effects of

rising incomes were likely present during this period, but they clearly were not strong enough to overcome the geopolitics of the Cold War and other dynamics that were driving the number, duration, and deadliness of conflicts upwards. When major power interventions ceased, the conflict-reducing impact of rising levels of economic development became apparent as conflict numbers began to fall and the number of new conflicts starting dropped sharply.

As noted previously, conflict numbers in the region had dropped from 13 in 1978 to five by the mid-1990s. We would also expect the effect of higher incomes to be reflected in an even greater reduction in civil war onsets. This is in fact what the data show. From 1951 to 1979, 12 new intrastate conflicts started; from 1980 to 2008, there were just three—a 75 percent reduction.

Why Rising Levels of Development Bring About Peace

Although there is a strong consensus in the research community that rising per capita incomes are associated with reduced risks of conflict, there is much less agreement as to why this should be the case. Income in itself is clearly not the driver—money is simply a medium of exchange. It is what is done with money, and the incentive structures that are associated with it, that matters. It is here that the disagreements lie.

Paul Collier and Anke Hoeffler argue that income levels are important because they determine the economic opportunity costs of joining a rebellion. When incomes are very low, the perceived benefits of joining a rebel group—especially for young unemployed males living on the edge of survival—may be high enough to outweigh the potential costs, which include getting captured, imprisoned, killed, or wounded.[132] The benefits of joining a rebel group include access to food, guns, excitement, comradeship, and the possibility of loot. As Collier puts it:

> Young men, who are the recruits for rebel armies, come pretty cheap in an environment of hopeless poverty. Life itself is cheap, and joining a rebel movement gives these young men a small chance of riches.[133]

But as Chris Blattman has pointed out, while plausible and having some empirical support, as a universal proposition this argument is not very compelling: "The people who riot or rebel are poor, unemployed young men. We can see that. The problem is that the people who don't riot are also poor, unemployed young men."[134]

THE EAST ASIAN PEACE: DIFFERENT ANALYTIC PERSPECTIVES

The East Asian civil peace has received relatively little attention in the scholarly community. What has been written has tended to focus on the abscence of international conflict in the region.

In the case of Northeast Asia, the focus of the scholarly work has primarily been the risk of interstate war. Realists have explained the absence of war in the subregion as resulting in large part from the deterrent effect of US forces in the region and the protective "nuclear umbrella" over Washington's allies in South Korea and Japan.[135]

Other researchers have pointed to increased elite interactions, and a related process of confidence-building among subregional powers, that are intended to reduce the risk of crises that escalate out of control.[136] The two explanations are complementary—deterrence strategies are not risk-free; confidence-building measures are designed in part to reduce the "security dilemma" risks associated with deterrence policies.[137]

A third—and related—theme in the literature on Northeast Asian security has been the question of whether or not China has become a status-quo power.[138] Here researchers, drawing on the liberal theories discussed in Chapter 1, have argued that as China has become more integrated into the global economy, it has gained a growing stake in the stability of the international system. This is evident in Beijing's growing and generally constructive involvement in multilateral fora, both at the regional and global level; in its aid and investment policies in the developing world; and in its growing participation in UN (United Nations) peace operations.

These developments support the contention that China is a status-quo military power with a vested interest in avoiding war.[139] Beijing can, of course, use its growing economic power as an instrument of political suasion and sometimes coercion. Indeed, the Chinese use their economic leverage to greater effect, over far greater distances, and at far less risk, than would be the case if they relied on coercive military power.

Analysts of security in Southeast Asia, by contrast, have focused on very different factors in explaining the 30-year absence of major interstate conflict in the subregion. Here the analysis has centred on the achievements of subregional institutions—notably the Association of Southeast Asian Nations (ASEAN) and on what has become known as the "ASEAN Way"—in reducing the level of conflict in the subregion.[140]

In the early years of the Cold War, the Southeast Asian subregion was a collectivity of states afflicted by violent ethnic conflicts, anticolonial struggles, communist insurgencies, and bitter intraregional territorial disputes.[141]

The central elements of the ASEAN Way are a strong norm against interference in the affairs of other regional states, informal elite networking, and the promotion of habits of consultation, dialogue, and consensus-building. But ASEAN's focus has been primarily on reducing the risk of interstate conflicts. It has been difficult for the organization to address intrastate conflicts at the subregional level because of the norm against intervening in the domestic affairs of member states.

In both Northeast and Southeast Asia, increased levels of economic interdependence have been associated with steadily rising levels of economic development at the national level. Economic development has become a paramount national goal for regional states whose leaders share a common interest in avoiding anything that threatens the trade and investment relationships on which development depends.

A 2007 econometric study by Benjamin E. Goldsmith found that "the importance of economic interdependence for reducing conflict in Asia [is] robustly confirmed."[142]

Proponents of the democratic peace thesis also point to the dramatic, though far from complete, growth in the number of democracies throughout the region. This again is another development associated with reduced risks of armed conflict.

We certainly do not discount the importance of these approaches, but they apply primarily to interstate wars that effectively came to an end in the region three decades ago.[143] Our analysis focuses on the dramatic reduction in the deadliness of warfare in the region—which none of the above approaches attempts to explain—and on the role of economic development in driving intrastate conflict numbers downwards.

Moreover, rebels are not necessarily motivated by narrow material self-interest as the opportunity-costs argument suggests. Country case studies make it clear that ideology, deeply held grievances, and the altruistic desire to create a more just society have also been major factors driving recruitment in many rebellions.[144]

Most recent research has focused on income per capita as a proxy variable for various elements of state capacity that determines the feasibility of rebellion rather than on the opportunity costs for poor unemployed young men. Here the argument, in essence, is that more affluent states have the resources to crush rebel groups, buy off their leaders, and address the grievances of their supporters. Poor states, which lack these resources, find it far more difficult to deter or otherwise prevent wars, or to stop those that cannot be prevented.

The state-capacity argument gained a growing following after the publication of James Fearon and David Laitin's seminal "Ethnicity, Insurgency and Civil War" article in the *American Political Science Review* in 2003.[145] A subsequent study by Fearon prepared for the World Bank's 2011 *World Development Report* tested the state capacity thesis directly by examining the association between the quality of governance measured by three separate datasets and the risk of conflict onsets. The tests revealed that the quality of governance was strongly associated with reduced risks of conflict onsets.[146]

Case studies show that ideology and deeply held grievances have been factors driving recruitment in rebellions.

Fearon and Laitin do not disagree that the opportunity costs for joining a rebellion may be one determinant of civil war. But they argue that "economic variables such as per capita income matter primarily because they proxy for state administrative, military, and police capabilities."[147] Here the focus is not on the incentives and disincentives for individuals to join rebel groups but rather on state strength—the ability of governments to deter or otherwise prevent wars, and win those that cannot be prevented.

"Ethnicity, Insurgency and Civil War" stresses the critical role of the coercive capacity of the state in determining the probability of civil war. "Most important for the prospects of a nascent insurgency," the authors argue, "*are the government's police and military capabilities and the reach of government institutions into rural areas.*"[148]

Coercive state power reduces the feasibility of rebellion. If rebels are denied the opportunity to mount successful insurgencies, then addressing rebel motives—particularly grievances—becomes unnecessary.

In this context, it is interesting to note that neither Fearon and Laitin nor Collier and Hoeffler have had much to say about conflict resolution strategies. The logic of their position is clear enough. If grievances are not a major cause of conflict, as these authors have maintained, then addressing them will not prevent wars or stop those that cannot be prevented. We return to this contentious issue in Chapter 4.

Why State Capacity Matters

Although Fearon and Laitin stress the importance of coercive state capacities in deterring and defeating insurgencies, their own research findings suggest that other capacities may be as, or more, important.

The problem for governments that confront the small rural insurgencies that are typical of Southeast Asia today lies not with any inability to defeat rebel forces in battle—even the weakest state armies in Southeast Asia are capable of this—but in locating them.[149] As long as the insurgents remain relatively few in number, they can be hard to find while posing no threat to the state. Given that the insurgents are so difficult to locate, and given that they represent no serious threat to public order, let alone the security of the state, governments have few incentives to embark on difficult and costly campaigns to defeat them. The result is an uneasy strategic equilibrium that can last for years.[150] This in part explains why the decline in conflict numbers in Southeast Asia levelled out in the mid-1990s.

The fact that locating insurgents, rather than defeating them, is the critical strategic challenge suggests, as noted above, that the military capability of states may not be as important as Fearon and Laitin argue. In this context, Cullen Hendrix notes that "the state's ability to put boots and arms in the field" may matter less than its ability to collect and manage information.[151]

However, collecting and managing security information—intelligence in other words—is only one of the elements of state capacity that can be used to help prevent conflicts and bring those that cannot be prevented to an end. And this is where the argument about the security impact of rising incomes becomes most relevant.

Economic development increases state capacity via increased tax revenues. These in turn provide states with the political and economic resources to prevent rebellions—by buying off grievances or through political co-optation—and to

an estimated 300,000 in all, crossed the Yalu and joined the fighting.[171] Some 425,000 troops fought under the UN flag, including approximately 178,000 Americans.[172] Overall, the communist side had well in excess of a million men under arms.

Once again the predictable effect of bringing tens of thousands of foreign troops and the transfer of huge numbers of major conventional weapons into the Korean theatre was a rapid escalation in the battle-death toll. Although estimates of the overall casualties vary, a thorough review of the sources suggests that the conflict resulted in around 1 million battle deaths.[173]

The Vietnam War (1965–1975)

Although most accounts of the US war in Vietnam focus on the period from 1965 to 1975, Washington's political and military involvement in South Vietnam had started much earlier. In 1955 a "US Military Assistance Advisor Group" took over responsibility for training South Vietnamese forces from the French.[174] In 1957 a new guerrilla insurgency started in the South, supported by the North.

America's military involvement in South Vietnam steadily increased in the early 1960s. By the end of 1963, there were some 16,000 US military "advisors" in the South. In March 1965 the first official combat troops arrived in Saigon. Over the next four years, US troop numbers climbed steadily, reaching a peak of 543,000 in April 1969, by which time more than 33,000 Americans had already been killed.[175] Political opposition to the war at home increased as the US body count rose.

In January 1969 peace talks began in Paris and the US started withdrawing its forces as part of a doomed "Vietnamization" plan to make Saigon take responsibility for running a war the US could not win. In January 1973 the Paris Peace Accords were signed, officially ending the war. Two months later the last American troops left Vietnam.

In early 1975 North Vietnam, assured of victory now that US troops had been withdrawn and the US Congress had banned any further US military involvement in Vietnam, stepped up its efforts to conquer the South.

On 29 April 1975, as the North Vietnamese army began its final assault on Saigon, the US was forced to mount a humiliating last-minute air evacuation of its remaining personnel and some South Vietnamese who had worked with the US.[176]

The estimated battle-death toll in the Vietnam War of more than 1.6 million—the largest of any war in the post-World War II period—was driven on the US side by a decade of sustained use of huge numbers of imported heavy conventional weapons that included bombers, tanks, long-range artillery, and rockets.

North Vietnam received massive supplies of similar matériel from Russia and China. The fact that the bombing tonnage dropped by US aircraft during the war was far greater than the total tonnage dropped by the US in all theatres of the war in World War II was indicative of the scale of the destruction.[177]

The impact of the war on the US military was significant. By war's end almost 3 million Americans had served in Vietnam, some 58,000 were dead—more than in Korea—and 150,000 had been seriously injured.[178]

The lesson US military leaders drew from their Vietnam experience was that fighting wars against foes that pose no direct military threat to the US, but generate large numbers of American fatalities, will inevitably lose elite and public support in the US and thus become unwinnable.

The Vietnam War was the last US military intervention in Southeast Asia.

After Vietnam

After the US quit Vietnam in 1975, and the short-lived Chinese border war with Vietnam came to an end in 1979, there was a dramatic change in the regional security climate. Major power interventions in the region effectively ceased. Northeast Asia has been essentially conflict-free ever since—apart from minor border clashes between Vietnam and China in the 1980s.

The armed conflicts that remain are relatively minor rural insurgencies in Southeast Asia that are being fought mostly with small arms and light weapons. The rebel groups involved in these conflicts have few sources of external support and the fighting tends to be sporadic and results in low battle-death tolls. In none of these conflicts do the rebels pose a serious threat to incumbent governments.

governments prevailed over surgents in some 67 percent of the civil conflicts that ended in formal victories.[179]

However, UCDP's stringent coding rules mean that the true extent of government victories is underestimated. A conflict termination is only coded as a victory if one warring party is "either defeated or eliminated, or otherwise succumbs to the power of the other through capitulation or public announcement."[180] But in many cases insurgents simply give up, stop fighting, and merge quietly back into civil society without being militarily defeated. These terminations are not counted as formal victories, but they are clearly de facto wins for the government.[181] It follows that the actual share of government wins from 1946 to 2007 should be even larger than the 67 percent that comes from counting formal victories alone.

While UCDP's coding rules tend to underestimate the number of actual government victories, the coding rules that Lyall and Wilson, and Arreguin-Toft rely on considerably over-estimate rebel victories—at least for the post-World War II period that is the focus of this chapter.

Lyall and Wilson count draws (which include peace settlements) as incumbent losses. But while it is true that peace agreements invariably involve concessions by the incumbent government, this does not mean the incumbent has been defeated—defeat would mean that the insurgents had seized power and had become the government. Draws, however defined, do not lead to a change of government and, given this, it is quite unclear why they should normally be considered insurgent victories. (The only exception is found with secessionist conflicts. Here of course rebels can gain independence—a form of victory—without the incumbent government being displaced. But secessionist victories are extraordinarily rare.)

Arreguin-Toft's coding rules overestimate weak actor victories to an even greater degree. Like Lyall and Wilson, he not only counts stalemates (draws) as strong actor defeats, but he also assumes that all ongoing conflicts are also defeats for the strong actors.

There is little evidence to support this latter assumption. The UCDP terminations data indicate that government losses to insurgents account for only 9 percent of all conflict termi-nations in the post-1946 period. We have no reason to believe that this share will grow dramatically when the conflicts being waged today come to an end. There is, in other words, no good reason to count ongoing wars as rebel victories.

The findings of these two studies, and our analysis of UCDP's terminations data, have important, but very different, security implications. If Lyall and Wilson and Arreguin-Toft

are correct and insurgents are winning most wars today, there may well be an emulation effect, with insurgent victories in one country encouraging further insurgencies elsewhere. There is ample evidence in the recent historical record to indicate that rebel success in one country tends to be emulated in other countries.[182]

If, on the other hand, the analysis based on the UCDP terminations data is correct, as we believe is the case, the historical evidence suggests that the high percentage of government victories may over time deter would-be rebels from starting new insurgencies. Since the end of World War II, failed insurgent strategies have tended to discourage emulation elsewhere—the failure of the Che Guevara-inspired guerrilla *foco* strategy in Latin America, and the weak and abortive neo-Marxist "urban guerrilla" campaigns in Europe in the 1960s and 1970s being cases in point.

Wars Without End?

As noted previously, East Asia has seen only three new intrastate conflicts in the last three decades. However, when we look at the number of conflicts that stop and then start again, a rather different picture emerges. No fewer than 22 of the 25 conflicts that started between 1980 and 2008 were reoccurrences.

What explains this pattern of conflict recurrence? There are several possible explanations, some general and some specific to the region:

- Armed conflicts tend to exacerbate the conditions that caused them in the first place, while the experience of war tends to heighten hostility between the warring parties.
- Insurgent groups may stop fighting for a period for purely tactical reasons—typically in order to regroup and rebuild the resources needed to continue the armed struggle more effectively at a later date.
- Many of the conflicts that have recurred in Southeast Asia have very low annual battle-death tolls. This means that small increases or decreases in fatalities can easily cause overall battle-death numbers to move above or below the 25-battle-deaths-per-year threshold that determines whether or not a conflict is recorded. When this happens, we see a pattern of conflict episodes formally stopping and then starting again but with very little real change on the ground.

But perhaps the most persuasive reason for the recur-rence of these minor conflicts is that while insurgents lack the power to defeat governments, governments often lack strong incentives to defeat the insurgents.

IS REPRESSION AN EFFECTIVE TOOL OF COUNTERINSURGENCY?

Writing in *Harper's Magazine* in February 2007, Edward Luttwak outlined what he called an "easy and reliable way of defeating all insurgencies everywhere."[183] All that is needed, he argued, is to "out-terrorize the insurgents, so that the fear of reprisals outweighs the [citizens'] desire to help the insurgents."[184]

The target of Luttwak's critique was the assumption—one that is central to the current US counterinsurgency doctrine—that government forces need to have popular support in order to defeat insurgents.[185]

Not so, says Luttwak, pointing out that for centuries rebels have been defeated by the use of violent repression. The repression often takes the form of barbaric collective punishments imposed on civilians in order to deter them from supporting the insurgents.

Counterinsurgent forces, according to this thesis, need obedience—not support—from the population in order to quell rebellions. And obedience can be coerced by resort to lethal violence.

Luttwak argues that willingness to use large-scale violent repression enabled the rulers of the Roman and Ottoman empires, and the Nazis, to control vast expanses of territory with minimal manpower:

> Terrible reprisals to deter any form of resistance were standard operating procedure for the German armed forces in the Second World War, and very effective they were in containing resistance with very few troops.[186]

It is far from clear, however, that "out-terrorizing the insurgents" was ever as effective as Professor Luttwak claims, not least because tactics that work in the short term are often counterproductive in the long term.[187]

During the Algerian war of independence, for example, France used brutal collective punishment tactics and widespread torture to successfully quell the armed nationalist resistance. But the tactics that the French military used were so barbaric that they caused widespread revulsion in metropolitan France where the political mood shifted in favour of withdrawal.

In July 1962, little more than two years after the rebel organization had been decisively crushed by the French military, Algeria gained its independence.

The French military had won an inglorious battle but had lost the war.

In April 2007 David Kilcullen, former counterinsurgency advisor to US General David Petraeus, challenged the core assumption of Luttwak's thesis: "The Nazis, Syrians, Taliban, Iranians, Saddam Hussein and others," he argued, "all tried brutalizing the population, and the evidence is that this simply does not work in the long term."

This was certainly true of the Roman, Ottoman, and Nazi empires, all of which collapsed despite—some would argue because of—their reliance on Luttwak's "easy and reliable way of defeating all insurgencies everywhere."

The case-study evidence from recent counterinsurgency campaigns supports Kilcullen's view. A new RAND Corporation report on the effectiveness of COIN (counterinsurgency) strategies based on 30 in-depth case histories found that:

> While some repressive COIN forces have managed to prevail, this analysis shows unambiguously that repression is a bad COIN practice. Only two of eight COIN winners used repression, and they still employed a pack of good COIN practices … Repression does win phases, but, in our data, the vast majority of phases won with repression preceded ultimate defeat.[188]

In a sense this is not surprising. Attempting to crush rebellions via large-scale indiscriminate and violent repression may sometimes stop armed rebellion in the short term, but will exacerbate the grievances that gave rise to the conflict in the first place. Repression is conducive neither to long-term stability nor to conflict resolution.

The evidence indicates moreover that states have been killing fewer civilians since the late 1990s.[189] Massive repression thus appears to be ineffective, except in the short term. It is also decreasingly common—and thus of shrinking strategic relevance in the late 1990s.

As noted earlier, small insurgent groups, often operating in remote areas, are very difficult to defeat. This is not because they are militarily powerful—they are not—but because they are often extremely difficult to locate. But while the fact that most insurgent bands are so small makes them difficult to find, it also ensures they can pose no military threat to the state.

Since these insurgent bands pose no real threat to the state, and little threat to public security more generally, governments may well choose to focus on containment rather than the costly campaigns needed to defeat them.[190]

Conclusion

Our examination of conflict trends in East Asia since World War II focused on the impact of major power interventions in the region, and on the impact of rising levels of economic development on the risk of war. We argued that the dramatic decline in the number of people killed in conflicts in the region since the mid-1970s was caused by the ending of major power interventions (indirect as well as direct) in regional conflicts.

On the other hand, the steady increase in levels of economic development across East Asia over the past 30 years, particularly in Southeast Asia, has enhanced the financial, political, administrative, and military capacities of governments relative to those of rural guerrilla organizations that typically operate outside the mainstream economy in remote, poverty-stricken rural areas.

As state incomes rise, other things being equal, governments will have more political and economic resources to prevent conflicts, buy off grievances, and co-opt adversaries, and more capable military forces to deter them. In the wars that cannot be prevented, the shift in the relative balance of resources that determines who will prevail in civil wars will also tend to favour governments.

Rising levels of economic development—and hence personal incomes—plus the remarkable increase in levels of democratization across the region has also enhanced the legitimacy of governments in the eyes of their citizens, reducing the incentives for individuals to join rebellions in the first place.

The evidence from East Asia supports the thesis that development is an important long-term force of conflict prevention. As we pointed out previously, the number of new intrastate conflicts between 1980 and 2008 was 75 percent less than in the previous 30-odd years.

The increased levels of trade and FDI in East Asia, which are both cause and effect of rising levels of economic development, have increased the level of regional economic interdependence. Economic interdependence is in turn associated with reduced risks of interstate warfare—as are increased levels of inclusive democracy.

The region has been free of interstate war for some 20 years.

The East Asian experience has interesting implications for the future of global security. According to the World Bank, per capita income has been growing in all regions of the world in recent years, in some more strongly than in others. Even the UN's (United Nation's) "least-developed" countries have on average experienced steady economic growth over the past decade.[191]

The dramatic decline in the number of people killed in conflicts is a result of the ending of major power interventions.

Across the developing world, growth rates, savings rates, and government reserves are up; inflation is down; remittances are increasing (and now exceed economic aid); and the share of global trade accruing to developing countries is rising.[192] The expectation is that per capita incomes across most of the developing world will continue to grow notwithstanding the impact of the current economic crisis. If this assessment is correct, it follows that, other things being equal, future governments in poor countries will—in general—become more capable of preventing, deterring, co-opting and defeating insurgencies, while citizens will have fewer reasons to join them. This should mean fewer wars.[193]

We stress here that we are talking about long-term trends and about the factors that reduce the probability of conflict. In the future, as in the past, the risk of conflict may increase in response to new sources of instability that are more powerful than the conflict-risk-reducing impact of increased levels of development.

In Chapter 4 our focus shifts back to the global level and to the causes of the sharp worldwide decline in intrastate conflict numbers since the end of the Cold War. Here we argue that the principal factor driving this decline has less to do with rising levels of economic development than with the dramatic upsurge of international activism, spearheaded by the UN and devoted to *peacemaking*—policies directed at stopping ongoing wars—and to *post-conflict peacebuilding*—policies whose strategic purpose is to prevent wars that have stopped from starting again.

Jacob Silberberg / Panos Pictures. HAITI.

CHAPTER 4

Explaining the Global Decline in Civil Wars

In this chapter we analyze the post-Cold War decline in intrastate conflict numbers that we described in the *Human Security Report 2005*. We advance two main explanations for this remarkable change.

The first examines the direct political impact of the end of the Cold War—an epochal change that removed a major source of conflict from the international system and helped end superpower proxy wars around the world. However, the net impact of this change on conflict numbers is difficult to determine because the end of the Cold War not only brought existing conflicts to an end but also triggered new ones.

Moreover, as we explain later, while of obvious historical importance, the direct impact of the end of the Cold War has diminished over time.

The second explanation for the decline in conflict numbers since the early 1990s focuses on the indirect effects of the ending of East-West hostilities. Here the key factor was the liberation of the UN (United Nations) from the paralyzing rivalries of Cold War politics. This change permitted the organization to spearhead an upsurge of international efforts to end wars via mediated settlements and seek to prevent those that had ended from restarting again.

As international initiatives soared—often fivefold or more—conflict numbers shrank. Indeed, high-intensity conflicts declined by some 80 percent between 1991 and 2008.

As noted in previous chapters, one of the most robust findings from quantitative research is that as national incomes—and hence state capacity—rise, the risk of new conflict onsets falls. The evidence also indicates that rising incomes are associated with shorter wars.[194] Given that average per capita incomes across the developing world—where most wars take place—have risen by some 40 percent since the end of the Cold War, we ask if these effects can help explain the decline in conflict numbers.

We also review three shifts in global norms that have driven:

- A dramatic increase in the number of democracies since the end of the Cold War.
- A growing rejection of the culture of impunity that protected gross abusers of human rights during the Cold War years.
- A sharp decline in the level of political discrimination against minority groups.

Each of these changes has made a contribution to reducing the number of conflicts; however, as we explain, determining their separate impact is very difficult.

The End of the Cold War

The worldwide decline in political violence that followed the end of the Cold War has been the subject of surprisingly little research. Not a single book or monograph—and only a handful of articles—has sought to explain it. The causes of peace, as we noted earlier, appear to interest scholars much less than the causes of war.

The starting point for our analysis is the end of the Cold War itself and its impact on the incidence of civil wars. This momentous, though largely unpredicted, event directly caused, or indirectly catalyzed, a series of changes that have had a major impact on global security.

By the end of the 1980s, the ideological confrontation that had divided the world into two hostile camps for some 40 years, and that had been a political force fuelling both international and civil wars, simply disappeared. The security significance of this change was profound. The geopolitics of the Cold War and the support that warring parties in so-called proxy wars received from one or other superpower had lengthened many civil wars and in some cases prevented their resolution.[195] Indeed, according to one study, conflicts that had a clear Cold War ideological dimension and received superpower support lasted three times longer than conflicts where this was not the case.[196]

The end of the Cold War set in motion changes that caused new conflicts.

There is no doubt that the ending of East-West ideological hostility removed an important driver of armed conflict from the international system. It also stopped the flow of resources from Washington, Moscow, and their allies, to warring parties in proxy wars across the developing world. For both superpowers, the assistance went beyond the provision of weapons to include education, indoctrination, training, on-the-ground advisors, and sometimes troops.[197] The ending of this assistance, together with the delegitimization of the communist model in the wake of the collapse of the Soviet Union, argues Ann Hironaka, "led to the end of nearly all the large-scale communist insurgencies in the world."[198]

But determining the extent to which these changes impacted the decline in armed conflict numbers in the 1990s is far from simple.

There is no dispute that the withdrawal of superpower support from clients in some proxy wars accelerated the ending of a number of conflicts—including those in Mozambique, Guatemala, El Salvador, Yemen, and Ethiopia. But the loss of external support was rarely a sufficient condition for peace, not least because the level of support was often minimal.

Take the case of the civil war in El Salvador. The end of the Cold War, and the withdrawal of the relatively modest level of Soviet and Cuban support for the rebels, meant that the US no longer had a major strategic interest in the outcome of the conflict or in continuing to provide political and military support to a regime that had an appalling human rights record.

But while the ending of superpower rivalry ensured that neither Washington nor Moscow was opposed to a negotiated settlement, neither was actively involved in promoting an agreement. The 1992 settlement was primarily a result of the unprecedented role the UN played in mediating the peace negotiations, verifying the terms of the agreement, and coordinating the subsequent post-conflict peacebuilding phase.[199] In other words, while the ending of East-West hostility may have been a necessary condition for peace in El Salvador, it was certainly not a sufficient one.

There are other reasons for being skeptical about claims that the end of the Cold War was the primary cause for the reduction of conflict numbers in the 1990s:

- While the direct impact of the end of the Cold War clearly helped bring some conflicts to an end, it also set in motion political changes that caused new conflicts to erupt— particularly in Eastern Europe and the former Soviet Union. The big increase in conflict onsets in the 1990s was also related to the political events unleashed by the withdrawal of superpower assistance to governments in the developing world. In other words, the direct impact of the end of the Cold War had the effect of both decreasing and increasing the number of conflicts. Determining the net effect of these changes would require a detailed analysis of individual cases that is beyond the scope of this *Report*.

- Some conflicts had never been affected by Cold War politics and in these cases the ending of Cold War hostilities was irrelevant. Examples include the conflict in Northern Ireland and the Chittagong Hill Tracts conflict in Bangladesh.

- There were some proxy wars where the warring parties had been affected by the cut-off of superpower support but where the fighting did not stop because other sources of support became available. In the case of Angola, for example, the regime had been supported by the Soviet Union and Cuba; the rebels by the US and South Africa. When the Cold War ended, most of the external support dried up, but the regime was able to rely on oil revenues to fund its war effort, while the rebels generated income from illicit diamond mining. The point here is that warring parties sometimes had domestic sources of revenue that could compensate for the loss of external support. For governments, these included oil and other economic rents, plus taxation. For rebel groups, possible revenue sources included "taxation" of local peasants, extortion of foreign companies, and control over illicit drug and gemstone production.

- Lastly, there have been a handful of communist rebel organizations—notably the Maoist-oriented Naxalite movement in India and the New People's Army in the Philippines—that fought their respective governments during the Cold War years and continue to do so today. These radical groups were influenced by Cold War politics, but they were never dependent on external aid from either the Soviet Union or China, so the end of the Cold War had no impact on their material ability to continue to wage war.

So, while the direct effect of the end of the Cold War certainly hastened the ending of a number of proxy wars, it alone cannot explain the decline in conflict numbers. And because it was a one-off event, its direct effects have diminished over time.

On the other hand, the indirect effects of the end of the Cold War—in particular the dramatically increased international commitment to peacemaking and peacebuilding—are even more salient today than in the 1990s.

An Explosion of International Activism

Since the end of the Cold War, the increase in the level of international activism aimed at reducing the incidence of political violence around the world has been astonishing. Importantly, the end of the Cold War transformed the UN. No longer paralyzed by the rivalries of the Cold War, the organization spearheaded an extraordinary upsurge of international activism directed at *peacemaking*—i.e., stopping ongoing wars—and *post-conflict peacebuilding*—i.e., preventing those that had stopped from starting again.

Despite the UN's many flaws, its universal membership and its Charter gave it a unique and legitimate leadership role in addressing a number of the global security challenges that emerged in the years that followed the end of the Cold War. But the UN did not act alone. Donor states, other international agencies, national governments in war-affected countries, and literally thousands of international and national NGOs (non-governmental organizations) not only supported the UN's efforts but played important peacemaking and peacebuilding roles on their own.

The increases in peacemaking and peacebuilding-related activities include the following:

- A fivefold increase in the number of diplomatic interventions intended to bring armed conflicts to a negotiated settlement in the 1990s relative to the 1980s.

- From 1991 to 2007, a tenfold increase in the number of Friends of the Secretary-General, Contact Groups, and other political arrangements that support peacemaking and post-conflict peacebuilding initiatives.
- From 1987 to 1994, a more than threefold increase in the number of UN peace operations.
- From 1989 to 2007, a more than twofold increase in the number of countries contributing troops to UN peace operations.
- A ninefold increase in the number of post-conflict disarmament, demobilization, and reintegration (DDR) programs from 1989 to 2008.
- A thirteenfold increase in the number of multilateral sanctions regimes between 1991 and 2008.

In some important areas—notably preventive diplomacy—we still lack reliable trend data.

It is not possible to determine which of these security-related initiatives has had the greatest overall effect—and of course the impact of different policies will vary from conflict to conflict. Multivariate regression analysis could, in principle, determine the average impact of different initiatives, but no such analysis has yet been attempted. Researchers undertaking such an exercise would confront formidable methodological challenges. Furthermore, assessments of success depend very much on the criteria used to determine it. These criteria can differ substantially and the higher the bar for success, the lower will be the success rate.

> Because the end of the Cold War was a one-off event, its direct effects have diminished over time.

The fact that the number of peacemaking and peacebuilding initiatives has increased while the number of conflicts has decreased does not, of course, mean that the former necessarily caused the latter. The case that peacemaking and peacebuilding reduce the incidence of armed conflict is, however, supported, not only by the statistical data but also by many individual case studies—and by the absence of compelling alternative explanations for the decline.

In the following sections we examine the impact of:

- Preventive diplomacy initiatives.
- Peacemaking initiatives.
- Peacekeeping operations, including DDR programs.
- Sanctions regimes.

THE REALIST CRITIQUE OF THE DECLINE OF WAR THESIS

In May 2008 Columbia University's Jack Snyder, a leading realist scholar, offered a skeptical assessment of what he described as "the end of war" thesis associated with the sharp decline in conflict numbers in the post-Cold War period.

Snyder argued that:

- It is inappropriate to extrapolate from short-term trends.
- The battle-death data that have been used to demonstrate that the deadliness of war is declining ignore *one-sided violence*—the intentional killing of civilians by governments and non-state armed groups.
- The battle-death data ignore the phenomenon of *indirect deaths*—i.e., fatalities from war-exacerbated disease and malnutrition.[200]

These are important arguments, but they do not detract from the case being argued in this *Report*.

First, we agree that it would be inappropriate to draw strong conclusions from conflict data for a short period—e.g., less than a decade. However, as noted elsewhere in this *Report*, the number of high-intensity conflicts has dropped by nearly 80 percent over a period of some 20 years. There was nothing remotely comparable to this decline during the Cold War years. Moreover, as we have argued in this chapter, the change is clearly related to forces unleashed by the ending of the Cold War and is unlikely to be reversed.

Second, it is quite true that the Uppsala Conflict Data Program (UCDP)/International Peace Research Institute, Oslo (PRIO) battle-death data do not include deaths from the targeted killing of civilians in wars. UCDP does, however, collect these data separately and makes them publicly available.

But the numbers killed by one-sided violence are relatively small compared with battle deaths and, for the period for which we have data, make little difference to the overall trends.[201] And notwithstanding many unsubstantiated claims to the contrary, there is no reliable evidence to support the suggestion that civilian deaths as a share of all war deaths have been increasing.[202]

Third, it is also true that indirect deaths from war-exacerbated disease and malnutrition are not included in the UCDP/PRIO battle-death counts and that the latter on their own provide an inadequate measure of the true human costs of war. We made precisely this point in the *Human Security Report 2005*.

But, contrary to Snyder, we do not believe that if the estimates of indirect death tolls were added to battle-death tolls (assuming that this were in fact possible) "the trend away from war would not look so compelling."

In fact, as we argue in Part II of this *Report*, indirect deaths have very likely declined more than battle deaths since 1946.

In his critique of "the end of war" thesis, Professor Snyder also touches on the state-capacity thesis associated with the work of James Fearon and David Laitin. This holds that as state capacity increases, the risk of war declines because states have more resources to buy off grievances and crush rebellions where negotiations fail or are impractical.[203]

Snyder accepts that there is a historical trend towards higher levels of state capacity, and that increased state capacity is associated with declining risks of conflict. But he argues that per capita economic growth—the most common proxy measure for increased state capacity—"is at best shaky in Africa, where much of the fighting has been."[204]

In fact, economic growth in Africa in the 1980s and early 1990s was worse than shaky—between 1985 and 1995, average GDP (gross domestic product) per capita in sub-Saharan Africa shrank by 1.1 percent a year.[205] But there has been a radical change since then. As a recent McKinsey and Company report noted, "real GDP rose 4.9 percent per year from 2000 through 2008, more than twice its pace in the 1980s and '90s."[206] And between 1999 and 2008, conflict numbers in the region declined by some 30 percent.[207]

Finally, we agree with Snyder that it makes little sense to claim that "war will go away soon." And indeed we do not know any scholars who make this case.[208]

The conditions that give rise to civil wars have changed, but certainly not enough to suggest that political violence is likely to end in the foreseeable future.

Preventive Diplomacy

Preventive diplomacy was defined in former UN Secretary-General Boutros Boutros-Ghali's influential 1992 *Agenda for Peace* report as involving "action to prevent disputes from arising between parties, [and] to prevent existing disputes from escalating into conflicts."[209]

Preventive diplomacy initiatives can include mediation; dispute resolution mechanisms; "good offices"; political assistance; diplomatic recognition or normalization; fact-finding and observer missions; public diplomacy or pressure; and the threat, or use, of diplomatic sanctions.[210] And, as UN Secretary-General Ban Ki-Moon has pointed out:

> [preventive diplomacy is a] core function of the United Nations and is central to the Secretary-General's role. The prevention of violent conflict is key to the Organization's Charter obligations to maintain international peace and security.[211]

There is, moreover, widespread agreement in the international community that "prevention is better than cure," that preventive diplomacy is highly cost-effective, and that failing to prevent wars creates "conflict traps" in poor countries that generate recurring warfare—and huge human and financial costs.[212]

Yet, despite what US Institute of Peace analyst Lawrence Woocher has described as "quite dramatic advances in rhetorical and declaratory support for conflict prevention" in recent decades, preventive diplomacy has been more talked about than practiced.

In November 2007 Ban Ki-Moon reported to the General Assembly that the UN's Department of Political Affairs (DPA) was so overstretched that there was "little time for the Department's officers to carry out the practice of preventive diplomacy or provide oversight to United Nations missions."[213]

This was a remarkable admission. The central mandate of the UN is to prevent the "scourge of war," yet here was a Secretary-General telling UN member states that the UN department with the primary responsibility for preventive diplomacy lacked the resources to undertake it.

Given that DPA has lacked the most basic resources that it needs to practice preventive diplomacy, it is unsurprising that this policy instrument is rarely practiced at the UN. However, DPA officers are not the only preventive diplomacy actors associated with the organization. In addition to the Secretary-General himself, there is a small army of Special Representatives of the Secretary-General (SRSGs) who have a range of important security roles in crisis-affected countries that can include preventive diplomacy. The number of SRSGs has increased more than fourfold since the end of the Cold War.[214] Few of them appear to have been involved in preventive diplomacy missions, however.

Nor is there any evidence that preventive diplomacy has been part of the agenda of the Friends of the Secretary-General, Contact Groups, and other informal groupings of states that have emerged to help end civil wars and to prevent wars that have ended from starting again.[215]

Perhaps the best evidence we have that preventive diplomacy missions are rarely attempted—or, if attempted, are ineffectual—comes from the Uppsala Conflict Data Program's (UCDP's) conflict onset and terminations data. As discussed in more detail in Part III of this *Report*, there were twice as many conflict onsets in the 1990s as in the 1980s. Many of these were restarts of older conflicts, but the number of completely new conflicts nearly doubled as well. The implications are obvious. If preventive diplomacy initiatives were being attempted in the chaotic 1990s, they were clearly not very successful. But there is little evidence to suggest that many such initiatives were in fact being attempted during this period.

Given the near-universal agreement that prevention is valuable and cost-effective, and given the repeated rhetorical endorsements of the virtues of preventive diplomacy, why has it been practiced so rarely—not least by the UN?

There are several reasons. First, the top priority of the UN Security Council, the Secretary-General, and DPA is always going to be crisis management, not conflict prevention. This is a matter of necessity, not choice. Neither the Security Council, nor the Secretary-General, nor DPA has any realistic option but to respond to crises. As a 2006 Secretary-General's report on conflict prevention noted, DPA's resource shortages have meant the department's workload has been "heavily driven by the exigencies of crisis response."[216] Preventive diplomacy almost never has the same degree of urgency.

Second, securing agreement from at-risk governments to deploy external preventive missions on their sovereign territory confronts formidable political barriers. As Barnett Rubin and Bruce Jones of the Center for International Cooperation have noted, preventive diplomacy:

> [is] the most politically problematic type of UN conflict prevention. The process treats both governments and opposition groups as parties to a conflict, rather than granting the government a monopoly on legitimate representation ... The appearance of taking sides becomes almost unavoidable. Even the most scrupulous neutrality of expression cannot disguise the

fact that the UN is treating as a political actor a group that the government may depict as criminal deviants.[217]

Third, as Rubin and Jones also point out, DPA not only lacks a strong field presence in crisis countries but was "not designed to have, and consequently lacks, the capacity to undertake the analysis needed for prevention."[218] Member states of the UN have repeatedly blocked attempts by the UN to create an in-house analytic capacity for DPA.

Finally, there are a range of bureaucratic impediments to implementing effective prevention policies. These include "a deeply embedded inability to coordinate based on differing mandates, governance structures, and funding mechanisms of different parts of the organization."[219]

However, the UN is not the only actor that pursues diplomatic initiatives to prevent conflicts from starting—or restarting. There are a number of "private diplomacy" organizations—discussed in more detail in the section on peacemaking—that also play an active role.[220]

Private diplomacy actors are not as constrained as international organizations and states when dealing with armed non-state actors, but here too the emphasis has been on mediating an end to ongoing conflicts rather than using diplomatic means to prevent conflicts from erupting in the first place.[221]

But the prospects for preventive diplomacy are not quite as negative as the above discussion might indicate. There is some case-study evidence to suggest that preventive diplomacy can succeed in practice.[222] Some of the more notable successes have been associated with the OSCE (Organization for Security and Co-operation in Europe), in particular the Office of the High Commissioner on National Minorities that, since the mid-1990s, has:

> helped to head off inter-ethnic conflicts in several Central and Eastern European countries such as Slovakia, the Baltic states, Albania, as well as Macedonia through informal diplomacy and crafting minority rights legislation that were adopted by the governments.[223]

There is also evidence that interest in preventive diplomacy is growing within the UN system. In 2008 DPA received funding for 50 new posts, which is enabling it to build in-house mediation capacity and to support mediation efforts in the field.[224] This capacity can in principle be used to support preventive diplomacy measures.[225]

During 2010 there was also evidence of increasing—though typically cautious—support for the idea of preventive

diplomacy from the Security Council. As Security Council Report, an independent organization, noted in July 2010:

> It seems that the Council is no longer quite so hesitant about the thematic issue of conflict prevention and may now be open in principle to more concrete language on the subject than was possible for much of the last decade. However, a key unresolved issue is whether members are also prepared to advance the issue of conflict prevention concretely in specific cases.[226]

In other words, there appears to be slow progress at the UN towards taking the idea of preventive diplomacy seriously. But it is still far from clear to what extent the Council will be prepared to push actively for preventive diplomacy initiatives in particular at-risk countries—or indeed how such initiatives might be received by the governments of these countries given ongoing concerns about sovereignty.

However, with some deficit-burdened donor states becoming concerned about the rapidly rising costs of peacekeeping, the case for preventive diplomacy with its minimal price tag may seem increasingly compelling. At the same time, a number of key African states are becoming increasingly vocal in their support of preventive diplomacy—a marked change from the situation a decade or more ago.[227]

If this modest progress continues, the rhetorical support for preventive diplomacy may eventually be matched by its actual use in states at risk of succumbing to conflict.

Peacemaking

Peacemaking is the UN's term for the use of external mediation to assist warring parties in ending conflicts through negotiated settlements. Most research on peacemaking has examined attempts to mediate interstate wars and, until very recently, there were no long-duration time-series data on attempts to end civil wars via diplomatic interventions. This changed with the recent release of a new dataset compiled by Patrick Regan and colleagues that recorded 438 peacemaking interventions in some 68 intrastate conflicts from 1945 to 1999.[228] The large majority of these interventions (352) were mediations, though 44 were offers—or requests—for mediation that were not taken up, while 23 involved multilateral forums.[229]

The new data provide the first real insight we have into post-World War II trends in diplomatic attempts to end intrastate conflicts via mediation.[230] Of the 153 intrastate conflicts between 1945 and 1999 recorded in the new dataset, 44 percent (68) experienced some form of diplomatic intervention.[231] The number of diplomatic interventions per conflict was highest in the Americas and sub-Saharan Africa; lowest in Asia and the Middle East.

Diplomatic interventions worldwide increased slowly from around 10 in the years between 1944 and 1949, to some 50 in the 1980s. Then in the 1990s the number shot up fivefold to more than 250. And as diplomatic interventions increased sharply in the 1990s, the number of military interventions fell.[232]

Regan's data show that the UN has been the most frequent conflict mediator since the end of World War II, with some 89 diplomatic interventions in 22 conflicts, followed by the US (56 interventions), and the Catholic Church (30). Of the 14 most active interveners, four were regional organizations and eight were national governments.

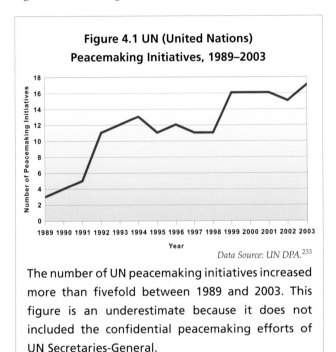

Figure 4.1 UN (United Nations) Peacemaking Initiatives, 1989–2003

Data Source: UN DPA.[233]

The number of UN peacemaking initiatives increased more than fivefold between 1989 and 2003. This figure is an underestimate because it does not included the confidential peacemaking efforts of UN Secretaries-General.

Although peacemaking is central to the mandate of the UN, and although the UN has been the most frequent mediator in civil wars since the end of World War II, DPA has not done a good job of recording its own peacemaking missions. However, data provided to the Human Security Report Project (HSRP) in 2004 indicate that the number of peacemaking missions increased at least fivefold between 1989 and 2002, as Figure 4.1 shows.[234] This is an underestimate, however, because the data do not include the various personal peacemaking initiatives undertaken in confidence by Secretaries-General.

As mentioned, regional organizations, private diplomacy actors, and individual states have also played an important—and increasing—role in peacemaking.

Regional organizations have advantages and sometimes liabilities as mediation actors. Their proximity and shared history with the countries in conflict means that they likely have a better understanding of the issues than distant international organizations like the UN. But they may also have political and economic interests in particular conflict outcomes that compromise their ability to act as impartial mediators.

The post-Cold War era has witnessed the rise of a new constellation of informal political organizations that seek to help end wars and prevent those that have stopped from starting again. These so-called Friends groups, noted briefly earlier, have been described by Teresa Whitfield, author of the most comprehensive account of the Friends' phenomenon, as:

> ad hoc, issue-specific minicoalitions of states and inter-governmental organizations that become involved in and provide support for the resolution of conflicts and the implementation of peace agreements.[235]

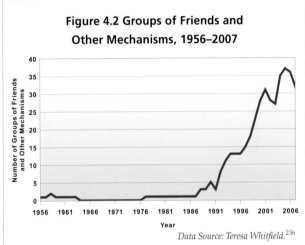

Figure 4.2 Groups of Friends and Other Mechanisms, 1956–2007

Data Source: Teresa Whitfield.[236]

The number of Friends groups and other mechanisms to support peacemaking and peacebuilding missions have increased dramatically since the end of the Cold War.

As Figure 4.2 shows, the number of active Friends groups increased dramatically in the post-Cold War years. And as Whitfield's description indicates, these so-called minilateral organizations are involved in supporting peacebuilding as well as peacemaking processes.

Friends groups typically play a supporting role in peacemaking efforts rather than being directly involved in the mediation process itself, but that support has often been of critical importance in achieving an eventual settlement.

WHY GRIEVANCES MATTER

The most-cited quantitative research on the causes of war explicitly rejects claims that grievances cause conflicts and has consequently paid little attention to peacemaking, peacebuilding, or other strategies that seek to resolve grievances. Clearly, if grievances do not drive conflicts then pursuing policies that seek to resolve them makes little sense.

Two main arguments have been advanced for rejecting grievance-based explanations for conflict onsets. Neither is compelling.

First, it is argued that grievances are ubiquitous, while wars are very rare. The implication is clear—if grievances really were a major driver of political violence, as so much of the case-study literature suggests, then the world should be suffering far more armed conflicts.

There is one obvious response to this objection, namely that some grievances are far more deeply felt than others and it is only those that are most deeply felt that are likely to lead to political violence.

Second, it is claimed that the statistical evidence does not support the grievance thesis. Study after study has failed to find any association between various measures of grievance and the onset of conflicts. These findings are highly problematic.

Grievances are psychological variables for which quantitative researchers have no direct measures. In attempting to get around this problem, they use measures for which there are global data—such as income inequality—as proxies for grievances. But this approach has been strongly criticized on the grounds that many of the measures that have been chosen to proxy grievances are inappropriate.[237]

There is, however, a more profound reason for contesting the claim that grievances do not matter— one that cannot be rebutted by creating better proxy measures, better cross-national data, or more sophisticated statistical significance tests.

Paul Collier and colleagues use nationwide data in seeking to determine the impact of grievance on the risk of war, as do James Fearon and David Laitin in their equally influential research.[238] With nationwide data, they can in principle measure the average impact of societal grievance on the risk of war.

But whole populations do not start wars—relatively small collectives of individuals do.

The proxy measures for grievance tell us about average levels of societal grievance—not about the grievances of the only individuals that really matter—i.e., the minority who start the wars. The fact that there is no association between societal levels of grievance and conflict onsets does not disprove grievance-based explanations.

Indeed Fearon and Laitin do not deny that grievances may motivate rebels. They argue instead that what determines whether or not war breaks out is opportunity. Absent opportunity, war is not feasible.

Opportunity and feasibility are largely determined by the capacity of states to deter and otherwise prevent wars. So it is not surprising that Fearon and Laitin's prescriptions focus on the need to build state capacity as a means of preventing civil wars while largely ignoring conflict resolution and peacemaking strategies.

An extreme hypothetical example illustrates the logic of Fearon and Laitin's thesis. Imagine a country where persecuted dissidents have been banished to an offshore island. Burning with a deep sense of grievance, the dissidents would seize any chance to engage the regime in armed struggle. But they are denied the opportunity to do so by the fact they are physically unable to leave the island. It is the lack of opportunity that prevents conflict—notwithstanding intense dissident grievances. But in other cases opportunity may be largely irrelevant and grievances critical.

Consider another hypothetical case—a society in which there is ample opportunity to start a conflict and even some prospect of victory but where the citizens harbour no grievances against the state. In this case, the absence of war arises not because the citizens have been deterred by the coercive power of the state but because they are not motivated to try and overthrow it.

Motivation and opportunity are necessary conditions for rebellion but neither is sufficient. Understanding what drives conflicts requires explanations that take both into account.

The post-Cold War world has also witnessed a remarkable upsurge in private diplomacy actors. A 2008 survey by the Crisis Management Initiative described the evolution and rapid growth of 14, mostly European, NGOs involved in peacemaking. Only two of these private diplomacy organizations were established before the end of the Cold War; 12 have been created since then.[239]

Private diplomacy initiatives, unlike UN-led peacemaking missions, are not constrained by the requirements of Security Council mandates or by pressure from powerful UN-member states. And private mediators "have the advantage of being able to engage early and with discretion with conflict parties who may be reluctant to engage with official actors."[240] But they rarely have the leverage of official peacemaking actors—whether the UN or governments.

How Successful Are Peacemaking Efforts?

It is remarkable how little is known about the success of peacemaking efforts. As Regan and his co-authors note in their study of more than six decades of peacemaking, "We know little about the effect of diplomatic initiatives on warring parties' decisionmaking or the record of external diplomatic efforts in the management of civil wars."[241]

The available evidence on the impact of peacemaking is fragmentary but suggestive.

A new and as yet unpublished 2010 study by Bernd Beber, which used a new mediation dataset, found that in approximately half the 35 high- and medium-intensity conflicts being waged around the world between 1990 and 2005, third-party mediation led to a "full or partial" settlement.[242]

Regan and colleagues find a similar relationship, but over a much longer period:

> If we consider full or partial settlements as successful outcomes, mediations were coded as ending successfully in 133 out of 352 cases (38%). Over 57% of mediations result in a ceasefire, and only 4% fail completely.[243]

In 2011 Frida Möller and co-authors reported on a rare quantitative study of regional peacemaking efforts—in Southeast Asia and Oceania. They found that as conflict management efforts increased in the region, so too did the number of conflict terminations. They concluded that there was "a strong positive relationship between mediation and agreements."[244]

Comparing peacemaking efforts in the first post-Cold War decade with the previous 10 years is particularly instructive. The Regan dataset shows that there was a fivefold increase in peacemaking efforts in the 1990s, compared with the 1980s. Over the same period, UCDP's conflict terminations dataset shows that the number of peace agreements increased sevenfold—up from three in the 1980s to 22 in the 1990s.[245]

Reaching a negotiated peace settlement is a major achievement, but in no sense a guarantee of sustained peace. The most common yardstick used to indicate the success—or "stability"—of peacemaking is a period of at least five years after the agreement is signed without the conflict recurring. Among the factors that determine the success or failure of peace settlements thus defined are the actual crafting of agreements and the degree of post-conflict support available to help implement them.

Private diplomacy actors rarely have the leverage of official peacemaking actors— whether the UN or governments.

The 1990s was a bad decade for the stability of peace agreements, with some 46 percent—almost twice the post-World War II average—breaking down within five years.

However, as Part III of this *Report* points out, the new millennium has witnessed what may turn out to be a substantial improvement in the stability of peace agreements—though it is far too early to determine whether it will prove durable. Between 2000 and 2003, only one of the seven new peace agreements failed within five years—a success rate of 86 percent—compared with a rate of just 55 percent in the 1990s.

This change suggests—no more—that today's peace agreements may be better timed, better crafted, and better supported than those of the turbulent 1990s.

Finally, we note that the potential for new peacemaking initiatives to further reduce the incidence of conflict is considerable. According to the Regan dataset, less than half (44 percent) of the civil wars between 1950 and 1999 saw external diplomatic interventions to help resolve them.[246] There is, in other words, great scope for new peacemaking initiatives to be pursued in the future.

Peacekeeping and Peacebuilding

Very few wars that break out in the current era are truly new. The majority of onsets in the new millenium are of conflicts that stopped at some stage and have started again. So, stopping conflicts from recurring once they have ended has become an increasingly important security goal for the

UN and other international actors. The term the UN uses to describe the policies it pursues to achieve this goal is *post-conflict peacebuilding*.

Peacebuilding has both a military and—increasingly—a civilian component. In principle, peacekeeping—the military component—provides the security needed for the implementation of civilian assistance programs that focus on helping war-affected countries rebuild their socio-economic, administrative, and political institutions.

The term *peace operation* is often used to describe the combined military peacekeeping and civilian peacebuilding effort.

The peace operations of the 1990s and subsequently were very different from the peacekeeping missions of the Cold War years, which often amounted to little more than the monitoring of ceasefires by small numbers of lightly armed peacekeepers. Today's peace operations tend to be large and highly complex exercises in state- and nation-building, with Security Council mandates that legitimize the use of force to protect civilians.

As Figure 4.3 indicates, between 1989 and 1994 the number of UN peacekeeping missions almost doubled and has since stabilized at a high level.[247]

As of 31 December 2010, there were a record 123,000 UN personnel serving in 16 peace operations on four continents. This represents a ninefold increase in UN peacekeepers since 1999.[248]

Figure 4.3 also shows that other international organizations such as NATO (North Atlantic Treaty Organization)

and the African Union (formerly known as the Organization of African Unity) have increased the number of their peace operations at an even greater rate.

The overwhelming majority of the studies that have examined the security impact of peace operations have concluded that they significantly reduce the probability that war will recur.

The first statistical analysis of the impact of peacebuilding was published in 2000 by Michael Doyle and Nicholas Sambanis. It concluded that an appropriately designed peace operation significantly improved the prospects for peace.[249]

In 2008 another major quantitative study by Page Fortna noted that "the risk of war resuming is much lower when peacekeepers are present than when belligerents are left to their own devices."[250] Where peacekeeping missions were deployed, the risk of war recurring was reduced by at least half compared with post-conflict countries where there was no peacekeeping operation.[251]

Lessons Learned

Notwithstanding the real successes, post-Cold War UN peacekeeping operations have suffered serious and much publicized failures. In 1999 a UN report was published under Secretary-General Kofi Annan's name that described the failure of the organization to prevent the massacre of thousands of Muslims who were in the UN-designated "safe haven" of Srebrenica in Bosnia in 1995. Written with atypical frankness, the report argued that the failure to stop the slaughter was due in large

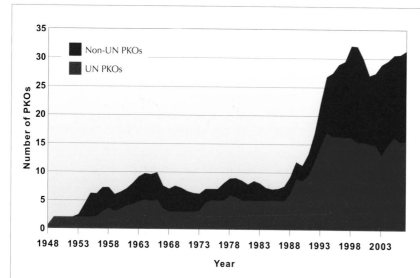

Figure 4.3 UN (United Nations) and Non-UN Peacekeeping Operations (PKOs), 1948–2007

The number of UN PKOs almost doubled between 1989 and 2007. There has been an even larger increase in the number of non-UN PKOs over the same period.

Data Source: Birger Heldt.[252]

Note: Figure 4.3 is a "stacked graph," meaning that the number of operations in each category is indicated by the depth of the band of colour. The top line shows the total number of operations of all types in each year.

part to the UN's commitment to the peacekeeping ethos of impartiality and its opposition to using force when confronted by blatant aggression.

That report, and another major investigation that examined the international community's even greater failure to stop the genocide in Rwanda in 1994, led Annan to initiate a full-scale review of peacekeeping operations in 2000. The *Brahimi Report*—so called because the investigation was led by former Algerian Foreign Minister Lakhdar Brahimi—was published in 2000. It criticized the UN for applying "best-case planning assumptions to situations where the local actors have historically exhibited worst-case behavior."[253]

Brahimi argued for greater emphasis on long-term peacebuilding programs to address root causes of conflict.

The *Brahimi Report* called for more realistic appraisals by the Department of Peacekeeping Operations (DPKO) of the situation on the ground where missions would be deployed, and stressed the need for appropriate mandates, sufficient resources, and intelligence in order to credibly deter violent behaviour and "to leave no doubt in the minds of would-be spoilers" about the consequences of their actions.[254] Above all, it warned of the grave risks of sending lightly armed peacekeepers where there was no peace to keep.

Brahimi's stress on the importance of ensuring that peacekeeping forces are appropriately resourced was supported by the findings of a second statistical study by Doyle and Sambanis on the effectiveness of UN peace operations that was published in 2006. The authors argued that:

> the greater the hostility, measured in terms of casualties, refugees, number of factions, type of war, and ethnic divisions, and the less the local capacity, measured in an underdeveloped and undiversified economy, the lower the probability of peacebuilding success, and the greater must international capacities be to increase that probability.[255]

Recognizing that simply preventing violence for the duration of the peace operation was rarely sufficient to prevent the outbreak of future conflict, Brahimi also argued for a much greater emphasis on long-term peacebuilding programs to address the root causes of the conflict and in so doing create the conditions for a sustainable peace. Central to

this goal was the need to strengthen state capacity and foster a climate for sustained economic development. In short, the report concluded:

> History has taught that peacekeepers and peacebuilders are inseparable partners in complex operations: while the peacebuilders may not be able to function without the peacekeepers' support, the peacekeepers have no exit without the peacebuilders' work.[256]

Continuing Challenges

Notwithstanding much reform and many real achievements, a decade after the publication of the *Brahimi Report*, UN peace operations still confront major challenges:

- The growth in the number and scope of missions has caused the organization to suffer from "overstretch," with a growing gap between commitments and the resources needed to meet them.[257]
- The quality of peacekeeping forces remains uneven and "has even worsened as many rich Western nations have followed US practice and become less willing to commit their armed forces to UN operations."[258] In addition to having inadequately trained personnel, many peacekeeping missions are short of appropriate communication and logistics equipment—and in some cases even more basic supplies.[259]
- Operational coordination between the UN Secretariat, missions in the field, local authorities, donor governments, international agencies, and local and international NGOs, and between the different national contingents of the multi-national peacekeeping forces is rarely satisfactory and remains a source of ongoing contention.[260]
- Deployment times of peacekeeping missions, particularly to sub-Saharan Africa, are often agonizingly slow, though the fault is not always that of the UN. Sometimes delays arise because of obstruction by the governments of the conflict-affected countries.[261]
- The sheer size of multidimensional peace operations means that they often have a distorting impact on local economies,[262] and there have been persistent—though sometimes exaggerated—problems with abuse and corruption within missions.[263]
- Finally, even though the UN constantly stresses the critical need to build local capacity in its peace operations in order to make progress self-sustaining, this ambition is rarely fully realized.[264]

DISARMAMENT, DEMOBILIZATION, AND REINTEGRATION

When civil wars come to an end, especially when they end in peace agreements rather than decisive victories, security is far from guaranteed and—as Part III of this *Report* demonstrates—there is a serious risk of the country succumbing to further conflict. One important means of reducing this risk is the effective disarmament and demobilization of insurgent forces and their reintegration into civil society.

The United Nations (UN) Disarmament, Demobilization, and Reintegration (DDR) Resource Centre defines DDR as a process that:

> aims to deal with the post-conflict security problem that results from ex-combatants being left without livelihoods or support networks, other than their former comrades, during the critical transition period from conflict to peace and development.[265]

Formal DDR programs have become a central element of the multidimensional peace operations that have proliferated since the end of the Cold War. In 2000 UN Secretary-General Kofi Annan described DDR programs as having "repeatedly proved to be vital to stability in a post-conflict situation."[266]

Figure 4.4 below reveals the rapid increase in the number of DDR operations since the end of the 1980s. In 1989 there were just two ongoing programs; in 2008 there were 18. While remarkable, this ninefold increase is not untypical of the increased international security activism in the wake of the Cold War.

As we can see from Figure 4.4, for most of the post-Cold War period DDR programs in sub-Saharan Africa have made up more than half of the worldwide total. This is not surprising since the region has also seen the greatest number of conflicts during this period—and a large number of UN peace operations.

DDR programs can take many different forms. In cases where the conflict ended because one party defeated the other decisively (Angola, 2002; Rwanda, 1994; Uganda, 1986; and Ethiopia, 1990s), the DDR process tends to be one-sided, relatively rapid, and coercive.[267]

In rare cases (Mozambique, 1992; Cambodia, 1991; Laos, 1962), agreements call for *both* government and rebel armies "to demobilize equally in order to integrate the same number of soldiers into a new national army."[268] But more often the focus is on the demobilization of rebel forces, with any government demobilization taking place subsequently.

DDR processes may be important, but they are also inherently challenging. As Macartan Humphreys and Jeremy Weinstein point out, years of violent armed struggle often mean that relationships between the warring parties are characterized by distrust and uncertainty. This means that:

> disarmament efforts, which aim to remove the means by which the war was fought, also leave factions and combatants vulnerable, without the weapons they would need to protect themselves if the other side reneges on an agreement.[269]

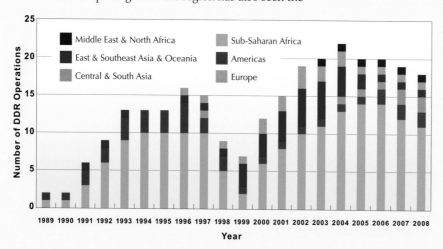

Figure 4.4 Disarmament, Demobilization, and Reintegration (DDR) Operations, 1989–2008

DDR operations are much more numerous than they were at the end of the Cold War. The vast majority of these operations have been in sub-Saharan Africa.

Data Source: Robert Muggah.[270]

These factors can provide powerful security incentives for the former warring parties to cheat on peace agreements—not least by understating the number of combatants and weapons.

This sort of cheating can be seen as a form of security insurance rather than as evidence of aggressive intent. But whatever the motive, if cheating is discovered, peace agreements are—at best—at risk; at worst the political fallout creates a new conflict spiral and fighting is renewed.

As Barbara Walter puts it, adversaries in these situations find it extraordinarily difficult *on their own* "to abide by the terms of a treaty that offers enormous rewards for cheating and enormous costs for being cheated upon."[271]

Walter argues that peace treaties often require external support to reassure the former warring parties that agreements—particularly with respect to disarmament—will be adhered to. The latter is precisely what UN-mandated DDR programs seek to achieve.

But there are serious equity issues at stake in many instances. Reintegration assistance is provided to former combatants but rarely to the often far larger number of conflict-displaced refugees and internally displaced persons returning to their homes after the fighting is over. In Liberia, for example, only 11 percent of post-conflict returnees were ex-combatants.[272] In some cases ex-combatants who perpetrated gross human rights violations in the course of the conflict have received reintegration assistance from the international community that their victims were denied. This has been a source of major concern in a number of countries where DDR programs have been implemented.

Determining the success of the reintegration phase of DDR programs—as against the disarmament and demobilization phases—is neither easy nor often attempted.

Humphreys and Weinstein note:

there have been few systematic efforts to evaluate the determinants of successful reintegration by ex-combatants after conflict … In particular, no studies have systematically compared the reintegration success of those who have and have not participated in demobilization and reintegration programs.[273]

The latter comparison was precisely what Humphreys and Weinstein undertook in Sierra Leone. Their findings were sobering. Individuals who had participated in the reintegration program did not reintegrate into civil society any better than those who had not. In other words, the reintegration phase of Sierra Leone's DDR program was a failure.

But the authors are careful to note that the fact that "there is little evidence that DDR programs were effective in Sierra Leone … does not mean that DDR programs are never successful."[274]

Indeed, in an analysis of the impact of the UN's DDRR[275] program in Liberia that used a very similar methodology to the study in neighbouring Sierra Leone, James Pugel found:

solid empirical evidence that the DDRR program in Liberia has indeed enabled a much better life for those ex-combatants who have completed their program of training when compared with those former fighters who chose not to register, preferring to reintegrate on their own.[276]

The Sierra Leone and Liberia evaluations of the impact of DDR programs were notable for their methodological rigour and reliance on data. This type of study remains the exception rather than the rule.[277] And because researchers have not gathered enough quantitative data, they have not been able to make meaningful cross-national comparisons of DDR program outcomes.

Part of the problem is that neither researchers nor practitioners have agreed on what might constitute success in a reintegration program.

A minimal, but important, criterion for success might seem to be whether conflict re-erupted following a DDR program—such programs are, of course, intended to reduce the risk of this happening.

But there are many reasons why conflicts may start again that have little to do with the effectiveness of a DDR program. And if no conflict erupted, it will rarely be possible to determine whether this was due to the success of the DDR program, to other peacebuilding initiatives, to the fact that the previously warring parties had simply lost their appetite for conflict, or to any of a host of other plausible explanations.

It is clear that the challenges that confront the effective deployment of peace operations remain formidable. But in one sense this makes the successes of peacekeeping and peacebuilding in reducing the risk that conflicts will reignite all the more remarkable.

Although few in the UN believe that the many problems that peace operations confront will be overcome in the near future, there is no reason for undue pessimism.

Resource constraints remain a serious problem in many areas. However, the level of funding per mission has actually increased considerably over the past two decades. While the number of UN missions has almost doubled since 1989, total peacekeeping expenditures have increased more than fivefold.[278] More and more countries are contributing troops to UN peace missions, reflecting the international community's growing commitment to peacebuilding. As Figure 4.5 indicates, the number of countries contributing troops to UN peace operations more than doubled between 1989 and 2007. The number of troop-contributors to non-UN missions has grown at a similar rate.

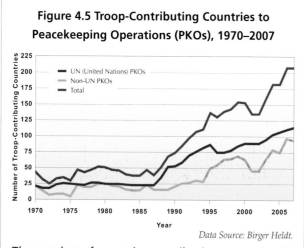

Figure 4.5 Troop-Contributing Countries to Peacekeeping Operations (PKOs), 1970–2007

Data Source: Birger Heldt.

The number of countries contributing troops to UN and non-UN PKOs has increased steeply in the last two decades.

Some donor governments, worried about soaring deficits at home, have fretted about peacekeeping's rising costs.[279] But, as Doyle and Sambanis have pointed out, the pay-off from peace operations is "a relative bargain."[280]

In 2007 the total UN peacekeeping budget was less than the US was spending in a single week in Iraq.[281] And while the UN's annual peacekeeping budget had soared to some $7.8 billion by mid-2009, this was still only half of 1 percent of global military expenditure, and only a small fraction of the defense budgets of most developed nations.[282] Considering the impact that peace operations have in reducing the risk of armed conflicts recurring, this would appear to be very good value for money.

Sanctions

As Figure 4.6 illustrates, the post-Cold War era has seen a dramatic increase in the number of sanctions regimes imposed by multilateral organizations, yet one more indication of the international community's increased activism in this period.

Sanctions have been used to coerce reluctant warring parties to join negotiations, to restrict the flow of arms to war zones, to pressure regimes to stop human rights abuses, and for many other purposes. They have been targeted mostly, but not exclusively, at governments in the developing world that are embroiled in civil wars, or are guilty of perpetrating gross human rights violations against their own citizens.

Notwithstanding the greatly increased resort to sanctions in the post-Cold War era, the evidence from a number of statistical analyses suggests that they are not a very effective means of coercing governments to change their behaviour.

Different datasets, methodologies, and criteria for success mean that statistical findings on the efficacy of sanctions regimes vary, but, whether the sanctions regimes are unilateral or multilateral, the findings are consistent enough to support the claim that in terms of coercing policy change in target regimes, sanctions are a weak policy instrument.

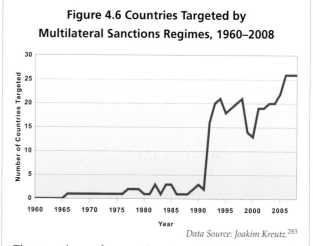

Figure 4.6 Countries Targeted by Multilateral Sanctions Regimes, 1960–2008

Data Source: Joakim Kreutz.[283]

The number of countries targeted by economic and political sanctions exploded after the end of the Cold War, going from just two in 1989 to 26 in 2008.

In what has been by far the most comprehensive and widely cited statistical study of US sanctions to date, the Washington-based Institute for International Economics examined 170 cases of economic sanctions imposed between 1915 and 2000 and found that they were "partially successful" in just 34 percent of cases.[284]

The success rate of sanctions imposed by the UN is little better. In a study of the effectiveness of 11 UN sanctions regimes, David Cortright and George Lopez determined that a maximum of just four cases (36 percent) could be judged as "partially successful" in producing compliance with the relevant UN resolutions.[285] The cases in question were Iraq, Yugoslavia, Libya, and to a lesser extent, Cambodia.

Conflict-affected countries under sanctions had shorter wars than countries that were not under sanctions.

A 2007 analysis by the Stockholm International Peace Research Institute (SIPRI) and Uppsala University's Department of Peace and Conflict Research examined 27 UN arms embargoes intended primarily to stop, or at the very least slow, the flow of arms to conflict zones.[286]

The success rate of these embargoes was not impressive either. The study was able to measure an "improvement in target behaviour" in just 25 percent of all observations.[287] In many cases, the embargoes had little effect—except perhaps to help bring the very idea of arms embargoes into disrepute.

The evidence suggests that sanctions have a positive impact in just 25 to 36 percent of cases, which raises an obvious question. Do these unimpressive findings mean that sanctions are such a weak policy instrument that they should be abandoned?

The short answer is no—and for several reasons.

In many cases where UN sanctions regimes have failed, the reason has little or nothing to do with any intrinsic flaws in sanctions strategy. A major reason for past failures has been that the Security Council has often put little or no effort into implementing, monitoring, or enforcing the regimes that they have imposed. As Cortright and Lopez point out, "lax enforcement has vitiated the potential impact of most arms embargoes."[288]

Had serious efforts been made to enforce the sanctions regimes the Council imposed on countries in sub-Saharan Africa in the 1990s—as they clearly could have been—then

the impact would surely have been greater. Here the problem lies not with sanctions, but the lack of will to enforce them.

The negative overall assessment of the efficacy of sanctions is also due in part to the fact that the criterion for success has become the degree to which sanctions regimes succeed in coercing target states to change their behaviour. But different measures of impact suggest that less pessimistic assessments are warranted.

One such alternative measure is the impact of sanctions on the length of wars. A recent study by Abel Escribà-Folch focused on 87 wars and used new data on sanctions to examine the association between the imposition of sanctions and the duration of civil wars.[289] Among the key findings of the study were that, other things being equal, conflict-affected countries under sanctions had shorter wars than countries that were not under sanctions, and the wars were also more likely to end in negotiated settlements. Escribà-Folch also found that in the average war-affected country under a multilateral sanctions regime, the fighting ended more quickly than did the average conflict in a country under a unilateral sanctions regime.[290]

Sanctions can also support the achievement of other security goals—from containing aggressor states to serving as instruments of deterrence. Both of these objectives, if realized, would tend to reduce the incidence of political violence, even if the target state failed to comply with Security Council resolutions.

To take one obvious example, the sanctions regime imposed on Iraq is widely believed to have failed. Saddam Hussein never conceded to key Security Council demands despite being subjected to the most draconian sanctions regime in modern history—one that imposed huge suffering on ordinary Iraqis.

Few would disagree that sanctions on Iraq failed to achieve their major objectives, yet the arms embargo component of the sanctions package was highly successful in preventing the regime from rebuilding its military capacity and again posing threats to its neighbours. Arms embargoes, in other words, have the potential to prevent, as well as shorten, conflicts.

With respect to the relationship between sanctions and the post-Cold War decline in conflict numbers, we would stress just two points.

First, as noted above, the Escribà-Folch study finds that where countries in conflict suffer the imposition of a sanctions regime, the duration of war will be shorter than in cases where sanctions are not applied. However, although this is an important finding, we should not place too much weight on it until it has been tested by further studies.

Second, even when the success rate of a particular security policy initiative is low, as is the case with the imposition of sanctions regimes, if the initiatives are numerous enough, the absolute number of successes may well be quite significant.

Today there is widespread consensus that the international community needs an instrument of suasion that lies between mere diplomatic censure on the one hand, and the use of force on the other. For this purpose—and notwithstanding the challenges—there is no real alternative to sanctions.

Other Possible Explanations for the Post-Cold War Decline in Conflict Numbers

The international initiatives discussed above have been directed at deterring wars, stopping those that cannot be prevented, and preventing those that have stopped from starting again. But there have been other changes associated with the end of the Cold War that may also have contributed to the decline in conflict numbers since the early 1990s.

The explosion of international peacemaking and post-conflict peacebuilding initiatives is central to any understanding of the decline in intrastate conflicts since the end of the Cold War. But these initiatives in turn need to be understood in the context of a broader shift in a range of security-related global norms that has taken place since the end of World War II. (We noted the evolution of the war-averseness norm in Chapter 1.) These evolving norms have provided a supportive context for the dramatic expansion of peacemaking and peacebuilding policies since the early 1990s, but may also have played an independent role in reducing the incidence of civil wars. It is the latter possibility that we address here.

In this section we consider the possible impact on the incidence of armed conflict in the post-Cold War period of three important shifts in global norms, namely:

- The ascendancy of democracy as the dominant norm of global governance—which is evident in the steep increase in the number of new democracies around the world over the past two decades.
- The increased salience of human rights norms evident in the more than fourfold increase in states with human rights prosecutions since the end of the Cold War.
- The sharp post-Cold War decline in the level of governmental discrimination directed at minority groups. This latter change is in turn related to the spread and deepening of the human rights and democracy norms.

We consider each in turn and finish with an examination of the possible impact of rising incomes on the incidence of armed conflict in the post-Cold War world.

Has the Democracy Revolution Driven Civil War Numbers Down?

At the end of World War II there were just 20 democracies (as defined by the Polity IV dataset) in the world. Today there are more than 90,[291] and democratic governance has become an entrenched global norm.

Chapter 1 pointed out that the increase in the number of democracies worldwide has been associated with a decline in international conflicts. Democratic peace theory suggests that this is because democracies almost never go to war against each other. And because the percentage of democracies in the international system has increased dramatically, the number of states that are never likely to fight each other has also increased.

But there is also persuasive evidence for a *democratic civil peace*—a peace that arises because inclusive democracies have much lower risks of succumbing to civil war than do autocracies and anocracies.[292] (*Anocracies* are regimes whose mode of governance is neither democratic nor authoritarian, but an unstable mix of both.)

Monty Marshall, director of the Polity IV Project, notes that anocracies "have been about six times more likely than democracies and two and one-half times as likely as autocracies to experience new outbreaks of societal wars."[293]

The finding that democracies have lower levels of violent conflict than nondemocracies is potentially relevant to explanations of the post-Cold War decline in armed conflict numbers because the number of democracies in the international system has almost doubled since the late 1980s.[294]

Given that inclusive democracies are at much lower risk of succumbing to war than either autocracies or anocracies, we would expect, other things being equal, that the post-Cold War doubling of the number of states with democratic governments would have tended to reduce the number of civil war onsets.

But while inclusive democracies may be at low risk of succumbing to armed conflict, the evidence indicates that the process of becoming a democracy increases the probability of a country suffering war. As a consequense, determining the extent of the impact of democratization on the risk of civil war is extremely difficult.[295]

The Deterrent Effect of Human Rights Prosecutions

In a recent issue of *International Studies Quarterly*, Hunjoon Kim and Kathryn Sikkink noted that human rights prosecutions "have been the major policy innovation of the late twentieth century designed to address human rights violations."[296] Their data show that the number of countries with prosecutions of perpetrators of human rights abuses has increased more than fourfold since 1989[297]—a change that has been aptly described as a "revolution in accountability."[298]

With respect to human rights abuses, Kim and Sikkink observe that "[p]rior to the 1970s, there was an almost zero likelihood that heads of state and state officials would be held accountable for past violations."[299] The resulting "culture of impunity" existed because, in the absence of prosecutions and punitive sanctions, there was no possibility of deterring rights violations.[300] But over the past two decades the number of prosecutions has increased dramatically, providing Kim and Sikkink with enough information to produce "the first full quantitative analysis on the impact of such prosecution on human rights practices."[301]

Sharp reductions in political discrimination should lead to reduced numbers of conflicts onsets.

The authors analyzed the impact of human rights prosecutions on 100 "transitional" countries. They examined three types of transition—political transitions to democracy, transitions from civil war, and transitions by state creation.[302] They do not include any human rights prosecutions in autocracies or democracies—and give reasons for these exclusions.

The key findings from the study were that:

transitional countries with human rights prosecutions are less repressive than countries without prosecutions [and] countries with more cumulative prosecutions are less repressive than countries with fewer prosecutions.[303]

Kim and Sikkink's findings appear to be directly relevant for conflict prevention since there is a striking correlation between increases in abuses of core human rights—notably those relating to assaults on physical integrity—and subsequent armed conflict onsets. As James Fearon has noted, when countries have a very poor human rights performance, this "is a *very* bad sign for a government: major civil conflict is then much more likely to begin."[304]

It follows that if human rights prosecutions reduce the risk of human rights abuses, they should also be associated with a reduced risk of future conflicts. The underlying argument here—one that aligns with grievance-based explanations of civil war onsets—is certainly plausible and may well be true. Fearon, however, points to a number of methodological challenges that caution against leaping too quickly to policy conclusions.[305] Although Kim and Sikkink's analysis controls for factors other than prosecutions that might affect their results, their findings need to be replicated before too much weight is placed on them.

The Decline in Discrimination Against Minority Groups

A third remarkable normative shift associated with the end of the Cold War has been evident in the decline in the level of discrimination directed by governments against ethnic and other minority groups around the world. Data from the Minorities at Risk Project indicate that between 1991 and 2004, the number of minority groups around the world that were being victimized by governmental discrimination almost halved, dropping from some 75 to 41.[306]

This finding has obvious relevance for global security. As a 2005 study by Victor Asal and Amy Pate noted, "there is abundant evidence that high levels of political discrimination are a key cause of violent ethnic conflict."[307] It follows that sharp reductions in political discrimination should lead to reduced numbers of conflict onsets.

In fact, the data presented by Asal and Pate's colleagues show that a significant decline in self-determination conflicts being waged around the world was associated with the downturn in governmental discrimination since the end of the Cold War. These types of conflicts dropped from 40 in 1991 to just 25 in 2004.[308]

In the case of the three normative shifts noted above, we see the impact of shifts in global security norms that have deepened since the end of the Cold War and that have helped drive increases in democratization, respect for human rights, and opposition to political and ethnic discrimination. In each case the normative shift is correlated with the decline in conflict numbers. This finding supports claims that the impact of shifting norms may have been a contributory cause of the decline in conflict numbers. It does not, of course, demonstrate this—correlation is not the same as causation.

Could Rising National Incomes Have Caused the Decline in Intrastate Conflict?

As noted previously, the most robust finding to emerge from the quantitative conflict literature over the past two decades has been that there is a strong association between GDP (gross domestic product) per capita—which is a proxy measure for state capacity—and the risk of intrastate conflict onsets. Other things being equal, the greater the capacity of the state, the lower the risk of war.

World Bank data indicate that global incomes did indeed rise following the end of the Cold War. In low- and middle-income countries—where most wars take place—average GDP per capita increased by almost 40 percent between 1989 and 2008.[309]

Other things being equal, the effect of this increase should have been a modest decrease in the number of conflict onsets. But this is not what happened—intrastate conflict onsets in the 1990s increased sharply. This suggests that although the post-Cold War increase in incomes may have had a conflict-onset-reducing impact, this impact was overwhelmed by more powerful forces that were driving conflict onsets upwards during the political turmoil that followed the end of the Cold War.

But rising incomes and state capacity are also associated with shorter wars,[310] and shorter wars mean more terminations. And as we know, terminations did increase in the 1990s. So, rising state capacity may be part of the explanation of that increase. But whatever the impact on the incidence of terminations, it is clear that it would have been very modest. We would therefore expect changes in income to have a substantial impact on the risk of conflict when measured over many decades, but only a minor impact over shorter periods.

Implications for Policy

We referred earlier to the major methodological and data challenges that would be involved in attempting to conduct quantitative analyses of all of the potential policy initiatives and structural changes that may have been drivers of the decline in conflict numbers in the post-Cold War era.

Our analysis has taken a very different approach—although we have cited econometric research findings where appropriate. Our approach has been driven in considerable part by descriptive statistics that have revealed the changing patterns of conflict since the Cold War and raised many of the questions that this chapter has sought to answer.

The evidence from various statistical studies cited here suggests that both the peacemaking initiatives (focused on mediating conflict settlements) and the peacebuilding initiatives (focused on peace operations) have been moderately successful in stopping wars and preventing them from restarting. And, as noted above, when policy initiatives have even moderate to low success rates, the absolute number of successes—i.e., wars stopped or prevented—will increase as the

number of initiatives increases. This is highly pertinent since, as we have seen, there have been dramatic increases in all forms of international security activism since the early 1990s.

This latter point also applies to the impact of sanctions—policy initiatives that have success rates varying between 25 and 36 percent and are widely regarded as ineffectual policy instruments for coercing change in the behaviour of target states. In the 1980s there were never more than three sanctions regimes in place in any year; in 2008 there were more than eight times that number. Even with a 25 percent success rate, this would have meant a substantial increase in the absolute number of successes. We also pointed out that sanctions can have positive security impacts—notably in shortening the length of wars—that have been largely overlooked in the sanctions literature.

The clear message for policy-makers is that international activism—primarily, but by no means solely, peacemaking and post-conflict peacebuilding—works. Indeed, we believe that it is the single most compelling policy-relevant explanation for the post-Cold War reduction in political violence around the world.

In our review of the causes of the decline in the number of intrastate conflicts since the early 1990s we also examined the direct impact of the end of the Cold War on conflict numbers. We suggested that while this extraordinary event clearly brought some conflicts to an end, it caused others to start. It is therefore impossible to determine the net effect without an in-depth investigation of all the relevant cases.

But it is clear that whatever the direct impact of the end of the Cold War on conflict numbers in the 1990s, this change no longer has any policy relevance. The political changes catalyzed directly by the end of East-West hostilities have ceased to be a cause of conflict, and there are no more proxy wars to be brought to an end by the withdrawal of superpower assistance to the warring parties. From the point of view of current and future security policies, the end of the Cold War, which was a one-off event and not a policy initiative, is of little consequence.

Conclusion

In the 60-plus years since the end of World War II, two powerful system-wide drivers of armed conflict—colonialism and the Cold War—have ceased to exist. Neither will return and at this time no obvious new system-wide threat to peace appears likely to replace them.

Some will argue that violent Islamist radicalism, as exemplified by al-Qaeda, already constitutes such a threat.

But, as we note in Part III, support for extremist Islamist ideologies has declined substantially throughout the Muslim world in recent years. Absent popular support, Islamist radicals cannot wage a successful "people's war," and without conventional armies—which no Islamist insurgents possess—overthrowing governments becomes a huge challenge. The radicals may possibly prevail in a small number of countries where state capacity is very weak, but it is highly unlikely that radical Islamist ideology can ever energize a sustained global campaign comparable to the anticolonial movement or the leftist insurgencies of the Cold War period.

There are several other reasons for cautious optimism regarding the global security future.

First, there is no real indication that the international community's commitment to peacemaking and peacebuilding is waning, notwithstanding the global economic crisis. As the authors of the authoritative *Annual Review of Peace Operations 2011* recently pointed out, 2010 was a year:

in which global peace operations continued to grow in overall levels of deployment *despite expectations that significant operational, political, and financial pressure would lead to downsizing.*[311]

Second, barring a major collapse of the global economy, incomes will almost certainly continue to grow throughout most of the developing world. Over the long term this will in turn continue to enhance state capacity which, almost all the statistical studies agree, reduces the risks of civil wars. International economic interdependence, which is associated with reduced risks of interstate war, will also continue to grow.

Third, the universalization of norms that help reduce the risk of conflict appears unlikely to be reversed.

None of these developments, of course, provides any guarantee that the security future, even in the short and medium term, will necessarily be benign. Conflict research, as discussed in Chapter 2, does not have a great record when it comes to predicting the security future—and wars have very disparate causes, many of which may be unaffected by the trends noted above.

In the short term we know that the 2011 political uprisings in the Middle East and North Africa may cause an increase in the number of conflict onsets—though it is unclear how long these conflicts will persist. Over the longer term, new security challenges will be posed by the combined impacts of climate change and population growth in the developing world. But at the very least the trends noted in this *Report* provide a powerful antidote to some of the more direly pessimistic predictions about the global security future.[312]

Finally, we note that in the two decades since the Cold War ended, the world has witnessed the creation of a new, but little-analyzed, global security architecture, one that is radically different from the bipolar security system of the Cold War years.

The new architecture comprises a loose but ever-expanding network of international organizations, donor and other governments, inter-agency committees, informal clusters of like-minded states like the Friends groups discussed previously, think-tanks, and large numbers of national and international NGOs.

The central rationale of the system is the reduction of political violence—in particular civil wars—around the world.

> The universalization of norms that help reduce the risk of conflict appears to be unlikely to be reversed.

The evolving mode of security governance that is associated with this new architecture does not eschew use of the military—uniformed peacekeepers play a central role in its missions. But its major security objectives—conflict prevention, peacemaking, and post-conflict peacebuilding—are undertaken primarily by nonmilitary means.

The pursuit of these objectives is grounded in a growing normative consensus that the international community has a responsibility to prevent war, to help stop wars that cannot be prevented, and to try and prevent those that have stopped from starting again.

This still emerging system of security governance has been, and remains, rife with coordination problems, disagreements over strategy, and unresolved tensions between international agencies, states, and NGOs. It is a system that is inherently inefficient and disputatious and—as Rwanda and Darfur remind us—prone to tragic failures. But the best evidence that we have suggests that its collective efforts have been a primary driver of the major decline in the deadliest forms of armed conflict since the end of the Cold War.

This is a considerable achievement.

PART I

ENDNOTES

CHAPTER 1

1. Uppsala Conflict Data Program (UCDP), Uppsala University, Uppsala, Sweden/Centre for the Study of Civil War, International Peace Research Institute, Oslo (PRIO), Armed Conflict Dataset v4-2009, http://www.prio.no/CSCW/Datasets/Armed-Conflict/UCDP-PRIO/ (accessed 16 November 2010).

2. Centre for the Study of Civil War, International Peace Research Institute, Oslo, (PRIO), Battle Deaths Dataset 3.0, http://www.prio.no/CSCW/Datasets/Armed-Conflict/Battle-Deaths/The-Battle-Deaths-Dataset-version-30/ (accessed 16 November 2010), updated from Bethany Lacina and Nils Petter Gleditsch, "Monitoring Trends in Global Combat: A New Dataset of Battle Deaths," *European Journal of Population* 21, no. 2–3 (2005): 145–166; UCDP/Human Security Report Project (HSRP), School for International Studies, Simon Fraser University, Vancouver, Canada.

3. Hans Morgenthau, *Politics Among Nations: The Struggle for Power and Peace* (New York: Knopf, 1948).

4. Kenneth Waltz, *Theory of International Politics* (Boston: McGraw-Hill, 1979); John Mearsheimer, *The Tragedy of Great Power Politics* (New York: Norton, 2001).

5. A. F. K. Organski and Jacek Kugler, *The War Ledger* (Chicago: University of Chicago Press, 1980).

6. Morgenthau and Waltz are the most influential scholarly proponents of the balance of power thesis.

7. John H. Herz, "Idealist Internationalism and the Security Dilemma," *World Politics* 2, no. 2 (January 1950): 157–180.

8. Michael D. Wallace, "Arms Races and Escalation: Some New Evidence," *The Journal of Conflict Resolution* 23, no. 1 (March 1979): 3–16.

9. John A. Vasquez, "What Do We Know about War?" in *What Do We Know about War?* ed. John A. Vasquez (Lanham, MD: Rowman & Littlefield Publishers, 2000), 344.

10. See Brett Ashley Leeds, "Do Alliances Deter Aggression? The Influence of Military Alliances on the Initiation of Militarized Interstate Disputes," *American Journal of Political Science* 47, no. 3 (July 2003): 427, for an extended discussion.

11. Ibid.

12. Jack S. Levy, "Alliance Formation and War Behavior: An Analysis of the Great Powers, 1495-1975," *The Journal of Conflict Resolution* 25, no. 4 (December 1981): 583–584.

13. Leeds argues that different alliances have very different purposes and that the failure to take this fact into account may explain the inconclusive findings in the major statistical studies. Some alliances are defensive and may well serve to prevent war, while others are coalitions of states bent on aggression. The probability of conflict will be far greater in the latter type of alliance than the former. However, Leeds argues that the important, but very different, relationships between alliance formation and the risk of war may be hidden by the very statistical methods that are intended to reveal them. Brett Ashley Leeds, "Do Alliances Deter Aggression? The Influence of Military Alliances on the Initiation of Militarized Interstate Disputes," *American Journal of Political Science* 47, no. 3 (July 2003): 427–439.

14. A. F. K. Organski and Jacek Kugler, *The War Ledger*; and Robert Gilpin, *War and Change in World Politics* (New York: Cambridge University Press, 1981).

15. William Brian Moul, "Balances of Power and Escalation to War of Serious Disputes among the European Great Powers, 1815-1939: Some Evidence," *American Journal of Political Science* 32, no. 2 (May 1988): 241–275.

16. Stuart Bremer, "Democracy and Militarized Interstate Conflict, 1816-1965," *International Interactions* 18, no. 3 (February 1993): 231–249.

17. Håvard Hegre, "Gravitating toward War: Preponderance May Pacify, but Power Kills," *Journal of Conflict Resolution* 52, no. 4 (August 2008): 566–589.

18. Ibid.

19. This includes involvement as a primary or secondary party in interstate and extrastate conflicts; UCDP/PRIO.

20. E. L. Katzenbach Jr., "Time, Space and Will: The Politico-Military Strategy Views of Mao Tse-tung," in *The Guerrilla and How To Fight Him*, ed. Lt. Col. T. N. Greene (New York: Frederick A. Praeger, 1962), 15.

21. Henry A. Kissinger, "The Vietnam Negotiations," *Foreign Affairs*, January 1969, 39.

22. For a detailed analysis of the strategy of asymmetric conflict see Andrew Mack, "Why Big Nations Lose Small Wars: The Politics of Asymmetric Conflict," *World Politics* 27, no. 2 (January 1975): 175–200.

23. Winston Churchill, speech at the Mansion House, London, UK, 9 November 1942.

24. Harold MacMillan, speech to members of both Houses of the Parliament of the Union of South Africa, Cape Town, 3 February 1960, Cabinet Memorandum, Prime Minister's African Tour, Note by the Secretary of the Cabinet, 12 April 1960, 155, http://filestore.nationalarchives.gov.uk/pdfs/small/cab-129-101-c-66.pdf (accessed 13 August 2010).

25. Kenneth Waltz, "Peace, Stability, and Nuclear Weapons," Institute on Global Conflict and Cooperation, Policy Paper No. 15, University of California, Berkeley, August 1995, 9, http://igcc.ucsd.edu/pdf/policypapers/pp15.pdf (accessed 6 August 2010).

26. Ronald Reagan, "Address before a Joint Session of the Congress on the State of the Union," 25 January 1984, The American Presidency Project, http://www.presidency.ucsb.edu/ws/index.php?pid=40205 (accessed 6 August 2010).

27. *Report of the International Commission on Nuclear Non-Proliferation and Disarmament: Eliminating Nuclear Threats: A Practical Agenda for Global Policymakers*, 2009, http://www.icnnd.org/reference/reports/ent/part-iii-6.html#deterrence (accessed 6 August 2010).

28. Waltz, "Peace, Stability, and Nuclear Weapons" (accessed 6 August 2010).

29. Nina Tannenwald, "Stigmatizing the Bomb: Origins of the Nuclear Taboo," *International Security* 29, no. 4 (Spring 2005): 5–49.

30. John Mueller, "The Escalating Irrelevance of Nuclear Weapons," in *The Absolute Weapon Revisited: Nuclear Arms and the Emerging International Order*, ed. T. V. Paul, Richard J. Harknett, and James J. Wirtz (Ann Arbor: University of Michigan Press, 2000), 77. Emphasis added.

31. Jack S. Levy, "Domestic Politics and War," *Journal of Interdisciplinary History* 18, no. 4 (Spring 1988): 662.

32. Polity IV Project at the Center for Systemic Peace, Maryland, USA, http://www.systemicpeace.org/polity/polity4.htm (accessed 15 November 2010).

33. Edward D. Mansfield and Jack Snyder, "Demographic Transitions and War: From Napoleon to the Millennium's End," in *Turbulent Peace: The Challenges of Managing International Conflict*, ed. Chester A. Crocker, Fen Osler Hampson, and Pamela Aall (Washington: United States Institute of Peace, 2001), 115.

34. Ibid., 114.

35. Ibid., 115.

36. See Vipin Narang and Rebecca M. Nelson, "Who are These Belligerent Democratizers? Reassessing the Impact of Democratization on War," *International Organization* 63, no. 2 (Spring 2009): 357–379. See also the response by Edward D. Mansfield and Jack Snyder, "Pathways to War in Democratic Transitions," *International Organization* 63, no. 2 (Spring 2009): 381–390.

37. John Mearsheimer, "Why We Will Soon Miss the Cold War," August 1990, http://teachingamericanhistory.org/library/index.asp?document=713 (accessed 6 August 2010).

38. Ibid.

39. Erik Gartzke, "The Capitalist Peace," *American Journal of Political Science* 51, no. 1 (January 2007): 166–191.

40. James Gwartney, Robert Lawson with Erik Gartzke, *Economic Freedom of the World: 2005 Annual Report* (Washington: The Cato Institute, 2005), 4.

41. John Mueller, *Capitalism, Democracy, and Ralph's Pretty Good Grocery* (Princeton: Princeton University Press, 1999), 245.

42. Solomon Polachek, Carlos Seiglie, and Jun Xiang, "Globalization and International Conflict: Can FDI Increase Peace as Trade Does?" American Economic Association, 2005, http://www.aeaweb.org/assa/2005/0109_0800_0204.pdf (accessed 6 August 2010). (The authors used the Kansas Events Data System (KEDS) as their source of conflict data.)

43. Ibid. (Unlike Gartzke, the authors found that democracy is associated with reduced risks of conflict.)

44. UNCTADstat, United Nations, http://unctadstat.unctad.org/ReportFolders/reportFolders.aspx?sCS_referer=&sCS_Chosen Lang=en (accessed 15 November 10).

45. The data presented in Figure 1.4 include FDI in the People's Republic of China that is disproportionately larger than that in other countries in the sample. Including China brings up the overall level of FDI in developing countries, but has virtually no effect on the trend.

46. See Allan Dafoe, "Statistical Critiques of the Democratic Peace: Caveat Emptor." *American Journal of Political Science,* forthcoming 2011; Ceren Altincekic, "FDI Peace: Which 'Capitalism' Leads to More Peace among Dyads?" (working paper, One Earth Foundation, 2009), http://www.oneearthfuture.org/siteadmin/images/files/file_41.pdf (accessed 6 August 2010).

47. John Mueller, "War Has Almost Ceased to Exist: An Assessment," *Political Science Quarterly* 124, no. 2 (Summer 2009): 300.

48. Michael Howard, *The Causes of Wars* (Cambridge: Harvard University Press, 1983), 9.

49. Steven Pinker, "A History of Violence; We're Getting Nicer Every Day," *The New Republic,* 19 March 2007, http://www.tnr.com/article/history-violence-were-getting-nicer-every-day (accessed 6 August 2010).

50. John Mueller, "Capitalism, Peace, and the Historical Movement of Ideas," *International Interactions* 36, no. 2 (April 2010): 180.

51. See Michael Howard, *The Lessons of History* (New Haven: Yale University Press, 1991); John Keegan, *A History of Warfare* (New York: Knopf, 1993).

52. Alexander Wendt, "Anarchy Is What States Make of It: The Social Construction of Power Politics," *International Organization* 46, no. 2 (March 1992): 391–425.

53. Kenneth Waltz, "Structural Realism after the Cold War," *International Security* 25, no. 1 (Summer 2000): 39.

CHAPTER 2

54. Other quantitative approaches are not covered here. They include game theory, explorations of the collective action problems associated with rebel recruitment and peace agreements, and power law theory.

55. There are some exceptions to these general rules. Some scholars, for example, examine global security developments using nonquantitative methodologies. While, as we point out later, *micro-quantitative* methods—which use quantitative techniques often in conjunction with population surveys at the local level and regional level—are being increasingly used to examine conflict dynamics in individual countries.

56. High-intensity conflicts are those in which there are 1,000 or more battle deaths per year. The Uppsala Conflict Data Program (UCDP), which provides the statistics used by the Human Security Report Project (HSRP), refers to these conflicts as "wars." Conflicts with 25 or more, but fewer than 1,000, deaths a year are referred to as "minor conflicts." The decline in all state-based armed conflicts between 1992 and 2003 was more than 40 percent. HSRP follows common usage here and uses the terms "civil war" and "intrastate conflict" interchangeably.

57. More specifically, regression analysis can reveal how the value of the dependent variable changes when any one of the independent variables is changed, while the other independent variables are *controlled*—i.e., held constant.

58. Some studies have conflict duration as the dependent variable.

59. James Fearon and David Laitin, "Integrating Qualitative and Quantitative Research Methods," in *The Oxford Handbook of Political Methodology*, ed. Janet M. Box-Steffensmeier, Henry E. Brady, and David Collier (New York: Oxford University Press, 2008), 756.

60. See Paul Collier and Anke Hoeffler, "Greed and Grievance in Civil War," *Oxford Economic Papers* 56, no. 4 (August 2004): 563–595.

61. Nicholas Sambanis and Paul Collier, eds., *Understanding Civil War: Evidence and Analysis*, vol. 1, *Africa*, vol. 2, *Europe, Central Asia, and Other Regions* (Washington: World Bank Publications, 2005).

62. Paul Collier, *The Bottom Billion: Why the Poorest Countries Are Failing and What Can Be Done about It* (Oxford: Oxford University Press, 2007).

63. Nathaniel Beck, Gary King, and Langche Zeng, "Improving Quantitative Studies of International Conflict: A Conjecture," *American Political Science Review* 94, no. 1 (March 2000): 21.

64. Håvard Hegre and Nicholas Sambanis, "Sensitivity Analysis of Empirical Results on Civil War Onset," *Journal of Conflict Resolution* 50, no. 3 (August 2006): 508–535.

65. Notably, Jeffrey Dixon, "What Causes Civil Wars? Integrating Quantitative Research Findings," *International Studies Review* 11, no. 4 (December 2009): 707–735.

66. Hegre and Sambanis, "Sensitivity Analysis of Empirical Results on Civil War Onset," 508–535 and Dixon, "What Causes Civil Wars? Integrating Quantitative Research Findings," 707–735.

67. Cullen S. Hendrix and Sarah M. Glaser, "Trends and Triggers: Climate Change and Civil Conflict in Sub-Saharan Africa" (paper presented at the international workshop on Human Security and Climate Change, Asker, Norway, June 2005), http://www.gechs.org/downloads/holmen/Hendrix_Glaser.pdf (accessed 2 September 2010), 4.

68. Michael D. Ward, Brian D. Greenhill, and Kristin M. Bakke, "The Perils of Policy by P-Value: Predicting Civil Conflicts," *Journal of Peace Research* 47, no. 4 (March 2010): 1–13.

69. James D. Fearon and David A. Laitin, "Ethnicity, Insurgency and Civil War," *American Political Science Review* 97, no. 1 (February 2003): 75–90.

70. The Fearon/Laitin model predicted none of the 107 wars under the 0.5 threshold above which civil wars are deemed to occur. Under the 0.3 and 0.1 thresholds, their model predicted 1 out of 107 and 15 out of 107 wars, respectively, but the higher predictive power comes at the cost of a greater number of false positives. See Ward, Greenhill, and Bakke, "The Perils of Policy by P-Value," 4.

71. Fearon and Laitin, "Integrating Qualitative and Quantitative Methods," 11.

72. Paul Collier, "Economic Causes of Civil Conflict and Their Implications for Policy," in *Leashing the Dogs of War: Conflict Management in a Divided World*, ed. Chester A. Crocker, Fen Osler Hampson, and Pamela Aall (Washington: United States Institute of Peace Press, 2007), 203.

73. Jack A. Goldstone et al., "A Global Model for Forecasting Political Instability," *American Journal of Political Science* 54, no. 1 (December 2009): 190–208.

74. Ibid.

75. Calculations for the comparison of success rates were undertaken in-house at HSRP.

76. Model specification determines which independent variables should be included in, or excluded from, the statistical model. Errors can arise when theoretically relevant variables are excluded or theoretically irrelevant variables are included. See Michael Patrick Allen, *Understanding Regression Analysis* (New York: Plenum Press, 1997). By "model" we mean a simplified mathematical representation of reality showing the interrelationships/associations between selected variables.

77. Christopher Blattman and Edward Miguel, "Civil War," *Journal of Economic Literature* 48, no. 1 (March 2010): 3–57.

78. Ward, Greenhill, and Bakke, "The Perils of Policy by P-Value," 1–13; Hegre and Sambanis, "Sensitivity Analysis of Empirical Results on Civil War Onset," 508–535; Nicholas Sambanis, "What Is Civil War? Conceptual and Empirical Complexities of an Operational Definition," *Journal of Conflict Resolution* 48, no. 6 (December 2004): 814–858.

79. Something is *endogenous* to a system if it is determined within the system, and *exogenous* if it is determined outside the system.

80. Michael Ross, "A Closer Look at Oil, Diamonds, and Civil War," *Annual Review of Political Science* 9 (June 2006): 265–300.

81. An additional point to note is that few influential papers in this literature test for interaction effects between the ostensibly independent variables, despite the fact that the qualitative literature on civil war indicates that these can be important in some cases.

82. Fearon and Laitin, "Integrating Qualitative and Quantitative Methods," 11.

83. Jeremy Weinstein, *Inside Rebellion: The Politics of Insurgent Violence* (New York: Cambridge University Press, 2007), 366.

84. Natural disasters—droughts, floods, earthquakes, for example—can also trigger conflict in high-risk situations. See Philip Nel and Marjolein Righarts, "Natural Disasters and the Risk of Violent Civil Conflict," *International Studies Quarterly* 52, no. 1 (April 2008): 159–185.

85. Doug Bond et al., "Integrated Data for Events Analysis (IDEA): An Event Typology for Automated Events Data Development," *Journal of Peace Research* 40, no. 6 (November 2003): 733–745.

86. Jack Goldstone, "Triggers of Instability: Random Events or Aids to Forecasting?" (paper presented at the annual meeting of the International Studies Association's (ISA) 50th Annual Convention, "Exploring the Past, Anticipating the Future," New York, February 2009), http://www.allacademic.com/meta/p_mla_apa_research_citation/3/1/2/6/7/p312671_index.html (accessed 10 September 2010).

87. Genocide Prevention Task Force, *Preventing Genocide: A Blueprint for U.S. Policymakers* (Washington: United States Holocaust Memorial Museum, The American Academy of Diplomacy, and the Endowment of the United States Institute of Peace, 2008): 21.

88. Goldstone, "Triggers of Instability" (accessed 10 September 2010).

89. See Jeffrey Checkel, "It's the Process Stupid! Process Tracing in the Study of European and International Politics," October 2005, http://www.arena.uio.no/publications/working-papers2005/papers/wp05_26.pdf (accessed 2 September 2010).

90. Graham Brown and Arnim Langer, "Dealing with Time in the Quantitative Study of Conflict" (Centre for Research on Inequality, Human Security and Ethnicity [CRISE], *Working Paper No. 66*, University of Oxford, 2009), 16.

91. Ibid., 18.

92. Sambanis, "What Is Civil War?" 814–858.

93. James D. Fearon, "Primary Commodity Exports and Civil War," *Journal of Conflict Resolution* 49, no. 4 (August 2005): 483–507.

94. Ibid. Reproducing the Collier/Hoeffler model, Fearon was able to include 16 of the 27 excluded cases by using a single country-year as the unit of analysis rather than the five-year period used by Collier and Hoeffler—the *Journal of Conflict Resolution* article contains a detailed rationale for doing this. Other things being equal, we would expect that the more complete, and thus more representative, dataset would generate more reliable results. The issue is re-examined in Paul Collier and Anke Hoeffler, "Resource Rents, Governance, and Conflict," *Journal of Conflict Resolution* 49, no. 4 (August 2005): 625–633. Here they focus more on resource rents than primary commodity dependence.

95. The authors had performed some robustness checks, but not the one that Fearon used.

96. Personal communication from Clionadh Raleigh of Armed Conflict Location and Events Data (ACLED) to HSRP Director Andrew Mack, 2 March 2009.

97. See Clionadh Raleigh and Håvard Hegre, "Introducing ACLED: An Armed Conflict Location and Event Dataset" (paper presented to the Conference on Disaggregating the Study of Civil War and Transnational Violence, San Diego, CA, 2005), 13–24.

98. This dataset, which is not yet complete, is being compiled by UCDP.

99. See, for example, Christopher Blattman, "From Violence to Voting: War and Political Participation in Uganda," *American Political Science Review* 103, no. 2 (May 2009): 231–247; Philip Verwimp, "Testing the Double-Genocide Thesis for Central and Southern Rwanda," *Journal of Conflict Resolution* 47, no. 4 (August 2003): 423–442; Ana M. Arjona and Stathis N. Kalyvas, "Rebelling against Rebellion: Comparing Insurgent and Counterinsurgent Recruitment" (paper presented at the Centre for Research on Inequality, Human Security and Ethnicity Workshop: Mobilisation for Political Violence What Do We Know? Oxford, UK, 2009), 4 and Macartan Humphreys and Jeremy Weinstein, "Who Fights? The Determinants of Participation in Civil War," *American Journal of Political Science* 52, no. 2 (April 2008): 436–455.

100. See http://www.hicn.org/index.html (accessed 2 September 2010) and http://www.microconflict.eu/ (accessed 2 September 2010).

101. Kristian Skrede Gleditsch, "Transnational Dimensions of Civil War," *Journal of Peace Research* 44, no. 3 (May 2007): 293–309.

102. Ibid.

103. For an audiofile description of the dataset, see http://www.utexas.edu/lbj/videos/05-17-2010/political-disorder-africa-new-dataset (accessed 2 September 2010).

104. See Doug Bond et al., "Mapping Mass Political Conflict and Civil Society: Issues and Prospects for the Automated Development of Event Data," *Journal of Conflict Resolution* 41, no. 4 (August 1997): 553–579; Phillip Schrodt and Omur Yilmaz, "Coding Sub-State Actors Using the CAMEO (Conflict and Mediation Event Observations) Actor Coding Framework" (paper presented at the annual meeting of the ISA's 49th Annual Convention, "Bridging Multiple Divides," San Francisco, CA, 2008). A new dataset associated with Project Civil Strife is being developed that "uses automated coding of English-language news reports to generate multi-actor political event data focusing on Southeast Asia. These data are used in statistical models to predict and explain political change." See http://smshel.people.wm.edu/Data/PCS.html (2 September 2010).

105. James Mahoney and Gary Goertz, "A Tale of Two Cultures: Contrasting Quantitative and Qualitative Research," *Political Analysis* 14, no. 3 (Summer 2006): 227–249.

106. J. W. Creswell, *Research Design: Qualitative, Quantitative, and Mixed Methods Approaches*, 3rd ed. (London: Sage Publications, 2009); Fearon and Laitin, "Integrating Qualitative and Quantitative Research Methods"; Barbara Walter, *Committing to Peace: The Successful Settlement of Civil Wars* (Princeton: Princeton University Press, 2001); and Sambanis and Collier, *Understanding Civil War*.

107. Sambanis and Collier, *Understanding Civil War*.

108. Fearon and Laitin, "Integrating Qualitative and Quantitative Research Methods," 766.

109. Ibid, 757.

110. Paul Collier, Anke Hoeffler, and Dominic Rohner, "Beyond Greed and Grievance: Feasibility and Civil War," *Oxford Economic Papers* 61, no. 1 (August 2009): 1–27.

CHAPTER 3

111. *East Asia* is used here to include both Northeast and Southeast Asia. Northeast Asia includes China, Japan, North and South Korea, Mongolia, and Taiwan. Southeast Asia includes Brunei, Burma, Cambodia, Indonesia, Laos, Malaysia, the Philippines, Singapore, Timor Leste, and Vietnam. See Stein Tønnesson, "What Is It That Best Explains the East Asian Peace since 1979? A Call for a Research Agenda," *Asian Perspective* 33, no. 1 (2009): 111–136.

112. Elsina Wainwright, "Conflict Prevention in Southeast Asia and the South Pacific," Center on International Cooperation, New York University (April 2010): 6, http://www.cic.nyu.edu/global/docs/wainwright_conflict_asia.pdf (accessed 20 October 2010).

113. The exception was the border war between China and Vietnam, which continued sporadically until the late 1980s, but the casualty figures were only a small fraction of the huge death tolls the region saw in earlier decades.

114. The Khmer Rouge defeated the then Cambodian government in 1975, but were subsequently ousted in 1978 in part as a consequence of the Vietnamese invasion in support of the anti-Khmer Rouge rebels.

115. Uppsala Conflict Data Program (UCDP), Uppsala University, Uppsala, Sweden/Centre for the Study of Civil War, International Peace Research Institute, Oslo (PRIO), Armed Conflict Dataset v4-2009, http://www.prio.no/CSCW/Datasets/Armed-Conflict/UCDP-PRIO/ (accessed 16 November 2010).

    The count of conflict years includes only countries that are independent as of 2008. For countries that gained independence from a colonial power or as a result of a war of secession, conflict years were counted for the colonial power as well as the future independent country.

    Note that the region displayed here is a sub-set of the HSRP region "East and Southeast Asia and Oceania" referred to in other parts of this *Report*, which includes the countries in Northeast and Southeast Asia shown in Figure 3.1 plus Oceania.

116. See Barry Buzan and Ole Wæver, *Regions and Powers: The Structure of International Security* (Cambridge: Cambridge University Press, 2003), 44. Emphasis added.

117. The most comprehensive of the extraordinarily few studies that have sought to explain the dramatic decline in the number and deadliness of armed conflicts in East Asia is Stein Tønnesson's "What Is It That Best Explains the East Asian Peace since 1979?"

118. Centre for the Study of Civil War, International Peace Research Institute, Oslo (PRIO), Battle Deaths Dataset 3.0, http://www.prio.no/CSCW/Datasets/Armed-Conflict/Battle-Deaths/The-Battle-Deaths-Dataset-version-30/ (accessed 16 November 2010), updated from Bethany Lacina and Nils Petter Gleditsch, "Monitoring Trends in Global Combat: A New Dataset of Battle Deaths," *European Journal of Population* 21, no. 2–3 (2005): 145–166; UCDP/Human Security Report Project, School for International Studies, Simon Fraser University, Vancouver, Canada.

119. The colonial territory of French Indochina was made up of present-day Cambodia, Laos, and Vietnam.

120. The conflict over Brunei's independence from the United Kingdom in 1962 resulted in only a few dozen battle deaths.

121. James Mayall and Cornelia Navari, eds., *The End of the Post-War Era: Documents on Great-Power Relations* 1968–75 (Cambridge: Cambridge University Press, 1980), 92. The Nixon Doctrine, also known as the Guam Doctrine, was announced in Guam in 1969 by President Nixon.

122. Richard Nixon, *No More Vietnams* (Westminster, MD: Arbor House Publishing, 1987).

123. The US has continued to maintain a sizable, though reduced, military presence in South Korea and Japan, but it abandoned its major military bases in the Philippines in the early 1990s.

124. China was particularly concerned to gain ASEAN's support for its goal of isolating Vietnam politically.

125. One communist insurgency remains in the subregion today, waged by the New People's Army in the Philippines. China stopped supplying it with aid in 1975.

126. David E. Cunningham, "Blocking Resolution: How External States Can Prolong Civil Wars," *Journal of Peace Research* 47, no. 2 (March 2010): 115–127.

127. The civilians killed in Bali, Jakarta, and other Islamist terror bombings are not counted as combat deaths.

128. The actual decline was from 13 to five ongoing conflicts from 1978 to 1995. The number of conflicts has remained at approximately the same level since then.

129. James Fearon, "Economic Development, Insurgency and Civil War," in *Economic Institutions and Civil War*, ed. Elhanan Helpman (Cambridge: Harvard University Press, 2008), 293.

130. Macartan Humphreys and Ashutosh Varshney, "Violent Conflict and the Millennium Development Goals: Diagnosis and Recommendations," First draft, background paper prepared for the meeting of the Millennium Development Goals Poverty Task Force Workshop, Bangkok, June 2004, http://www.columbia.edu/~mh2245/papers1/HV.pdf (accessed 15 November 2010), 9.

131. Angus Maddison, "Statistics on World Population, GDP and Per Capita GDP, 1-2008 AD," http://www.ggdc.net/maddison/content.shtml (accessed 15 November 2010).

    Maddison aggregated data for 24 small economies under the category "24 small East Asian countries." However, the list mostly comprises countries that HSRP classifies as being in Oceania. Thus, this figure excludes these "24 small East Asian countries." However, including them would produce a virtually identical graph.

132. Paul Collier and Anke Hoeffler, "Greed and Grievance in Civil War," *Oxford Economic Papers* 56, no. 4 (August 2004): 563–595.

133. Paul Collier, *The Bottom Billion: Why the Poorest Countries are Failing and What Can Be Done About It* (New York: Oxford University Press, 2007), 20.

134. Christopher Blattman, "Can Youth Employment Programs Foster Social Stability in Africa?" (paper presented to the World Bank Africa Management Retreat, April 2010), http://chrisblattman.com/files/2010/09/Blattman-Can-youth-employment-reduce-social-instability-April-2010.pdf (accessed 21 October 2010), 3.

135. See William T. Tow, *Encountering the Dominant Player: U.S. Extended Deterrence Strategy in the Asia-Pacific* (New York: Columbia University Press, 1991).

136. Vinod Aggarwal and Min Gyo Koo, "An Institutional Path: Community Building in Northeast East Asia," in *The United States and Northeast Asia: Debates, Issue, and New Order*, ed. John Ikenberry and Chung-in Moon (Lanham, MD: Rowan and Littlefield, 2007), 285–307.

137. Chung-in Moon and Seung-Won Suh, "Identity Politics, Nationalism and the Future of Northeast Asian Order," in *The United States and Northeast Asia: Debates, Issue, and New Order*, ed. John Ikenberry and Chung-in Moon (Lanham: Rowan and Littlefield, 2007), 194.

138. See Alastair I. Johnstone, "Is China a Status-Quo Power?" *International Security* 27, no. 4 (Spring 2003): 5–56.

139. On a few issues—most obviously Taiwan—the Chinese have made it clear that they are prepared to use force regardless of the economic costs.

140. ASEAN, which was created in August 1967, is now made up of 10 countries: Brunei, Burma, Cambodia, Indonesia, Laos, Malaysia, Philippines, Singapore, Thailand, and Vietnam. Brunei joined in 1984, Vietnam in 1995, Laos and Burma in 1997, and Cambodia in 1999. See ASEAN, "Overview," http://www.aseansec.org/64.htm (accessed 27 October 2010). Timor Leste has expressed its intention to apply for membership.

141. See Amitav Acharya, *Constructing a Security Community in Southeast Asia: ASEAN and the Problem of Regional Order* (New York: Routledge, 2001), 4.

142. Benjamin E. Goldsmith, "A Liberal Peace in Asia?" *Journal of Peace Research* 44, no. 1 (January 2007): 5–27.

143. The border war between China and Vietnam carried on well into the 1980s, but the casualty figures were only a small fraction of the huge death tolls the region saw in earlier decades.

144. See Elizabeth Wood, *Insurgent Collective Action and Civil War in El Salvador* (Cambridge: Cambridge University Press, 2003); and Paul Collier and Nicholas Sambanis, *Understanding Civil War: Evidence and Analysis* (Washington: World Bank, 2005).

145. James Fearon and David Laitin, "Ethnicity, Insurgency and Civil War," *American Political Science Review* 97, no. 1 (February 2003): 75–90.

146. See James D. Fearon, "Governance and Civil War Onset" (background paper for the World Development Report 2011, Washington, DC, 31 August 2010), http://wdr2011.worldbank.org/sites/default/files/pdfs/WDR%20Background%20 Paper_Fearon_0.pdf (accessed 19 January 2011).

147. Ibid., 76.

148. Ibid., 80. Emphasis in original.

149. Fearon, "Economic Development, Insurgency and Civil War," 318.

150. Ibid., 319.

151. Cullen S. Hendrix, "Measuring State Capacity: Theoretical and Empirical Implications for the Study of Civil Conflict," *Journal of Peace Research* 47, no. 3 (May 2010): 273–285.

152. Note that the conflict terminations data referred to here are at the *dyadic* level—i.e., they relate to the outcomes of conflicts between pairs of warring parties as opposed to conflict terminations that can include several actors on each side. A number of the insurgent victories were in fact military coups—i.e., revolts from within the government—not cases where a rebel group overthrew the state.

153. Richard Stubbs, "ASEAN Plus Three: Process and Performance Legitimacy" (paper presented at the 2nd Annual Meeting of the GARNET Network, Coventry, United Kingdom, 17–19 September 2007).

154. A recent econometric analysis by Clayton Thyne found that states that provide public goods effectively—the study focused on educational and health policies—have a reduced risk of succumbing to conflict. See Clayton L. Thyne, "ABC's, 123's and the Golden Rule: The Pacifying Effect of Education on Civil War, 1980–1999," *International Studies Quarterly* 50, no. 4 (December 2006): 733–754; and David C. Gompert and John Gordon IV, "War by Other Means: Building Complete and Balanced Capabilities for Counterinsurgency," RAND Corporation, 2008, 96, http://www.rand.org/pubs/monographs/2008/RAND_MG595.2.pdf (accessed 21 October 2010).

155. Andrew J. Nathan, "Political Culture and Diffuse Regime Support in Asia" (working paper series no. 43, Asian Barometer Project Office, Taipei, Taiwan, 2007), 2, http://www.asianbarometer.org/newenglish/publications/workingpapers/no.43.pdf (accessed 21 October 2010).

156. Ibid. In highly democratic Japan where the standard of living is far higher than in China, but where the economy has stalled over the last 20 years while China's has boomed, the level of support for the government is very low.

157. Martin C. Libicki, "Eighty-Nine Insurgencies and Endings," in *War by Other Means: Building Complete and Balanced Capabilities for Counterinsurgency* (Santa Monica: RAND Corporation, 2008), 391, http://www.rand.org/pubs/monographs/2008/RAND_MG595.2.pdf (accessed 21 October 2010).

158. Ibid., 385.

159. Indeed, the state-capacity argument advanced by Fearon and Laitin and others only makes sense if one assumes that government resources increase at a faster rate than do those of insurgents when national income is increasing. In some cases, of course, rebels may secure external funding or gain access to lootable resources—diamonds in Sierra Leone and Angola, and other gemstones and timber in Cambodia, for example. This could counter the increased resources that accrue disproportionately to governments as the level of national development increases.

160. Jason Lyall and Isaiah Wilson III, "Rage against the Machines: Explaining Outcomes in Counterinsurgency Wars," *International Organization* 63, no. 1 (January 2009): 67–106.

161. Ibid.

162. Ivan Arreguin-Toft, "How the Weak Win Wars: A Theory of Asymmetric Conflict," *International Organization* 26, no. 1 (Summer 2001): 93–128.

163. Arreguin-Toft's dataset includes some interstate wars; both the Arreguin-Toft and Lyall and Wilson datasets include cases like Vietnam where insurgents are fighting external powers.

164. Ibid., 97.

165. Bethany Lacina and Nils Petter Gleditsch, "Monitoring Trends in Global Combat: A New Dataset of Battle Deaths," *European Journal of Population* 21, no. 2–3 (2005): 154.

166. The wars of liberation from colonial rule in Southeast Asia took place between 1946 and 1962, and included struggles by Indonesian nationalists against the Dutch, by the Communist Party of Malaya against the British, and by Vietnamese nationalists against the French.

167. Spencer Tucker, *Vietnam* (Lexington: University Press of Kentucky, 1999), 57.

168. Douglas Pike, *Vietnam and the Soviet Union, Anatomy of an Alliance* (Boulder, CO: Westview Press, 1987), 106.

169. Lacina and Gleditsch, "Monitoring Trends in Global Combat," 154.

170. Mark O'Neill, "Soviet Involvement in the Korean War: A New View from the Soviet-era Archives," *OAH Magazine of History* 14, no. 3 (Spring 2000): 20–24.

171. United States Army Center of Military History, "The Korean War: The Chinese Intervention 3 November 1950–24 January 1951," 3 October 2003, http://www.history.army.mil/brochures/kw-chinter/chinter.htm (accessed 8 October 2010).

172. Ibid.

173. Lacina and Gleditsch, "Monitoring Trends in Global Combat," 154. In a recent update, the figures have been adjusted slightly downwards, with a best estimate of 995,000.

174. Major General George S. Eckhardt, *Vietnam Studies: Command and Control 1950–1969* (Washington, DC: Department of the Army, 1991), 11.

175. See The History Place, "The Vietnam War: The Bitter End: 1969–1975," 1999, http://www.historyplace.com/unitedstates/vietnam/index-1969.html (accessed 26 October 2010).

176. Ibid.

177. Andrew Wiest, *The Vietnam War* (Oxford: Osprey Publishing, 2002), 70.

178. Anne Leland and Mari-Jana Oboroceanu, *American War and Military Operations Casualties: Lists and Statistics* (Washington, DC: Congressional Research Service, 26 February 2010), http://www.fas.org/sgp/crs/natsec/RL32492.pdf (accessed 26 October 2010).

179. The RAND study noted earlier, which used a somewhat different definition of the term "conflict" to that used by UCDP, found that governments won in 53 percent of conflicts that terminated in a victory. See Gompert and Gordon, *War by Other Means* (accessed 21 October 2010). The UCDP conflict terminations data referred to here and in what follows are at the *dyadic* level and are not comparable with the conflict terminations data discussed in Chapters 4 and 10 of this *Report*, which are at the *conflict* level—i.e., they may include conflicts between a state and *more than one* non-state armed group. At the conflict level, the share of government wins over insurgents is almost 70 percent of all formal victories.

180. Joakim Kreutz, UCDP *Conflict Termination Dataset Codebook: Version 2.1* (Uppsala, Sweden: Uppsala University, Department of Peace and Conflict Research, September 2008), http://www.pcr.uu.se/digitalAssets/15/15902_Codebook_conflict_termination_2.1.pdf (accessed 20 October 2010).

181. UCDP counts a conflict episode as terminated if the battle-death toll falls below 25 a year. Not all conflicts that stop because battle-death numbers fall below this threshold are de facto government victories, of course. In some cases, the fighting stops because insurgents are simply taking time out to regroup and re-arm to fight again another day. But conflicts that stop because they fall below the threshold *and* do not start up again can reasonably be described as de facto government victories. In the case of East Asia between 1980 and 2008, almost half of the intrastate conflict dyads that became inactive because their battle-death toll fell below 25 in a year have not resumed fighting; at the conflict level the figure is 30 percent.

182. Steven Metz, "Counterinsurgency: Strategy and the Phoenix of American Capability," Strategic Studies Institute, United States Army War College, 1 February 1995, http://www.strategicstudiesinstitute.army.mil/pubs/display.cfm?pubID=333 (accessed 20 October 2010).

183. Edward Luttwak, "Dead End: Counterinsurgency Warfare as Military Malpractice," *Harper's Magazine*, February 2007, http://www.harpers.org/archive/2007/02/0081384 (accessed 25 October 2010).

184. Ibid.

185. Ibid.

186. Ibid.

187. Dave Kilcullen, "Edward Luttwak's 'Counterinsurgency Malpractice,'" *Small Wars Journal Blog*, 15 April 2007, http://smallwarsjournal.com/blog/2007/04/edward-luttwaks-counterinsurge-1/ (accessed 25 October 2010).

188. Christopher Paul, Colin P. Clarke, and Beth Grill, *Victory Has a Thousand Fathers: Sources of Success in Counterinsurgency* (Santa Monica: RAND Corporation, 2010), 97, http://www.rand.org/pubs/monographs/2010/RAND_MG964.pdf (accessed 25 October 2010).

189. See the UCDP/HSRP one-sided violence dataset.

190. James Fearon, "Why Do Some Civil Wars Last So Much Longer than Others?" *Journal of Peace Research* 41, no. 3 (2004): 275–301.

191. World Bank, *World Development Indicators (WDI) & Global Development Finance (GDF)*, World databank, http://databank. worldbank.org/ddp/home.do?Step=12&id=4&CNO=2 (accessed 20 October 2010).

192. Commission on Growth and Development, *The Growth Report: Strategies for Sustained Growth and Inclusive Development*, 2008, http://cgd.s3.amazonaws.com/GrowthReportComplete.pdf (accessed 20 October 2010).

193. One corollary is that we would expect that future wars will cluster in states that have weak institutions of governance and low levels of legitimacy.

CHAPTER 4

194. There are far fewer studies of civil war duration than there are of civil war onset. Among the most cited of the former are Paul Collier, Anke Hoeffler, and Måns Söderbom, "On the Duration of Civil War," *Journal of Peace Research* 41, no. 3 (May 2004): 253–273; James D. Fearon, "Why Do Some Wars Last So Much Longer than Others?" *Journal of Peace Research* 41, no. 3 (2004): 275–301.

195. Ann Hironaka, *Neverending Wars: The International Community, Weak States, and the Perpetuation of Civil War* (Cambridge: President and Fellows of Harvard College, 2005), 106.

196. Ibid., 50.

197. Stathis N. Kalyvas and Laia Balcells, "International System and Technologies of Rebellion: How the Cold War Shaped Internal Conflict," *American Political Science Review* 104, no. 3 (August 2010): 415–429.

198. Hironaka, *Neverending Wars*, 124.

199. Charles T. Call, "Assessing El Salvador's Transition from Civil War to Peace," in *Ending Civil Wars: The Implementation of Peace Agreements*, eds. Stephen John Stedman, Donald Rothchild, and Elizabeth Cousens (Boulder, CO: Lynne Rienner, 2002), 384.

200. Jack Snyder, "The End of War? Not So Fast" (paper prepared for The End of War: A Conference in Honor of Randall Forsberg, City College of New York, New York City, May 2008).

201. The one obvious exception here is the genocide in Rwanda.

202. See Human Security Report Project, "The Myth of Civilian War Deaths," in *Human Security Report 2005: War and Peace in the 21st Century* (New York: Oxford University Press, 2005), 75.

203. James D. Fearon and David A. Laitin, "Ethnicity, Insurgency and Civil War," *American Political Science Review* 97, no. 1 (February 2003): 75–90.

204. Snyder, "The End of War? Not So Fast."

205. Tatyana P. Soubbotina with Katherine A. Sheram, *Beyond Economic Growth: Meeting the Challenges of Global Development* (Washington, DC: The World Bank, 2000), 24.

206. Charles Roxburgh et al., *Lions on the Move: The Progress and Potential of African Economies* (San Francisco: McKinsey & Company, 2010), 1. Economic growth rates have continued to rise since 2008.

207. This supports the claim that increased state capacity decreases the risk of war. It in no sense demonstrates it, of course, since there are other possible explanations for the decline in conflicts in this period.

208. John Mueller has argued that war, as traditionally defined, may indeed be obsolescent, but he does not deny that what most conflict researchers define as armed conflict persists in very poor countries. However, he distinguishes what he sees as violent "predation" from more traditional conceptions of warfare. See John Mueller, "Policing the Remnants of War," *Journal of Peace Research* 40, no. 5 (September 2003): 507–518.

209. UN Security Council, *An Agenda for Peace, Preventive Diplomacy, Peacemaking and Peace-keeping*, Report of the Secretary-General pursuant to the statement adopted by the Summit Meeting of the Security Council, 31 January 1992, http://www.unrol.org/files/A_47_277.pdf (accessed 20 December 2010).

210. Lawrence Woocher, "Preventing Violent Conflict: Assessing Progress, Meeting Challenges," *Special Report* no. 231 (Washington: United States Institute of Peace, 2009), 12.

211. Report of the Secretary-General, *Proposed Programme Budget for the Biennium 2008–2009* (New York: United Nations General Assembly, 2 November 2007), 2.

212. Once a country succumbs to conflict, its risk of again relapsing into conflict if the fighting stops increases sharply. This creates so-called conflict traps. These arise because the structural causes of war—notably weak state capacity—and the level of hostility between warring parties are intensified by the destruction wrought by prolonged wartime violence. See Paul Collier et al., *Breaking the Conflict Trap: Civil War and Development Policy* (Washington: World Bank, 2003), 4.

213. Report of the Secretary-General, *Proposed Programme Budget*, 26.

214. SRSG Database created by Manuel Fröhlich, Friedrich-Schiller-University Jena (http://www.iog.uni-jena.de) as part of a project funded by the German Foundation for Peace Research (DSF); Manuel Fröhlich et al., "Mapping UN Presence. A Follow-Up to the Human Security Report," *Die Friedenswarte. Journal of International Peace and Organization* 81, no. 2 (2006): 13–23.

215. Theresa Whitfield, author of a study of Friends groups, has reviewed the security role played by these groups under three broad headings: peacemaking (stopping ongoing wars); post-conflict peacebuilding (preventing wars that have stopped from starting again); and preventive diplomacy. Her findings were instructive. While Friends groups were involved in peacemaking and post-conflict peacebuilding in approximately equal numbers, there was no evidence that any were involved in preventive diplomacy missions. Teresa Whitfield, *Friends Indeed? The United Nations, Groups of Friends, and the Resolution of Conflict* (Washington: United States Institute of Peace, 2007): 286–295.

216. Report of the Secretary-General, *Progress Report on the Prevention of Armed Conflict* (New York: United Nations General Assembly, 18 July 2006), 26.

217. Barnett R. Rubin and Bruce D. Jones, "Prevention of Violent Conflict: Tasks and Challenges for the United Nations," *Global Governance* 13 (July–September 2007): 391–408.

218. Ibid., 404.

219. Ibid., 392.

220. See Antje Herrberg and Heidi Kumpulainen, eds., *The Private Diplomacy Survey 2008: Mapping of 14 Private Diplomacy Actors in Europe and America* (Brussels: Initiative for Peacebuilding, 2008).

221. The effectiveness of preventive diplomacy, when practiced, is difficult to determine for two reasons. First, when it succeeds, nothing happens. Proving the counterfactual, i.e., that if there had not been a preventive initiative there would have been war is extremely difficult. Second, it will frequently be just as difficult to attribute the nonhappening to the diplomatic initiatives rather than other factors.

222. See various case studies in David Carment and Albrecht Schnabel, eds., *Conflict Prevention: Path to Peace or Grand Illusion?* (New York: United Nations University Press, 2003).

223. Michael S. Lund and Lisa Schirch, "The Roles of Non-Military Programs Within a Comprehensive Preventive Approach to Terrorism and Insurgencies" (statement given before the House Armed Services Committee: Subcommittee on Terrorism, Unconventional Threats, and Capabilities, Washington, DC, 7 May 2009), 7.

224. See UN Department of Political Affairs, "Politically Speaking: Bulletin of the United Nations Department of Political Affairs," Spring 2009, http://www.un.org/wcm/webdav/site/undpa/shared/undpa/pdf/dpa_ps_2009_spring.pdf (accessed 12 December 2010).

225. DPA preventive diplomacy intiatives sometimes include attempting to prevent the escalation of existing conflicts.

226. Security Council Report, "Preventive Diplomacy and Conflict Prevention," *Security Council Report Update Report*, 14 July 2010, 3.

227. Security Council Report, "Preventive Diplomacy."

228. Patrick M. Regan, Richard W. Frank, and Aysegul Aydin, "Diplomatic Interventions and Civil War: A New Dataset," *Journal of Peace Research* 46, no. 1 (2009): 135–146.

229. Ibid. There were also five cases of withdrawal of diplomatic representation.

230. Ibid. Another new dataset on mediation in intrastate conflicts has been compiled by Jacob Bercovitch, Karl DeRouen, and Paulina Popieszna. It was discussed at the annual conference of the International Studies Association in New Orleans, LA, in February 2010. It is not yet in the public domain, however.

231. Regan, Frank, and Aydin, "Diplomatic Inventions."

232. Ibid.

233. UN Department of Political Affairs, 2003, unpublished data.

234. The data came originally from a UN official who was then in the Department of Political Affairs.

235. Whitfield, *Friends Indeed?*, 285.

236. Ibid.

237. Laurie Nathan, "'The Frightful Inadequacy of Most of the Statistics': A Critique of Collier and Hoeffler on Causes of Civil War," Crisis States Discussion Paper no. 11 (London: Development Studies Institute [DESTIN], London School of Economics, 2005).

238. See Paul Collier and Anke Hoeffler, "Greed and Grievance in Civil War," *Oxford Economic Papers* 56, no. 4 (August 2004): 563–595 and James D. Fearon and David A. Laitin, "Ethnicity, Insurgency and Civil War," *American Political Science Review* 97, no. 1 (February 2003): 75–90.

239. Herrberg and Kumpulainen, *Private Diplomacy Survey*. The study was undertaken for the European Union-funded Initiative for Peace Building.

240. Teresa Whitfield, "External Actors in Mediation," in Mediation Practice Series (Geneva: Henry Dunant Centre for Humanitarian Dialogue, February 2010), 10.

241. Regan, Frank, and Aydin, "Diplomatic Interventions," 136.

242. Bernd Beber, "The (Non-)Efficacy of Multi-Party Mediation in Wars Since 1990" (essay written at New York University, August 2010), 15. The dataset included interstate conflicts but these were only a very small percentage of all conflicts in this period.

243. Regan, Frank, and Aydin, "Diplomatic Interventions," 140.

244. Frida Möller, Karl DeRouen Jr., Jacob Bercovitch, and Peter Wallensteen, "The Limits of Peace: Third Parties in Civil Wars in Southeast Asia, 1993–2004," in *Unraveling Internal Conflicts in East Asia and the Pacific: Incidence, Consequences, and Resolutions*, eds. Jacob Bercovitch and Karl DeRouen Jr. (Plymouth: Lexington Books, 2011), 60. There are, as we pointed out in Chapter 3, other factors that help explain the decline in armed conflicts in Southeast Asia, notably rising state capacity and increased state legitimacy. These long-term changes reduced both the incentives and opportunities for armed conflict and, in some cases, created conditions conducive to effective peacemaking as well. The point here is simply that explanations that focus on long-term socio-economic changes whose effects are conducive to peace, and explanations that focus on mediation processes that lead to peace settlements, are complementary, not contradictory.

245. Not all of these peace agreements involved international mediation, but the overwhelming majority certainly did.

246. Regan, Frank, and Aydin, "Diplomatic Interventions," 142.

247. The large number of conflict recurrences we see today is not a result of failed peacebuilding efforts. As the data presented in Chapter 10 indicate, the conflicts that recur are predominantly those in which there is neither a decisive victory nor a peace agreement, and certainly not a peacekeeping mission.

248. United Nations Department of Peacekeeping Operations, "Background Note: United Nations Peacekeeping," UN Factsheet, January 2011, http://www.un.org/en/peacekeeping/documents/backgroundnote.pdf (accessed 5 February 2011).

249. Michael W. Doyle and Nicholas Sambanis, "International Peacebuilding: A Theoretical and Quantitative Analysis," *The American Political Science Review* 94, no. 4 (December 2000): 779–801.

250. Virginia Page Fortna, *Does Peacekeeping Work? Shaping Belligerents' Choices after Civil War* (Princeton: Princeton University Press, 2008), 173. For further research that confirms the general stabilizing effects of peacekeeping operations, see Paul Collier, Anke Hoeffler, and Måns Söderbom, "Post-Conflict Risks," *Journal of Peace Research* 45, no. 4 (July 2008): 461–478; Håvard Hegre, Lisa Hultman, and Håvard Mokleiv Nygård, "Evaluating the Conflict-Reducing Effect of UN Peace-keeping Operations" (paper presented to the 2010 Annual Meeting of the American Political Science Association, Washington, DC, 2–5 September 2010), and Joakim Kreutz, "How and When Armed Conflicts End: Introducing the UCDP Conflict Termination Dataset," *Journal of Peace Research* 47, no. 2 (March 2010): 243–250.

251. Fortna, *Does Peacekeeping Work?*, 173.

252. Dr. Birger Heldt, Folke Bernadotte Academy, Sandöverken, Sweden.

    Note that the graph shows the average number of peacekeeping operations per month for each year.

253. UN Security Council, "Report of the Panel on United Nations Peace Operations," Report to the UN General Assembly, 21 August 2000, x.

254. Ibid., 9.

255. Michael W. Doyle and Nicholas Sambanis, *Making War and Building Peace: United Nations Peace Operations* (Princeton: Princeton University Press, 2006), 335.

256. UN Security Council, "Report on Peace Operations," 5.

257. See UN DPKO and Department of Field Support, "A New Partnership Agenda: Charting a New Horizon for UN Peacekeeping," July 2009, http://www.un.org/en/peacekeeping/documents/newhorizon.pdf (accessed 20 December 2010).

258. James Dobbins, "The UN's Role in Nation-building: From the Belgian Congo to Iraq," *Survival* 46, no. 4 (Winter 2004–2005): 81–102.

259. On critical equipment shortages for peacekeeping operations—from strategic airlift to night operations capabilities—see UN DPKO and Department of Field Support, "A New Partnership Agenda."

260. The UN has sought to address the coordination challenge by introducing the idea of "integrated missions," with mixed success and strong opposition from some humanitarian agencies. See Erin A. Weir, "Conflict and Compromise: UN Integrated Missions and the Humanitarian Imperative," Kofi Annan International Peace Keeping Training Center (KAIPTC) Monograph, no. 4 (June 2006), http://reliefweb.int/sites/reliefweb.int/files/resources/1EE897418FD9945CC12571CE003EB 9F8-KAIPTC-Jun2006.pdf (accessed 20 December 2010), 36.

261. Center on International Cooperation, *Annual Review of Global Peace Operations 2007* (Boulder: Lynne Rienner, 2007).

262. Michael Carnahan, William Durch, and Scott Gilmore, "Economic Impact of Peacekeeping" (report prepared for the UN Department of Peacekeeping Operations, New York, NY, March 2006).

263. Sharon Wiharta, "The Legitimacy of Peace Operations," in *Stockholm International Peace Research Institute (SIPRI) Yearbook 2009: Armaments, Disarmament and International Security* (Oxford: Oxford University Press, 2009), 111.

264. Addressing this concern, a new report undertaken for the UN by an advisory group led by former Under-Secretary General for Peacekeeping, Jean-Marie Guehenno, has proposed a radical change to the way the UN provides civilian peacebuilding capacity to peace operations. Rather than relying heavily on outside expertise, the UN should, the report argues, draw more on the civilian capacities of conflict-affected countries themselves, "with international capacity the mechanism of last resort." UN News Service, "Nimbler UN, Global Partners Needed to Build Stability in Post-conflict States—Report," press release, 7 March 2011, http://www.un.org/apps/news/story.asp?NewsID=37700&Cr=post-conflict&Cr1= (accessed 8 March 2011).

265. UN DDR Resource Centre, The UN Approach to DDR, "Integrated Disarmament, Demobilization and Reintegration Standards: Level 2 Concepts, Policy and Strategy of the IDDRS," 1 August 2006, http://www.unddr.org/iddrs/02/#6 (accessed 20 April 2011).

266. Macartan Humphreys and Jeremy M. Weinstein, "Demobilization and Reintegration," *Journal of Conflict Resolution* 51, no. 4 (August 2007): 531–567.

267. UN Office of the Special Adviser on Africa, "Overview: DDR Processes in Africa" (paper presented at the Second International Conference on DDR and Stability in Africa, Kinshasa, Democratic Republic of Congo, June 2007), 7, http://www.un.org/africa/osaa/speeches/overview.pdf (accessed 20 April 2011).

268. Barbara F. Walter, *Committing to Peace: The Successful Settlement of Civil Wars* (Princeton: Princeton University Press, 2002), 20.

269. Jeremy Weinstein and Macartan Humphreys, "Disentangling the Determinants of Successful Demobilization and Reintegration" (Center for Global Development Working Paper no. 69, Washington, DC, September 2005), 3.

270. Robert Muggah, "The Emperor's Clothes?" in *Security and Post-Conflict Reconstruction: Dealing with Fighters in the Aftermath of War* (New York: Routledge, 2009), 7.

271. Walter, *Committing to Peace*, 161.

272. James Pugel, "Measuring Reintegration in Liberia: Assessing the Gap between Outputs and Outcomes," in *Security and Post-Conflict Reconstruction: Dealing with Fighters in the Aftermath of War*, ed. Robert Muggah (New York: Routledge, 2008), 87.

273. Humphreys and Weinstein, "Demobilization and Reintegration," 532.

274. Ibid., 563.

275. DDR programs are increasingly being referred to as DDRR programs, i.e., disarmament, demobilization, rehabilitation, and reintegration programs.

276. James Pugel, United Nations Development Programme, "What the Fighters Say: A Survey of Ex-Combatants in Liberia," April 2007, 69, http://www.lr.undp.org/UNDPwhatFightersSayLiberia_Finalv3.pdf (accessed 11 February 2011).

277. The study of the reintegration of former child soldiers in northern Uganda by Christopher Blattman and Jeannie Annan is another rare example of a methodologically sophisticated survey-based analysis—one that challenges many common assumptions about the impact of conflict on the prospects for successful integration. See Christopher Blattman and Jeannie Annan, "Child Combatants in Northern Uganda: Reintegration Myths and Realities," in *Security and Post-Conflict Reconstruction: Dealing with Fighters in the Aftermath of War*, ed. Robert Muggah (New York: Routledge, 2008).

278. Michael Renner, "Peacekeeping Expenditures in Current vs. Real Terms: 1947–2005," Global Policy Forum, http://www.globalpolicy.org/images/pdfs/Z/pk_tables/currentreal.pdf (accessed 11 February 2011).

279. Richard Gowan, "Will UN Peacekeeping Fall Victim to Budget Cuts?" *The Globalist*, 23 September 2010, http://www.theglobalist.com/storyid.aspx?StoryId=8708 (accessed 20 December 2010).

280. Doyle and Sambanis, *Making War and Building Peace*, 350.

281. Timothy E. Wirth, "UN Peacekeeping: A Bargain and an Opportunity" (testimony to the Committee on Foreign Affairs Subcommittee on International Organizations, Human Rights and Oversight, United States House of Representatives, Washington, DC, 13 June 2007) http://www.globalsecurity.org/military/library/congress/2007_hr/070613-wirth.htm (accessed 10 December 2010).

282. The data for the UN peacekeeping budget are from UN Department of Peacekeeping Operations. Global military expenditure in 2009 is estimated to have been $1,531 billion; see Sam Perlo-Freeman, Olawale Ismail, and Carina Solmirano, "Military Expenditure," in *Stockholm International Peace Research Institute (SIPRI) Yearbook 2010: Armaments, Disarmament and International Security* (Oxford: Oxford University Press, 2010), 178.

283. Joakim Kreutz, Department of Peace and Conflict Research, Uppsala University, Uppsala, Sweden; updated from Joakim Kreutz, "Hard Measures by a Soft Power? Sanctions Policy of the European Union," Bonn International Center for Conversion Paper 45, 2005, http://www.bicc.de/uploads/pdf/publications/papers/paper45/paper45.pdf (accessed 25 November 2010).

The graph includes UN, European Union, and OSCE sanctions regimes.

284. Gary Clyde Hufbauer et al., *Economic Sanctions Reconsidered*, 3rd ed. (Washington: Peter G. Peterson Institute for International Economics, 2007), 158. A study by the United States Institute of Peace found that US-imposed sanctions had a success rate of between 25 and 33 percent. See Robert J. Art and Patrick M. Cronin, eds., *The United States and Coercive Diplomacy* (Washington: United States Institute of Peace, 2003).

285. David Cortright and George A. Lopez, "Learning from the Sanctions Decade," *Global Dialogue* 2, no. 3 (Summer 2000), http://www.worlddialogue.org/content.php?id=90 (accessed 17 December 2010).

286. See Damien Fruchart et al., "United Nations Arms Embargoes: Their Impact on Arms Flows and Target Behaviour," report by SIPRI and the Special Program on the Implementation of Targeted Sanctions at the Department of Peace and Conflict Research at Uppsala University, November 2007.

287. Fruchart et al., "United Nations Arms Embargoes," 33–34. Note that these embargoes have also been included in the total of the other UN sanctions regimes discussed earlier. This separate discussion is included here because arms embargoes have some unique features.

288. David Cortright and George A. Lopez, eds., *Smart Sanctions: Targeting Economic Statecraft* (Lanham: Rowman and Littlefield Publishers, 2002), 18.

289. Abel Escribà-Folch, "Economic Sanctions and the Duration of Civil Conflicts," *Journal of Peace Research* 47, no. 2 (March 2010): 129–141.

290. Ibid.

291. See Monty G. Marshall, "Polity IV Project," http://www.systemicpeace.org/polity/polity4.htm (accessed 10 December 2010). Note that the Polity IV dataset only includes countries with a population size of 500,000 or greater.

292. Håvard Hegre et al., "Toward a Democratic Civil Peace? Democracy, Political Change, and Civil War, 1816–1992," *American Political Science Review* 95, no. 1 (March 2001): 33–48.

293. See Monty G. Marshall, "Global Trends in Democratization," in *Peace and Conflict 2005: A Global Survey of Armed Conflicts, Self-Determination Movements, and Democracy*, eds. Monty G. Marshall and Ted Robert Gurr (College Park, MD: Center for International Development and Conflict Management, 2005), 17.

294. Marshall, "Polity IV Project" (accessed 10 December 2010).

295. Determining the net impact of the increase in the number of democratic countries on the risk of conflict is difficult because the number of anocracies—the mode of governance that has the highest risk of war—has also increased over the past two decades. For a discussion of these issues, see Monty G. Marshall, "Global Trends in Democratization," 17.

296. Hunjoon Kim and Kathryn Sikkink, "Explaining the Deterrence Effect of Human Rights Prosecutions for Transitional Countries," *International Studies Quarterly* 54, no. 4 (December 2010): 939–963.

297. Ibid.

298. Chandra Lekha Sriram, "Revolutions in Accountability: New Approaches to Past Abuses," *American University International Law Review* 19, no. 2 (2003): 310–429.

299. Kim and Sikkink, "Explaining the Deterrence Effect of Human Rights," 943.

300. The deterrent effect of punishment has been the subject of considerable debate in the research community, particularly with respect to the deterrent effect of punishments in domestic legal systems where almost all the research has been undertaken. Kim and Sikkink note with respect to the latter that the evidence indicates that it is the *probability* of punitive sanctions, rather than their *severity*, that determines the deterrent effect.

301. Kim and Sikkink, "Explaining the Deterrence Effect of Human Rights," 940.

302. Ibid. See footnote 12 on page 946 of that paper for an explanation of how the authors used the Polity IV dataset to determine the coding criteria for the three categories.

303. Ibid., 941.

304. James Fearon, "Governance and Civil War Onset," in *World Development Report 2011* (Washington: World Bank, 2010), 25. Emphasis in original. A key question is: Are core human rights violations an independent cause of civil war or merely an early manifestation of it? This is an important methodological caveat, but even if human rights violations are not an independent cause of civil war, knowing that any increase in their frequency could still provide early warning of impending conflict is a potentially relevant finding for policy-makers.

305. James D. Fearon, "Governance and Civil War Onset" (background paper for the World Development Report 2011, Washington, DC, 31 August 2010), http://wdr2011.worldbank.org/sites/default/files/pdfs/WDR%20Background%20Paper_Fearon_0.pdf (accessed 19 January 2011). As we noted in Chapter 2, the conflict-related quantitative research literature is replete, not only with methodological challenges, but also with studies that have divergent findings—indeed consensus is the exception rather than the rule.

306. To be included in the dataset, minority groups had to have a membership of at least 100,000 or constitute 1 percent of the national population of the country in question. See Victor Asal and Amy Pate, "The Decline of Ethnic Political Discrimination, 1950–2003," in *Peace and Conflict 2005: A Global Survey of Armed Conflicts, Self-Determination Movements, and Democracy*, eds. Monty G. Marshall and Ted Robert Gurr (College Park: Center for International Development and Conflict Management, 2005), 29, 33.

307. Asal and Pate, "The Decline of Ethnic Political Discrimination, 1950–2003," 33.

308. Deepa Khosla, "Self-Determination Movements and Their Outcomes," in *Peace and Conflict 2005: A Global Survey of Armed Conflicts, Self-Determination Movements, and Democracy*, eds. Monty G. Marshall and Ted Robert Gurr (College Park: Center for International Development and Conflict Management, 2005), 25.

309. World Bank, World Development Indicators & Global Development Finance, http://databank.worldbank.org/ddp/home.do?Step=12&id=4&CNO=2 (accessed 13 December 2010). The figure presented here is for low- and lower-middle-income countries.

310. Håvard Hegre, "The Duration and Termination of Civil War," *Journal of Peace Research* 41, no. 3 (May 2004): 243–252.

311. Center on International Cooperation, announcement of the publication of the *Annual Review of Global Peace Operations 2011*, http://www.cic.nyu.edu/peacekeeping/annual_review_11.html (accessed 24 February 2011). Emphasis added. The authors of the annual review warn, however, that "the international community's unwillingness to mandate new operations amid fiscal constraints … mean that the era of large-scale growth in global peace operations may be coming to a close."

312. See, for example, Robert S. McNamara and James G. Blight, *Wilson's Ghost: Reducing the Risk of Conflict, Killing, and Catastrophe in the 21st Century* (New York: Public Affairs, 2001); and Norman Podhoretz, *World War IV: The Long Struggle against Islamofascism* (New York: Vintage Books, 2007).

Fredrik Naumann / Panos Pictures. AFGHANISTAN.

THE SHRINKING COSTS OF WAR

Part II examines the startling decline in the deadliness of warfare over the last 60 years and provides a critical review of the assertion that some 5.4 million people died as a result of the war in the Democratic Republic of the Congo between 1998 and 2007.

PART II

THE SHRINKING COSTS OF WAR

Introduction

INTRODUCTION

Part II of this *Report* examines the human costs of war in the post-World War II period—not just the direct deaths from bombs and bullets, but the larger toll from indirect deaths from war-exacerbated disease and malnutrition.

Chapter 5 reviews the ways in which indirect deaths can be estimated and explores the various factors that drive them.

Chapter 6 presents our most counterintuitive finding—namely that nationwide mortality rates have actually declined during the overwhelming majority of high-intensity armed conflicts since the 1970s. Paradoxical though this finding seems, the facts are indisputable. Well over 100 surveys indicate that under-five mortality rates (U5MRs) declined during periods of warfare in some 90 percent of country-years in war between 1970 and 2008.

A major World Bank study published in 2008 suggests that these findings are not limited to U5MRs. The World Bank's researchers found that median adult and infant mortality rates also decline in wartime.

Common sense suggests that because wars kill people, the extra deaths should cause national mortality rates to increase, not decrease. In fact, today's armed conflicts rarely generate enough fatalities to reverse the long-term downward trend in peacetime mortality that has become the norm for most of the developing world. Three interrelated developments account for this contrarian trend.

First, more than three decades of highly successful international efforts to promote public health in developing countries have led to a steady reduction in peacetime mortality rates. The enduring effects of these efforts have led to another—mostly unnoticed—change, namely the saving of large numbers of lives in wartime. International efforts to increase immunization coverage, which have saved millions of lives worldwide over the past two decades, have sharply reduced child mortality rates—in times of war, as well as times of peace.

Second, wars generate far fewer deaths on average today than they did in the past, largely because the nature of warfare has changed. In contrast to the Cold War years, relatively few of today's conflicts involve interventions by major powers, or prolonged engagements between huge armies equipped with heavy conventional weapons. The low-intensity conflicts of the post-Cold War era are almost always fought within, not between, states. Rebel armies are typically small, mostly equipped with small arms and light weapons, and are rarely keen to engage in major battles. As a consequence, death tolls are generally low.

Third, there has been a substantial increase in the level and scope of humanitarian assistance since the end of the Cold War. Aid per displaced person in war-affected countries has increased more than threefold over the past two decades. It has also become more cost-effective, benefitting in many cases from peacetime developments in public health programs.

The Human Security Report Project's (HSRP's) finding that mortality rates decline in most wars stands in sharp contrast to the survey-derived claim by the well-regarded International Rescue Committee (IRC) in 2008 that an astonishing 5.4 million people have died as a consequence of the fighting in the Democratic Republic of the Congo.

In what is the most comprehensive analysis to date of the IRC's findings, Chapter 7 of this *Report* challenges the IRC's 5.4-million estimate, arguing that it is far too high.[1]

Given that the practice of estimating the number of excess war deaths—or total war deaths—via retrospective mortality surveys is so prone to error, and given that the effects of some of these errors become greater the longer wars last, Chapter 8 makes a strong case for seeking alternative approaches to estimating the human costs of war.

However, the caution against using surveys for the specific purpose of estimating nationwide excess deaths is emphatically not an argument against the utility of nationwide population surveys more generally. These remain a critically important instrument for creating an evidence base for needs assessments for UN and non-UN peace operations, for monitoring, and for impact evaluation. Estimates of nationwide excess mortality tolls are not needed for any of these purposes.

Chapter 9, the final chapter in Part II, examines the World Health Organization-affiliated Health as a Bridge for Peace program, whose proponents argue that health professionals have a role to play in conflict prevention via education, in seeking to stop ongoing wars via what the UN calls "peacemaking," and in post-conflict peacebuilding, where the key security goal is to prevent wars that have stopped from starting again.

CHAPTER 5

Deadly Connections: Wartime Violence and Indirect Deaths

Over the past decade, humanitarian organizations and conflict researchers have paid increasing attention to the phenomenon of *indirect deaths*—those fatalities from war-exacerbated disease and malnutrition that would not have occurred had there been no war.[2]

There is general agreement in the research community that the violence that generates deaths on the battlefield is an important driver of indirect deaths, and that the latter are significantly greater in number than the former. But despite the growing interest and a handful of nationwide mortality surveys undertaken to determine excess war death tolls in Iraq, the Democratic Republic of the Congo (DRC), Kosovo, and elsewhere, the number of indirect deaths generated by today's wars remains mostly unmeasured—and thus unknown.

Data for global, regional, and national direct—or violent—death tolls caused by combat are available, however, and some scholars have suggested there is a consistent ratio between direct death tolls from violent injuries and those from war-exacerbated disease and malnutrition, implying that, if we have data for the former, we will be able to calculate the latter.

A much-cited article in the *British Medical Journal* noted in 2002, for example, that "for at least a decade, the ratio of indirect to direct conflict deaths has been quoted as 9:1."[3] But the article went on to point out that this figure had never been

supported by any reported empirical data. Nor could it have been—no such data existed.

In a study of Africa's wars published in 1994, Reginald Green claimed that "lack of food and of medical services, combined with the physical stress of flight, kill about twenty times as many human beings as do bombs, bullets and cold steel."[4] This, too, was a claim for which there was a complete lack of compelling evidence.

More recently, the wide-ranging *Global Burden of Armed Violence* report, published by the Geneva Declaration Secretariat, argued that for every person who died violently in wars around the world between 2004 and 2007, another four died from war-exacerbated disease and malnutrition.[5] The report did not claim there was a consistent ratio between the two, simply that on average, the indirect-to-direct war death ratio was 4:1. This ratio is certainly not implausible, but the evidence base used to calculate it is far too narrow and uncertain to engender any confidence in its accuracy.

Moreover, even if an average ratio between indirect and direct deaths could be accurately determined, this would tell us nothing about individual countries. There are, in fact, huge variations in the indirect/direct death ratios between countries afflicted by conflict.[6] In wars in relatively developed countries, for example, there are remarkably few indirect deaths; in poor-country wars, by contrast, they greatly outnumber direct deaths.

Yet, while the extent of indirect death tolls in warfare remains largely unknown, humanitarian organizations know a great deal about the relationship between war and the vulnerability of war-affected poor-country populations to malnutrition and deadly disease.

Data from hundreds of small needs-assessment surveys carried out by humanitarian agencies and NGOs (nongovernmental organizations) in refugee and internally displaced person (IDP) camps indicate that just four "killer diseases"—acute respiratory infections (ARIs); malaria; diarrheal diseases; and measles—are responsible for most indirect deaths in conflict zones (see The Four Killer Diseases in this chapter). Malnutrition increases the susceptibility of individuals—particularly children—to these diseases and is an important cause of death in its own right.

The Drivers of Disease in Wartime

War-affected populations are far more susceptible to disease than those in peacetime. This is not surprising.

> As the *Human Security Report 2005* noted:

> Wars destroy property, disrupt economic activity, divert resources from health care... Crowded into camps, susceptible refugees fall ill from infectious diseases and contribute to the further spread of these diseases...

> Wars increase exposure to conditions that, in turn, increase the risk of disease, injury and death. Prolonged and bloody civil wars usually displace large populations—either internally or across borders...

> Bad food, contaminated water, poor sanitation and inadequate shelter can combine to transform camps into vectors for infectious disease—measles, respiratory disease and acute diarrhoea—while malnutrition and stress compromise people's immune systems. Diseases rampant in refugee camps easily spread to wider populations...

> Prevention and treatment programs, already weakened by the wartime destruction of health care infrastructure, simply cannot cope with new threats posed by mass population displacements...

> Civil wars also deplete the human and fixed capital of the health care system. Heavy fighting often destroys clinics, hospitals and laboratories, as well as water treatment and electrical systems.[7]

This extract from the first *Human Security Report* accurately describes how major wars can drive up indirect death tolls. But most conflicts that have been waged since the end of the Cold War have been relatively minor and have killed far fewer people than the major wars of the Cold War period. Their impact on population health has been much less extensive and severe than the impression created in the literature—including the above passage.

There is broad consensus within the humanitarian and research communities about the factors that affect—positively or negatively—the risk of death from disease and malnutrition. These include the following:

- The geographical scope and intensity of the fighting—the latter being measured by the number of violent deaths, the former often by the percentage of the national territory afflicted by serious violence.
- The number of individuals displaced who become either refugees or—more commonly—IDPs.[8]
- Increased stress and exposure to new strains of disease, both of which are associated with displacement.
- Reduced access to health services as a consequence of conflict.
- Loss of livelihoods.
- Access to potable water, sanitation, and shelter.
- Timely humanitarian assistance.
- The preconflict health status of the war-affected population.
- The physical and psychological resilience of populations in war-affected areas.

The impact of these factors on population health differs markedly from conflict to conflict. And as we argue in Chapter 6, there are good reasons to believe that a combination of low-cost but highly effective pre-war health interventions, less-deadly wars, and increased humanitarian assistance to war-affected populations has considerably reduced the ratio of indirect to direct death tolls in today's wars compared with those of the Cold War era.

Measuring Indirect War Deaths

As noted earlier, warfare generates two related but quite different death tolls. Direct deaths, as the term suggests, are those that result directly from injuries caused by military operations. They include not only combatants but civilians caught in the crossfire. Indirect deaths are those that result from war-exacerbated disease and malnutrition. Excess deaths are the total number of deaths—both direct and indirect—that would not have occurred had there been no war.

Measuring direct deaths is quite straightforward in theory, though often challenging in practice. Direct death data have been collected for *state-based conflicts*, i.e., those in which

THE FOUR KILLER DISEASES

The deadliest disease clusters associated with wars in poor countries are malaria, diarrheal diseases, acute respiratory infections (ARIs), and measles. Widespread in many developing countries in peacetime, these diseases are notable not only for their deadly impact but also because they can be treated simply and at a remarkably low cost.

Fatalities from communicable diseases typically increase during periods of political violence, sometimes dramatically, with children, refugees, and internally displaced persons (IDPs) being particularly vulnerable.

An analysis of 46 retrospective mortality surveys undertaken for the Human Security Report Project by the Paris-based research centre Epicentre found that, overall, malaria was the disease that caused the most deaths in conflict and post-conflict zones, followed by diarrheal disease, ARIs, and measles.[9] The incidence of particular diseases varied significantly from one conflict to another, however.

Malaria

The deadliest killers in many war zones are malaria-carrying anopheles mosquitoes. Endemic in much of the developing world, malaria causes fever, headaches, chills, and vomiting. Without prompt treatment it is often fatal, particularly among children under five. Displaced populations, often stressed, malnourished, and frequently sleeping in the open, are particularly vulnerable to infection.

Although low-cost treatment options have shrunk in recent years due to the growing resistance of malarial parasites to traditional antimalarial drugs, the costs of the new therapies remain affordable for most humanitarian agencies.

Diarrheal Diseases

Diarrhea is often the first deadly disease to strike war-affected populations. In locations that lack access to safe drinking water, are overcrowded, and have poor sanitation, cholera, dysentery, and other intestinal infections can spread rapidly and with devastating effect. Mortality rates from diarrheal diseases tend to be highest at the onset of complex emergencies before adequate humanitarian assistance becomes available. In the wake of the genocide in Rwanda, an estimated 50,000 Rwandan refugees in eastern Zaire (now the Democratic Republic of the Congo) died in July 1994 following outbreaks of cholera and shigellosis.[10] The crude mortality rate was one of the highest ever recorded among refugees or IDPs.[11]

Oral rehydration salts or intravenous solutions are used to rehydrate those afflicted by diarrhea, while antibiotics are used to treat cases of cholera and shigellosis.[12]

ARIs

Pneumonia, influenza, and tuberculosis, which are caused by airborne bacteria and viruses, spread easily in crowded living conditions, and people suffering from malnutrition and increased levels of stress are particularly susceptible to infection.

Treatment and prevention of ARIs vary according to the disease. Low-cost antibiotics are usually effective against the bacterial infections associated with pneumonia.[13] Vaccination is the primary preventive measure against influenza and can reduce flu mortality by up to 80 percent, and sometimes even more depending on the risk level of the group in question.[14]

Treating tuberculosis during complex emergencies is challenging, in part because some strains of the disease become resistant to antibiotics if treatment is interrupted.[15] However, timely and appropriate treatment can lead to an 85 percent cure rate.[16]

Measles

Despite the recent reductions in global mortality rates from measles, the disease remains a major cause of death in the developing world. In war zones, where displaced persons are often stressed and initially gathered in overcrowded camps, a significant proportion of the population can become infected, with children once again at the greatest risk of dying. In the Gode District of Ethiopia during the conflict and drought in 1999 and 2000, for example, measles was a major cause of death among children under 14 years old.[17]

Preventing measles via vaccination is easier and cheaper than treating it, and vaccination programs are now routine in refugee and IDP camps, where crowding would otherwise greatly increase the risk of contagion. The average cost of the measles vaccine for a child is USD 0.60–1.00.[18] Immunization programs have been extraordinarily effective. Between 2000 and 2007, the global measles mortality toll dropped by 74 percent.[19]

The central message of nearly two decades of research on the four disease clusters that put war-affected populations at greatest risk is that they are all treatable—and that the cost of saving countless lives is very small indeed.

a government is one of the warring parties, since 1946. Estimating indirect deaths poses a far greater challenge.

When soldiers are killed in combat and civilians are caught in the crossfire, their deaths are—in principle at least—both easy to count and unambiguously attributable to the wartime violence. A combatant shot on the battlefield is clearly a victim of war and can be reported as such. But individuals who succumb to malaria during the course of the same conflict are not necessarily victims of the war because they might well have died of the same disease had there been no fighting.

Mortality rates are the most important measure of population health.

It is rarely possible to determine whether or not a particular individual who dies of disease in wartime perished because of factors associated with the war. It is hypothetically possible, however, to determine statistically how the overall mortality rate has increased during the war relative to the pre-war period. The difference between the peacetime and wartime rate—the *excess* mortality rate—can be used to determine the excess death toll provided that the population size and population growth rate are known. When the causes of death—violence versus disease and malnutrition—are also known, it is then possible to distinguish the direct from indirect death tolls.

Measuring Indirect Death Tolls with Surveys

In poor countries affected by war, effective health surveillance systems rarely exist and estimates of mortality rates from disease and malnutrition are usually derived from health surveys. Such surveys have become the standard means for humanitarian agencies and NGOs to assess humanitarian needs and track the health status of populations receiving assistance in war-affected communities.

Among other things, these surveys typically measure adult and/or child mortality rates and the causes of death—nonviolent, as well as violent. Mortality rates are the single most important measure of population health in regions affected by warfare; in these regions, survey data usually reveal rates that are many times higher than in peacetime.

The information these local surveys provide is critically important for the assessment of humanitarian needs but cannot be used to determine the impact of war-driven disease and malnutrition on mortality levels nationwide. This is because conditions in refugee and IDP camps—where most surveys are carried out—are not representative of the nation as a whole. Indeed, they are usually highly unrepresentative.

When initially established, camps may not be able to provide adequate services for the displaced persons who crowd into them. For this reason, camp mortality rates are often considerably higher initially than the national average. But once camps become properly established and displaced populations gain access to adequate nutrition, live-saving health services, clean water, and basic sanitation, mortality rates drop rapidly, often to below the nationwide pre-war rate.

To determine national mortality rates—and hence death tolls—researchers can employ nationwide retrospective mortality surveys. Only a few such surveys—in Iraq, Kosovo, East Timor, the DRC, and elsewhere—have been carried out with the specific intent of estimating excess death numbers.

The procedure that researchers follow in order to estimate the excess death toll is relatively straightforward:

- *Select* a sample population to be interviewed that is sufficiently large and representative of the population of the country as a whole.
- *Ask* respondents if any members of their household died during the war—and if so, how. The responses provide a record of the number of deaths in the sample population and their cause, e.g., whether from violence or disease.
- *Determine* the mortality rate for the sample population—usually measured in terms of deaths per 1,000 persons surveyed per month, or deaths per 10,000 persons per day.
- *Assume* the mortality rate for the national population will be approximately the same as that of the sample—though all extrapolations have a margin of error.
- *Estimate* the national pre-war mortality rate—usually referred to as the *baseline* mortality rate. (Note: This is the most challenging part of the process.)
- *Determine* the excess mortality rate from the direct and indirect effects of wartime violence by subtracting the pre-war mortality rate from the survey-derived wartime rate.
- *Estimate* the excess death toll. This is relatively simple to calculate provided the excess mortality rate, the size of the national population, and the population growth rate for the period covered by the survey are all known.
- *Assess* the causes of death. When survey respondents are asked about the cause of death, the data can be disaggregated to reveal what percentage of deaths were from violent versus nonviolent causes.

However, what is straightforward in principle can be extremely challenging in practice. Confidence in the accuracy of nationwide death toll estimates is reduced by different forms of bias that impact all such surveys, and by the often significant uncertainties with respect to pre-war mortality rates, population size, and growth rates.[20]

In Chapter 7 we show how inappropriate estimates of baseline mortality rates can lead to a dramatic exaggeration of excess death tolls.

Nationwide mortality rates mostly decline during periods of war.

In Chapter 8 we argue that the conventional treatment of the baseline mortality rate (i.e., the assumption that had there been no war it would have remained constant) is highly problematic and can be a further source of major error in estimating excess death tolls.

Conclusion

This chapter has examined some of the challenges that confront efforts to estimate the number of indirect deaths from war-exacerbated disease and malnutrition. We noted the widespread agreement within the humanitarian community that, in wars in poor countries, i.e., the majority of wars today, indirect death tolls are far greater than tolls from war-related violence. But we also noted there is no consensus as to the extent of these deaths, nor indeed as to what the average ratio of indirect to direct deaths might be. As a consequence, indirect deaths around the world remain uncounted and—except in a few high-profile conflicts as in Darfur and the DRC—largely unnoticed.

In Chapter 6 we turn to a critically important, deeply counterintuitive, and largely unrecognized phenomenon—namely that nationwide mortality rates mostly decline during periods of war.

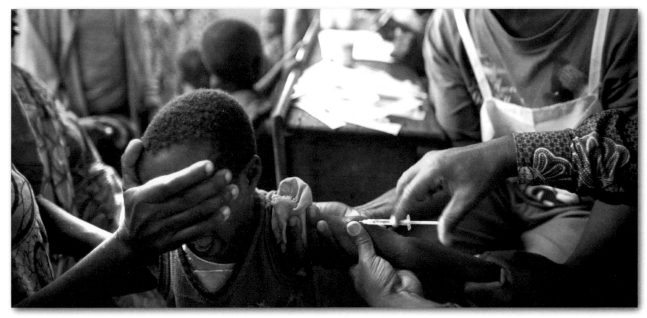

CHAPTER 6

The Paradox of Mortality Rates that Decline in Wartime

In this chapter we examine a seemingly paradoxical finding that has attracted virtually no attention in either the conflict research or humanitarian communities, let alone the media—namely that since 1970, nationwide mortality rates in most countries have actually declined during periods of war.

The data reviewed here—which take into account indirect deaths from war-exacerbated disease and malnutrition, as well as deaths from injuries caused by violence—suggest that the human costs of warfare may not be as great as many people believe—and much of the literature suggests.

The prepublication version of The Shrinking Costs of War contained a review of trends in under-five mortality rates (U5MRs) in conflict-affected countries in sub-Saharan Africa. Here, we review the U5MR trend data for all countries that experienced war during the period from 1970 to 2008.[21] In the overwhelming majority of cases, mortality rates declined during wartime.

The explanation for this apparent paradox turns out to be relatively straightforward. First, the long-term forces that have been driving mortality rates down in the developing world in peacetime continue to have an impact in wartime. Second, the relatively small and geographically concentrated armed conflicts that are typical of the current era rarely lead to enough excess deaths to reverse the long-term downward trend in peacetime mortality. Third, increased and increasingly

effective humanitarian assistance has had remarkable success in driving down mortality rates—especially from disease and malnutrition—in wartime.

Mortality Rates in War

There is comparatively little reliable information collected on trends in adult mortality in the developing world, where most wars take place; by contrast, there is a great deal of information on the (related) trends in child mortality.

As noted in Chapter 5, only a handful of retrospective mortality surveys have been carried out expressly to measure death tolls (for adults, as well as children) due to warfare. But national population health surveys that collect data on child mortality are regularly undertaken throughout the developing world by US Demographic and Health Surveys (DHS), UNICEF (United Nations Children's Fund), and, most recently, WHO (World Health Organization). The surveys from all three organizations cover periods of warfare, but they do not estimate excess war death tolls.

The U5MR is a particularly sensitive indicator of the indirect costs of war. In humanitarian emergencies, children tend to die earlier and—proportionate to their share of the national population—in larger numbers than adults. They are sometimes described as the "canaries in the coal mine" of conflict mortality.[22]

Given that the U5MR is a highly sensitive indicator of the extent of indirect war deaths, and given that no one doubts that organized violence in poor countries drives up the incidence of malnutrition and deadly diseases to which young children are particularly vulnerable, we might expect U5MRs to increase in countries afflicted by war.

Yet nationwide U5MRs, as measured by DHS, UNICEF, and other surveys, mostly decline not only in peacetime but also during periods of high-intensity armed conflict.[23] As we note later, recent research from the World Bank suggests that this pattern also holds for adult and infant mortality.

In reporting these counterintuitive findings, we stress that we do not for a moment dispute the overwhelming evidence that conflict-exacerbated disease and malnutrition lead to sharply increased death tolls in war zones and among conflict-displaced populations. But for most—not all—countries, war zones encompass only a relatively small part of the national territory, and warfare directly affects only part of the population.

Trends in Under-Five Mortality in War

The Human Security Report Project (HSRP) examined the trend in under-five mortality for the period from 1970 to 2008 in every country that experienced 1,000 or more battle deaths from state-based armed conflict in a given year. What we found is there were extraordinarily few instances in which national mortality rates increased during war.

Table 6.1 presents the data on the number of country-years in war in which the U5MR increased between 1970 and 2008. A *country-year in war* is defined as a calendar year in which a country experienced 1,000 or more battle deaths. We record an increase in the U5MR when the rate for a country is higher than it was in the preceding year.

It is very clear from Table 6.1 that over the past four decades, remarkably few wars were accompanied by increases in under-five mortality. In fact, the U5MR increased in only 25 of the 477—or 5 percent—of country-years in war.[24]

In Table 6.2 the focus is on countries rather than country-years. Here, the data show that worldwide, just eight countries (15 percent) experienced increases in U5MRs in wartime.

Six out of these eight countries were in sub-Saharan Africa (Mozambique, Republic of the Congo, Rwanda, Sudan, Uganda, and Zimbabwe); one was in East and Southeast Asia (Vietnam); while the other was in Europe (Russia). The six sub-Saharan African countries accounted for 88 percent of the country-years in war in which under-five mortality increased.

Tables 6.1 and 6.2 demonstrate unequivocally that for some four decades, armed conflict has very rarely been deadly enough to reverse the near-universal downward trend in nationwide U5MRs.

Table 6.1 Increases in the Under-Five Mortality Rate (U5MR) by Country-Year in War, 1970–2008

Region	Number of Country-Years in War	Number of Country-Years in War in which the U5MR Increased	Percentage of Country-Years in War in which the U5MR Increased
Sub-Saharan Africa	155	22	14.19
Americas	65	0	0.00
Central & South Asia	96	0	0.00
East & Southeast Asia & Oceania	76	1	1.32
Europe	13	2	15.38
Middle East & North Africa	72	0	0.00
Global	477	25	5.24

Data Sources: PRIO; UCDP/HSRP Dataset; IACMEG.[25]

A country-year in war is a year in which a country experienced 1,000 or more battle deaths from state-based armed conflict.
An increase in the U5MR is recorded when the best estimate of the U5MR for a country is higher than it was in the preceding year.

Over the last four decades, surprisingly few countries have experienced increases in the nationwide U5MR during war. Indeed, the U5MR increased in only 5 percent of country-years in war. In three regions of the world—the Americas, Central and South Asia, and the Middle East and North Africa—no war generated enough deaths to cause the U5MR to increase. Even in sub-Saharan Africa, the most war-prone region, and the region with the highest U5MRs, only 14 percent of country-years in war witnessed increases in the U5MR.

Table 6.2 Increases in the Under-Five Mortality Rate (U5MR) during War by Country, 1970–2008

Region	Number of Countries that Experienced at Least One Year of War	Number of Countries that Experienced an Increase in the U5MR during War	Percentage of War-Affected Countries with an Increase in the U5MR during War
Sub-Saharan Africa	14	6	42.86
Americas	8	0	0.00
Central & South Asia	9	0	0.00
East & Southeast Asia & Oceania	6	1	16.67
Europe	4	1	25.00
Middle East & North Africa	11	0	0.00
Global	52	8	15.38

Data Sources: PRIO; UCDP/HSRP Dataset; IACMEG.[26]

A country that experienced war is a country that had 1,000 or more battle deaths from state-based armed conflict in a given year.

An increase in the U5MR is recorded when the best estimate of the U5MR for a country is higher than it was in the preceding year.

Here, the focus is on countries rather than country-years in war. But the pattern is similar. Very few countries experienced increases in U5MR during wartime between 1970 and 2008. Sub-Saharan Africa has the highest percentage of countries in which warfare is associated with an increase in the U5MR. But even here, less than half of the countries in question saw increases. Worldwide, just 15 percent of war-affected countries experienced increases in U5MR rates in wartime.

Figure 6.1 shows the trends in U5MRs in a number of countries around the world. The under-five mortality trend data are taken from the consensus estimates of the Inter-Agency Child Mortality Estimation Group (IACMEG), which are, in turn, compiled from data drawn from DHS, UNICEF, other surveys, and census data. The conflict data are from the Uppsala Conflict Data Program (UCDP), as well as the International Peace Research Institute, Oslo (PRIO).

Figure 6.1 is not representative of most countries in conflict—three out of seven of the countries show increases in U5MRs during war. The most dramatic example is Rwanda where the genocide killed an estimated 8 to 9 percent of the population in just a few months. This was the deadliest period of organized violence experienced by any country since the end of World War II.[27] In Russia, another country that experienced an increase in under-five mortality, the increase predated the war and was related to a general increase in mortality throughout the country.

However, what Figure 6.1 reveals is that in some high-intensity and long-duration wars, like those in Afghanistan, Colombia, and Ethiopia, U5MRs continue to decline.

These findings are so counterintuitive that they inevitably give rise to questions about the reliability of the data used to generate them. There is, in fact, little reason to doubt that the overall trends are correct, although it is quite true that the "best fit" trend lines are made up of survey (and sometimes census) data that often have wide confidence intervals—that is, they are subject to a considerable degree of uncertainty.[28] We cannot therefore be confident that any particular mortality measure on the best fit trend line will be accurate. But the data are accurate enough to confirm the average trend in child mortality—i.e., that rates almost always decline in periods of warfare.

The Human Costs of War in Global Perspective

In addition to the survey data, there have been a small number of studies that have sought to measure the *global* impact of war on population health. Most of these studies use WHO's Disability-Adjusted Life Year (DALY)—an indicator of the number of healthy years of life lost—rather than simply mortality rates to measure the health impact of war. The key findings of this research are reviewed later in this chapter (see Political Science Estimates of the Human Costs of War).

In 2008 the *World Bank Economic Review* published a major study by Siyan Chen, Norman Loayza, and Marta Reynal-Querol on the worldwide impact of warfare on a range of economic, political, and social variables in war-affected countries.[29]

Part of the study was devoted to examining the impact of war on adult male and female mortality, and infant mortality, rather than under-five mortality. The authors counted only those conflicts in which there were at least 1,000 battle deaths in a given year, and they used World Bank mortality rates as their main indicator of population health. The article compares median adult and infant mortality trends for the war-affected countries for a seven-year period before the fighting broke out, and for seven years after a conflict had ended.

The authors found that both median adult and infant mortality declined before, after, and during periods of warfare—the same trend revealed in the under-five mortality data reviewed earlier.[30]

The World Bank article reveals that war-affected countries have far higher pre-war mortality rates than regional control countries that are not affected by war, though in both cases median mortality rates decline at similar rates. This suggests that factors other than war—notably levels of poverty-related disease and malnutrition—remain important drivers of mortality in times of war as well as peace.

Data on adult mortality rates in poor countries are often derived from the under-five mortality data for the country in question. Where this is the case, the adult mortality rate will clearly track the child mortality rate quite closely. However, a new study from the Institute for Health Metrics and Evaluation (IHME) at the University of Washington suggests that, contrary to what has commonly been assumed, adult mortality rates may in some cases diverge from child mortality rates. The IHME findings, which are based in part on new data taken from sibling survival surveys, indicate that adult male mortality rates sometimes increase in wartime even when child mortality rates are falling. These findings are based on a relatively small sample of countries, and are subject to considerable uncertainty, but they pose a challenge to the findings of the World Bank study.[31]

Why Mortality Rates Decline in Wartime

Armed conflict not only causes violent deaths but also population displacement, stress, malnutrition, and loss of access to health services, all of which greatly increase the susceptibility of individuals to fatal diseases. This raises an obvious question: Why do nationwide mortality rates decrease rather than increase during periods of warfare—particularly with respect to the most vulnerable members of society—children under five?

In fact, mortality rates, from disease as well as violence, do increase—often dramatically—in and around war zones, as literally hundreds of epidemiological surveys demonstrate.

But if this is the case, why do these fatalities appear to have so little impact on nationwide mortality trends?

The answer is twofold. First, the enduring impact of what UNICEF calls the "revolution in child survival" has been driving down peacetime U5MRs in developing countries for more than three decades. Second, the impact of war deaths on national mortality rates is much less than was the case with the major wars of the Cold War years, and less than is assumed in much of the literature. This is in part because today's armed conflicts generate far fewer deaths on average than those of the past, and because they are more geographically concentrated—the latter being a function of smaller armies with limited power projection capacities. In short, the impact of war deaths has not been great enough to reverse the long-term decline in nationwide mortality rates—except in a very small minority of cases.

The extent of the improvement in health outcomes in the developing world—of adults as well as children—over the past 50-plus years has been extraordinary. As a 2007 report from the Center for Global Development noted, "one of the greatest human accomplishments has been the spectacular improvement in health since 1950, particularly in developing countries."[32]

The 2008 *World Bank Economic Review* study cited earlier argues that conflict-affected countries "have been able to participate in international progress, despite the war. This is arguably a testament to the beneficial impact of medical innovations… and the international campaigns to promote them."[33]

The "Revolution in Child Survival"

In most conflict-affected countries, child mortality due to war-exacerbated disease and malnutrition—by far the greatest cause of child deaths in wartime—has been substantially reduced by the enduring impact of a range of low-cost, nationwide, public health interventions in peacetime.

These interventions are part of long-term global campaigns waged by WHO and UNICEF to reduce child mortality that have been directed in large part against infectious and parasitical diseases. Critical elements in these campaigns have been the Expanded Programme on Immunization, launched by WHO in 1974, and UNICEF's "revolution in child survival" initiative launched in 1982.

According to UNICEF:

Immunization coverage of infants for the six major vaccine-preventable diseases—diphtheria, measles, pertussis, polio, tetanus and tuberculosis—rose from less than five per cent in 1974 to more than 75 per cent in 2006.[34]

FIGURE 6.1

Periods of War and Under-Five Mortality Rates (U5MRs), 1970–2008

With few exceptions, U5MRs in countries around the world have declined during periods of war. This finding holds even in long and high-intensity wars—such as those in Afghanistan, Colombia, and Ethiopia.

Periods of intense violence in countries with relatively small populations, such as that in Rwanda in the mid-1990s, are sometimes associated with increases in U5MRs. Increases in mortality can also predate a period of war, as was the case in Russia in the early 1990s.

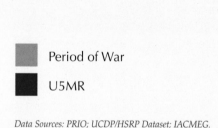

Period of War

U5MR

Data Sources: PRIO; UCDP/HSRP Dataset; IACMEG.

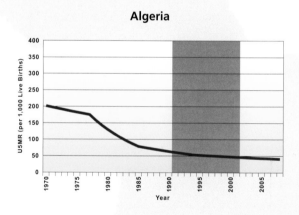

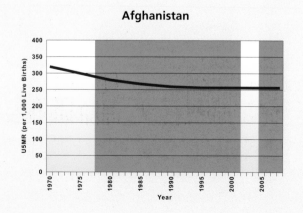

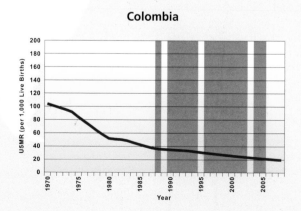

A period of war is a year, or series of years, in which a country experienced state-based armed conflict that resulted in 1,000 or more battle deaths per annum.

Ethiopia

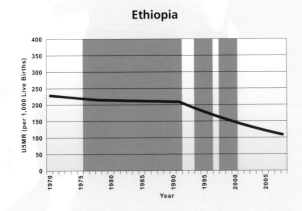

Rwanda

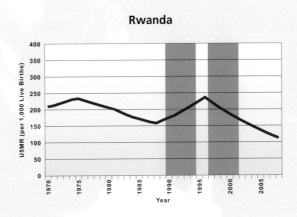

Russia/USSR

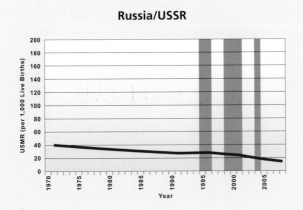

Vietnam

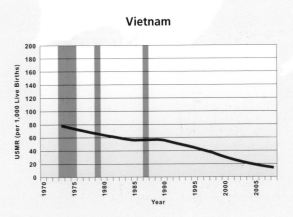

THE REVOLUTION IN CHILD SURVIVAL

The "revolution in child survival" had its genesis some 30 years ago when the then executive director of UNICEF (United Nations Children's Fund), James P. Grant, launched a new initiative to cut child mortality rates.

UNICEF's main targets were the infectious diseases that posed the greatest threat to children under five.[35] The new strategy stressed prevention—notably immunization against preventable diseases—as well as low-cost treatment.[36]

The key policy elements in the campaign were summarized in the acronym "GOBI":

Growth monitoring to keep track of child well-being in a regular and systematic manner.

Oral rehydration therapy to combat diarrhea.

Breastfeeding to provide essential nutrients in the child's early stages of development.

Immunization against tuberculosis, diphtheria, whooping cough, tetanus, polio, and measles.

Subsequently, three more components were added to the GOBI strategy: food supplementation, family spacing, and female education—"GOBI" then became "GOBI-FFF."[37]

Working with the World Health Organization and a broad coalition of nongovernmental organizations, UNICEF's campaign has had a dramatic impact—child mortality rates in the developing world have declined by more than half since 1960.[38] In 1960, the earliest year for which global data on child deaths are available, an estimated 20 million children died; by 2008, the figure was under 9 million. The revolution in child survival, in other words, has helped save millions of lives.

Poverty does not necessarily prevent countries from sharply reducing the rate at which their children die. In almost a third of the 50 least developed countries, mortality rates declined by 40 percent or more between 1990 and 2006.[39]

In sub-Saharan Africa, progress has been considerably slower than in other regions.[40] According to a 2003 study published in the UK journal *The Lancet*, 41 percent of the estimated 10.8 million child deaths worldwide in 2000 were in sub-Saharan Africa.[41] African children continue to die merely because they lack access to simple, inexpensive, and proven life-saving prevention and treatment programs.

The authors of a subsequent *Lancet* study in the same series focused on the 42 countries that generate 90 percent of child deaths—almost 10 million in 2000—and estimated that with universal coverage of basic health interventions, this toll could be reduced by two-thirds.[42] Thus, notwithstanding the successes to date, it is clear there is great scope for further progress.

It is also clear that in most countries that have made major progress in driving down child mortality, national governments, often under pressure from local communities, have played a critical role.

The ongoing revolution in child survival helps explain the apparent paradox of child—and by implication, adult—mortality rates that decline in wartime.

It does so in several ways.

First, children who are healthy and well nourished immediately prior to a war are likely to be more resistant to disease and malnutrition in wartime than those who are not.

Second, as noted elsewhere in this chapter, peacetime health campaigns—for mass immunization, for example—often continue to have a beneficial and enduring impact even in periods of conflict.

Third, much of the research on improving child health in poor countries in peacetime has helped improve the efficacy of humanitarian assistance in war zones and in post-conflict situations. This, in turn, has helped reduce wartime and post-conflict mortality rates.

Fourth, in most of today's conflicts, warfare has a serious direct impact only on a relatively small part of the national territory. In territory unaffected by serious violence, basic health services will often still be provided.

Fifth, in a substantial number of wars, it has been possible for so-called Days of Tranquility to be negotiated with rebel groups. These temporary truces permit health workers to carry out mass immunization programs on children in conflict zones.

Last, the promotion of child health, even in war-affected countries, has widespread support both at home and among donors and international agencies. It is relatively inexpensive, enhances the legitimacy of national governments, and is popular with the citizens whose needs it meets.

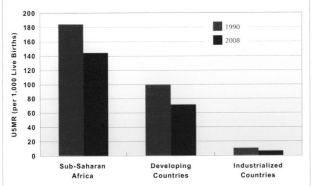

Figure 6.2 Under-Five Mortality Rates (U5MRs): Sub-Saharan Africa, Developing Countries, and Industrialized Countries, 1990 and 2008

Data Sources: UNICEF.[43]

Although U5MRs remain significantly higher in sub-Saharan Africa than the developing world average, even here there have been marked improvements over the last two decades.

By some estimates, immunization alone has saved up to 1 million lives a year on average over the past two decades.[44]

The worldwide impact of the revolution in child survival is clearly evident in the declines in under-five mortality revealed in Figure 6.2. The graph shows that while sub-Saharan Africa's U5MRs are much higher than the developing country average, they have still declined appreciably since 1990. (The decline has, in fact, been underway at least since child mortality estimates first became available in the 1960s.)

The discussion in this section has focused thus far on declines in child mortality. But it is important to note that the available data on adult mortality rates in poor countries, though less reliable, suggest that these too have generally followed a similar downward trend.

According to one leading demographer:

Adult mortality appears to have been falling throughout the developing world from the 1960s to the 1990s, on average by about one percent per annum for males and two percent per annum for females, though the HIV/AIDS epidemic undoubtedly will reverse these gains in countries that are substantially affected.[45]

Mortality rates decline during periods of warfare in part because immunization in peacetime saves lives in wartime. War's impacts increase the susceptibility of children to infectious diseases, but the long-lasting protection provided by immunization programs in peacetime significantly reduces the risk of succumbing to infection once the violence starts. Immunization against measles, for example, provides lifetime protection against contracting the disease, though other vaccines require booster shots to provide continued full protection.

Changes in nonmedical health practices in peacetime can also save lives in wartime. In sub-Saharan Africa, exclusive breastfeeding rates more than doubled between 1990 and 2004—from 15 to 32 percent, in part as a consequence of international and national advocacy campaigns.[46] This is important because breastfeeding infants strengthens their immune systems and reduces the risk that they will die from diarrhea and acute respiratory infections (ARIs). Both diseases are major killers of children in wartime.[47]

This changing practice has also reduced wartime mortality because, as WHO has pointed out, "Infants aged 0-5 months who are not breastfed have seven-fold and five-fold increased risks of death from diarrhoea and pneumonia, respectively, compared with infants who are exclusively breastfed."[48]

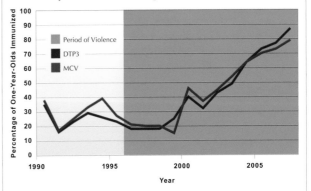

Figure 6.3 Organized Violence and Immunization Coverage in the Democratic Republic of the Congo (DRC), 1990–2007

Data Sources: PRIO; UCDP/HSRP Dataset; WHO Statistical Information System.[49]

In the DRC, immunization coverage increased dramatically between 1996 and 2007, despite the ongoing violence.

The Impact of Immunization Campaigns

Coverage of the critically important immunization programs can even increase in countries experiencing armed conflict. As Figure 6.3 shows, in the Democratic Republic of the Congo (DRC) immunization coverage in 1990, according to WHO, was 35 percent for diphtheria, tetanus, and pertussis (DTP3) and 38 percent for measles (MCV). By 2007 the coverage had increased to 87 and 79 percent, respectively.[50] The critical point to note here is that immunization coverage grew steadily throughout the most intense periods of warfare. In 1998 and 1999, the conflict in the DRC was the deadliest in Africa. This remarkable change may help explain why, according to the 2007 DHS survey, U5MRs have not risen since the war started.

In some countries, immunization in war zones is enabled by negotiated ceasefires–sometimes known as Days of Tranquility—that permit health workers access to children deep in rebel territory who would otherwise not have been treated. Humanitarian ceasefires have been successfully negotiated in Afghanistan, Angola, the DRC, El Salvador, Guinea-Bissau, Iraq, Lebanon, the Philippines, Sierra Leone, Sri Lanka, Sudan, and Tajikistan.[51]

Some of the international initiatives to save the lives of children in conflict zones have been extraordinarily ambitious. For example, in Somalia, a country not only wracked by organized violence but without a functioning central government for many years, UNICEF and WHO embarked in late 2008 on a massive campaign in partnership with local authorities and NGOs to provide every Somali child under five with "immunization against measles, diphtheria, whooping cough, tetanus and polio; Vitamin A supplementation; nutritional assessments; de-worming; … oral rehydration salts and water purification tablets."[52]

There have been relatively few population health surveys conducted in Somalia, but even in this largely ungoverned and violence-afflicted country, some progress has been made in improving child health. Data from the most recent individual surveys on the IACMEG website, childmortality.org, show an uneven downward trend in the U5MR.[53]

All such estimates are affected by substantial uncertainty, with the potential for error likely to be greatest in conflict-affected countries, so the extent of the decline in mortality in Somalia is certainly debatable. But unless the population health surveys that have been undertaken are all fundamentally flawed, the evidence suggests that even here the overall trend in child mortality has been downwards.

While the efforts of UNICEF, WHO, and other international agencies, donors, and NGOs have played a critically important role in the revolution in child survival, the decline in child mortality throughout the developing world also owes a great deal to the parallel efforts of national governments to promote life-saving advances in health care; to the more general diffusion of child-saving knowledge among populations in developing countries—the promotion of breastfeeding, for example—and to general improvements in living standards.

The Impact of Humanitarian Assistance

The "beneficial impact of medical innovations" on wartime mortality, to which the *World Bank Economic Review* article noted earlier refers, is evident not only in the long-term effect of improved access to basic health services in developing countries in peacetime but also in the shorter-term impact of humanitarian action in reducing death tolls from war-exacerbated disease and malnutrition.

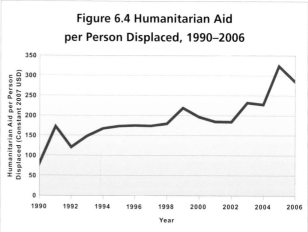

Figure 6.4 Humanitarian Aid per Person Displaced, 1990–2006

Data Sources: Phil Orchard; Global Humanitarian Assistance.[54]

Humanitarian assistance per displaced person more than tripled between 1990 and 2006, contributing significantly to the reduction in wartime mortality.

The impact of humanitarian assistance on wartime mortality has increased for two reasons. First, the level of assistance has risen dramatically. As Figure 6.4 shows, the dollar value of humanitarian aid per displaced person has more than tripled since the end of the Cold War.

But humanitarian assistance is not simply better funded today, it is also more effective.

Writing in *The Lancet* in 2004, Peter Salama and colleagues noted that:

> Major advances have been made during the past decade in the way the international community responds to the health and nutrition consequences of complex emergencies. The public health and clinical response to diseases of acute epidemic potential has improved, especially in camps. Case-fatality rates for severely malnourished children have plummeted because of better protocols and products.[55]

Epidemiological surveys taken in refugee and internally displaced person camps reveal that mortality rates among displaced people who have access to basic humanitarian assistance—health services, nutrition, shelter, and access to clean water and sanitation—can decline very rapidly,[56] often falling to the pre-war rate or even lower within four to six months. Sometimes the reduction in mortality is even more rapid. In 1997, for example, the death rate of Rwandan refugees in the Ndjoundou refugee camp in the Republic of the Congo dropped from almost 11 deaths per 10,000 per day to 0.5 deaths per 10,000 per day in some seven weeks.[57] This huge decline saved many lives.

POLITICAL SCIENCE ESTIMATES OF THE HUMAN COSTS OF WAR

In 2003 the *American Political Science Review* published the first-ever quantitative estimate of the global impact of civil wars on population health. Hazem Adam Ghobarah, Paul Huth, and Bruce Russett's influential article, "Civil Wars Kill and Maim People—Long after the Shooting Stops," reviewed the manifold ways in which intrastate warfare exposed civilian populations to increased risks from a range of killer diseases while reducing access to health services at precisely the time they are most needed.[58]

The World Health Organization's Disability-Adjusted Life Year (DALY), which measures years of healthy life lost, was used as their indicator of population health. The authors' statistical analysis of data from 177 countries controlled for the effects of health expenditure, income inequality, and other factors likely to impact health outcomes.

The authors collated battle death data from some 51 civil wars being waged around the world between 1991 and 1997. To exemplify the "hidden costs" of conflict, they sought to calculate the delayed impact of the civil war deaths in terms of DALYs in 1999.

The key finding of the study was that countries experiencing civil wars between 1991 and 1997 incurred an additional burden of disease and disability in 1999 from the indirect and lingering effects of the earlier conflicts.

In a subsequent article published in 2004 that used more refined data, the authors estimated that some 12 million years of healthy life were lost in 1999 by the citizens of the countries who had been afflicted by war between 1991 and 1997. These are years of healthy life that would not have been lost had there been no wars.[59]

These estimates are subject to considerable uncertainty because most wars take place in countries where health data are poor to nonexistent—the DALY estimates reflect this uncertainty.

Two subsequent macro-quantitative studies published in 2005 and 2006 provided support for these findings. In 2005 Quan Li and Wen Ming reported that intrastate conflict had "a very large immediate effect on both male and female mortality rates," but added, "it does not have strong or robust lingering effects for both genders."[60]

But early in 2009 Matthew Hoddie and Jason Smith presented findings that arrived at a rather different conclusion. In a study published in *International Studies Quarterly*,[61] the authors relied on a very similar statistical methodology to determine the human costs of war to that used by Ghobarah and his colleagues, but they employed different battle death datasets.

Running regressions with the widely used data recorded by the International Peace Research Institute, Oslo (PRIO), the authors found that war did *not* have the expected negative impact on population health. Indeed, half of their findings indicated that war was associated with *improving* health outcomes—although it is important to note that almost none of these findings were statistically significant.

When they ran their regressions with mortality data from a second dataset—this time that of the Political Instability Task Force—they again found that "the magnitude of battle deaths does not appear to be a strong determinant of a country's post-conflict public health performance."[62] In fact, their statistical analysis showed that in nine of the 10 age/gender categories, health outcomes had *improved* in the aftermath of war. This result is in line with our finding that child mortality rates improve nationwide in wartime.

None of these latter findings were statistically significant, however, which means that we cannot assume that, *in fact*, health outcomes improved—the reported improvements could have occurred by chance. Equally important, the study found no evidence that, on average, health outcomes *worsened* as a long-term consequence of warfare—which is what most of the literature on indirect deaths assumes.

Humanitarian assistance, in other words, has been an important factor in reducing the incidence of indirect war deaths, which, in turn, reduces the impact of war on nation-wide mortality rates.

The Changing Nature of Warfare

As we noted earlier, two long-term changes in the global system help explain the apparent paradox of mortality rates that decline in wartime. The first is the decades-long reduction in mortality rates in peacetime. The second is the dramatic, though highly uneven, fifty-plus-year reduction in mortality rates in wartime.

The first part of this chapter noted how low-cost, but highly effective, health interventions have driven down child mortality rates in peacetime and have had a major impact in wartime as well. We now turn to the impact of changes in the nature of warfare that have driven down overall mortality rates—from both direct and indirect deaths—in wartime.

The major armed conflicts of the Cold War years—the Chinese civil war, the Korean War, the French and American wars in Indochina, the Iran-Iraq War, and the Soviet war in Afghanistan—all generated massive annual death tolls. These wars typically involved military intervention by the great powers and were mostly fought with very large armies, with at least one side deploying heavy conventional weapons. Long-range bombardment of cities from the air, or by artillery, was common and resulted in huge numbers of deaths and injuries. Mobile warfare tactics, plus the fact that one or both sides usually had effective long-range power-projection capabilities, meant that the fighting typically ranged over very large areas of the national territory causing immense disruption in the process.

Changes in the nature of warfare have driven down mortality rates from both direct and indirect deaths in wartime.

The poor-country wars of the post-Cold War era by contrast are typically fought with small arms and light weapons and by relatively small rebel armies that tend to avoid major engagements. In many cases insurgent groups seek protection by operating from remote, underpopulated, mountainous regions, or in dense forests. As such they pose little threat to government forces which, for this reason, have few incentives to engage them militarily.

Warring parties on both sides often resort to indiscriminate violence and sometimes target civilians rather than their ostensible enemies. But the size of rebel armed forces, their disinclination—or inability—to engage in prolonged high-level combat, or to project power over long distances, as well as the lack of incentive for governments to mount large-scale campaigns against them, mean that such conflicts generally kill far fewer people than the major wars of the Cold War era. The Rwandan genocide remains the horrific exception to this rule.[63]

The changing nature of warfare has also reduced the geographical extent of wartime violence. In the predominantly low-intensity conflicts that characterize the post-Cold War era, insurgents rarely have the technical capability—aircraft and medium-range missiles—to project military power over long distances, or sufficiently large armies to conduct nation-wide military operations. As a consequence, the area directly impacted by fighting is relatively small in most conflict-affected countries. In fact, a recent review of 11 conflicts in sub-Saharan Africa, conducted by the Armed Conflict Location and Event Data (ACLED) project, found that, on average, only 12 percent of the national territory of war-affected countries is impacted by serious violence.[64]

Fighting in one region of a country may have no impact on livelihoods in other regions.

In Uganda, for example, the conflict involving the Lord's Resistance Army has been in the poor and relatively under-populated north, while the south of the country has remained unaffected. In Sudan's two civil wars, the violence has been concentrated in the south and in the west (Darfur) of the country. In the DRC, the fighting has been mostly in the eastern provinces. Similar patterns are evident in wars in the rest of the developing world.

Given that the economies in these mostly poor, war-affected countries are often based on subsistence agriculture, organized violence in one region of a country may well have little or no impact on livelihoods—which are important determinants of mortality—in other regions. So, while mortality rates from disease and malnutrition may be very high in the areas directly affected by violence, the impact of these deaths on nationwide mortality rates will often be relatively small—and frequently within the margin of error of attempts to measure them.

The Worldwide Decline in Battle Deaths

The decline in the deadliness of warfare is very clear in the trend data on the number of battle deaths per conflict per year by decade—a key indicator of the deadliness of armed conflicts. The data indicate that in the new millennium, the average conflict killed 90 percent less people each year than did the average conflict in the 1950s. Figure 6.5 shows the trends.

A more fine-grained measure of the deadliness of warfare over time is the average number of battle deaths per million of the world's population per year. Figure 6.6 illustrates the annual trend data.

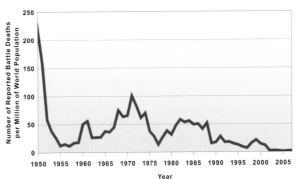

Figure 6.6 Battle Deaths per Year per Million of World Population, 1950–2007

Data Sources: PRIO; UCDP/HSRP Dataset; UN World Population Prospects.[66]

The trend in battle deaths per million of the world's population per year provides a more detailed picture of how the deadliness of war has changed over time. Unlike Figure 6.5, this graph takes into account the large increase in population over the past 50-plus years.

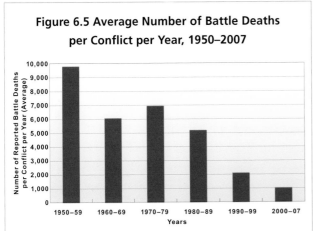

Figure 6.5 Average Number of Battle Deaths per Conflict per Year, 1950–2007

Data Sources: PRIO; UCDP/HSRP Dataset.[65]

There has been a clear, though far from consistent, decline in the deadliness of armed conflict since the end of the Korean War. In the 1950s, the average armed conflict killed nearly 10,000 people a year; by the new millennium, the average had fallen to just over 1,000.

Indirect Death Tolls Have Also Declined

The large and highly destructive wars of the Cold War era not only generated very high battle-death tolls but also displaced large numbers of people, disrupted health services, destroyed housing, reduced access to potable water, and massively disrupted livelihoods. These changes, in turn, increased indirect death tolls from war-driven disease and malnutrition.

For much of the Cold War period there were few countervailing forces reducing indirect death rates. Immunization rates were very low in most war-affected populations during this period, and humanitarian assistance was minimal. The situation today is very different. Conflict-affected populations in the post-Cold War period have benefitted from both peacetime health interventions and increased and increasingly effective humanitarian assistance.

The impact of these changes on battle-death tolls and indirect death tolls is well illustrated by comparing the human costs of the Korean War, the deadliest war during the Cold War, with that of the deadliest conflict in Africa in the 1990s—the war in the DRC that started in 1998.

In the Korean War, an estimated 1.7 percent of the combined population of the two Koreas died from wartime violence in 1950. In the DRC, the death toll was somewhere between less than one-tenth of 1 percent to roughly one-fifth of 1 percent of the population.[67] The most violent year of the Korean War, in other words, was proportionately eight to over 20 times more deadly than that in the DRC in terms of battle deaths.

The two Koreas also suffered a much greater indirect death toll relative to their combined population than did the DRC. According to one report, some 5 to 6 million people died from starvation during the course of the Korean War.[68] Over four years this would amount to some 4 to 4.5 percent of the population per year on average—an extraordinary toll. The IRC claims there have been some 5 million indirect deaths in the DRC between 1998 and 2007.[69] This estimate is almost certainly too high, as we demonstrate in Chapter 7, but even if it were true, it would amount to an average annual death rate of approximately 1 percent of the DRC's population for the period. This suggests that, in terms of indirect deaths, the

Korean conflict was some four to four and a half times deadlier than that in the DRC.

The exact number of indirect deaths in the Korean War and the DRC conflict can certainly be contested, but there can be no doubt that the war in Korea was far more deadly than that in the DRC.

Conclusion

As noted earlier, the apparent paradox of mortality rates that decline in wartime is easily resolved. Mortality rates in poor countries mostly decline in peacetime, and, since 1970, wars have rarely been deadly enough to reverse the downward trend. Warfare is less deadly in large part because wars today are fought with smaller armies, fewer engagements, and lesser weapons systems, and so kill far fewer people on the battlefield and generate far less societal destruction than those of the Cold War era.

Changes in the nature of warfare also mean that there are fewer deaths from war-induced disease and malnutrition—smaller wars mean lower levels of displacement, societal disruption, and stress that increase the vulnerability of war-affected populations to disease. But additional factors help explain the decline in indirect war death tolls. These include improvements in population health in peacetime that help

reduce the vulnerability of children to disease in wartime, and the dramatic increase in the level and effectiveness of humanitarian assistance to war-affected countries.

Although there are no global trend data on the extent of deaths from war-exacerbated disease and malnutrition around the world, a compelling case can be made that they have declined to an even greater degree than battle deaths.

For more than three decades dramatic increases in immunization coverage and nonmedical interventions, such as the campaigns to increase breastfeeding, have provided enduring protection for hundreds of thousands of children in wartime who would likely otherwise have succumbed to disease.

But none of these life-saving interventions have any real impact on death rates from war-related injuries. This means that, contrary to the views of some scholars, death rates from disease have very likely declined more than death rates from injury.

In the next chapter, we review the most comprehensive analysis ever undertaken on the human costs of a contemporary armed conflict—the IRC's survey-based investigation of excess deaths in the DRC. The extraordinary findings of this much-publicized study present a sharply different picture of the human costs of war to that presented in this chapter.

CHAPTER 7

The Death Toll in the Democratic Republic of the Congo

Claims that national mortality rates decline during periods of warfare are not only deeply counterintuitive but they also stand in sharp contrast to the findings of the largest, most widely cited, and most influential research project ever undertaken on the human costs of war.

In 2008, after carrying out and analyzing five retrospective mortality surveys in the Democratic Republic of the Congo (DRC), researchers at the International Rescue Committee (IRC) concluded that some 5.4 million people died between 1998 and 2007 who would not have died had there been no war.[70] The IRC estimated that more than 90 percent of the victims perished from war-exacerbated disease and malnutrition, or other nonviolent causes. Indeed, the IRC's findings suggest that by 2007, less than 1 percent of war-related fatalities were due to violence.

This huge death toll arises, according to the IRC, because the mortality rate in the DRC increased dramatically after the war started in 1998. They note that it dropped in 2001 but has remained significantly higher than the IRC's assumed pre-war—"baseline"—mortality rate of 1.5 deaths per 1,000 per month ever since.

While no one doubts the death rate in the DRC is tragically high, the analysis of the IRC's data and methodology presented in this chapter indicates that a number of key assumptions made by the organization's researchers are highly questionable

and that the claim that 5.4 million Congolese have died as a result of the war cannot be sustained.

The IRC is a New York-based humanitarian organization with operations in many parts of the developing world and a long history of engagement in the DRC. In its three nationwide surveys carried out in 2002, 2004, and 2007, IRC researchers used standard survey methodology, selected large samples, and reported appropriate confidence intervals for their mortality estimates. The US Centers for Disease Control and, subsequently, the Burnet Institute at the University of Melbourne, Australia, were consulted on the methodology used to undertake the surveys.

The surveys in 2000 and 2001, were, however, compromised by questionable methodological assumptions. And, while they clearly reveal very high levels of mortality in parts of the eastern region of the DRC, we argue that the excess death estimates they produced should be rejected.

The IRC's findings on mortality in the DRC have become widely known and accepted and have attracted none of the public controversy that has surrounded war death estimates for Iraq and Darfur. They have been published in the influential UK journal *The Lancet*, and have been cited in other peer-reviewed journals, as well as by governments, international agencies, the media, and many NGOs (nongovernmental organizations).[71]

The IRC's reputation, and the publicity that has attended the launches of its reports on the situation in the DRC, have ensured that its findings have gained widespread media attention for a humanitarian crisis that had long been neglected. Its research has also helped increase public understanding of the indirect impact of wartime violence on population health.

Moreover, there is no doubt the IRC's tireless and effective advocacy has helped focus the attention of the US government and other major donors, as well as the UN (United Nations) Security Council, on the violence in the DRC. "Following the release of the 2000 survey results, total humanitarian aid increased by over 500% between 2000 and 2001. The United States' contribution alone increased by a factor of almost 26."[72]

The number of peacekeepers in the country has also increased substantially. Indeed, with a force of 20,255 uniformed personnel on the ground, the DRC is now host to the UN's biggest peacekeeping force.[73]

The IRC's research-informed advocacy has, in other words, had a considerable impact not only in the global media but also on donors and international agencies.

Two Challenges to the IRC's Findings

Although the extraordinary figure of 5.4 million excess deaths has attracted little public controversy, two recent reports in the public domain, both released in French, have produced mortality estimates that are sharply at odds with those of the IRC. Neither has received much media attention in the English-speaking world.

In October 2008 two Belgian demographers, André Lambert and Louis Lohlé-Tart, published a critique of the IRC's findings that drew on demographic data collected between July 2005 and February 2006 for the voter registration process in the DRC, together with data from the national census in 1984 and a demographic survey taken in 1956.[74] Their estimate of the excess death toll between 1998 and 2004 was some 200,000—just one-twentieth of the IRC's 3.9 million excess death estimate for the same period.[75]

Both the Belgian study and the IRC assume very high mortality levels in the DRC from 1998 to 2004, but the critical difference is the IRC assumes a dramatic jump in the mortality rate after the war starts. Indeed, it is this sudden increase from a very low—we believe too low—baseline mortality rate that creates the IRC's huge cumulative excess death toll. By contrast, the Belgian study assumes that mortality rates are high before, as well as during and after, the war.

The Belgian study has, in turn, been criticized by other demographers both on methodological grounds and because there was insufficient information provided in the paper to permit independent replication of its findings. The publication of the paper triggered a review of its methodology and that of the IRC by the World Health Organization-affiliated Health

and Nutrition Tracking Service (HNTS).[76] HNTS reviewers were critical of some of the methodological assumptions and the lack of information provided in the Belgian study, but they also criticized the IRC's methodology.[77]

The second challenge to the IRC's estimates comes from a survey undertaken in the DRC in 2007 by the authoritative Demographic and Health Surveys (DHS).[78] The DHS data indicate that the DRC's under-five mortality rate (U5MR)—the most sensitive indicator of the indirect costs of war—is dramatically lower than that reported by the IRC for the same period.[79] Since the IRC found that children made up 47 percent of all excess deaths in the DRC during the final survey period, the child mortality rate is clearly an important factor in the overall mortality estimate.

For the 2006 to 2007 period, the IRC's survey data indicate that the nationwide child mortality rate is 5.00 under-five deaths per 1,000 per month. The DHS estimate for this period is 148 deaths per 1,000 live births over a five-year span.[80] This translates into 2.63 deaths per 1,000 children per month—a little over half the IRC's estimate.[81] Both estimates cannot be correct.

However, as with the earlier discussion of the Belgian study, our point here is not to determine which of the estimates is correct. It is simply to note that the IRC's fatality estimates, while not publicly controversial, have not only been challenged but are much higher than those of the other studies.

Questioning the IRC's Methodology

The analysis that follows reviews the methodology used in all five of the IRC's surveys. It argues that key assumptions used by the researchers to estimate excess death tolls are incorrect, and that these errors had the effect of unwarrantedly increasing the excess death toll estimates.

The first and second surveys covered only the war-affected eastern part of the DRC—the three subsequent surveys were nationwide.

The first survey was conducted in 2000 and covered a 22-month period from the beginning of the most intense episode of fighting in August 1998.[82] It found that some 1.7 million people who had died in the eastern part of the country would not have died had there been no war. However, as we explain below, the methodology used to arrive at this estimate is highly problematic because the areas to be surveyed were not chosen appropriately.

The second survey was carried out in March and April 2001. It had a recall period of some 15 months from January 2000 to March 2001. Its findings—along with interpolated excess death estimates from the nonsurveyed period covering

April 2000 to December 2000—boosted the cumulative excess death toll estimate for the two survey periods to 2.5 million, of which 350,000 were violent deaths. As with the first survey, the findings of the second survey were compromised because the areas to be surveyed were not chosen in a way that ensured that they were representative of the region as a whole.

The primary problem with the three nationwide surveys that were conducted in 2002, 2004, and 2007 was the IRC's reliance on a baseline mortality rate that was too low.

In reaching its cumulative nationwide excess death estimate of 5.4 million for the period covered by all five surveys, the IRC added the excess death tolls from the first two surveys to those of the subsequent three surveys.

Readers may wonder how the IRC could calculate nationwide excess war death toll estimates for 1998 to 2001, given the two surveys taken in this period only provided fatality data for the war-affected eastern part of the country.

The short answer is the IRC assumed the violence was concentrated in the east and there were no excess war deaths in the west of the country over this period.[83] From this it follows that the excess war death toll for the east of the country in this period will also be the nationwide excess death toll.

In the analysis that follows, we focus on the IRC's own estimates, as well as the methodology and assumptions that underpin them.

In All the Surveys the Baseline Mortality Rate Is Too Low

In determining the excess death toll, the baseline mortality rate is critically important. If it is too low, the excess death toll will be too high.

The IRC uses the sub-Saharan average of 1.5 deaths per 1,000 per month as its baseline mortality rate for all but the very last survey when the sub-Saharan average drops to 1.4.[84] Using the sub-Saharan African average mortality rate as a comparator—to indicate how high death rates were in the east of the DRC compared with the rest of sub-Saharan Africa, for example—would have been both instructive and appropriate. Using it as a measure of the pre-war mortality rate in the DRC itself makes little sense.

The IRC argues that the sub-Saharan African average mortality rate is a conservative choice for pre-war DRC—i.e., it is higher than previous estimates drawn from data from the 1984 census and two UNICEF (United Nations Children's Fund) surveys that covered periods before the war started. But, the IRC never explains why it believes that the sub-Saharan African average is an appropriate measure of the

pre-war mortality rate for a country that is far from average in sub-Saharan Africa.

The DRC languishes at the bottom of most development indicators for sub-Saharan Africa. It suffered a devastating 20-year economic decline from the mid-1970s that reduced its GDP (gross domestic product) per capita from more than USD 300 to just a third of that figure by 1998. Foreign aid was withdrawn almost completely in the early 1990s, and Mobutu Sese Seko's hopelessly inept and corrupt government had collapsed in total disarray by 1997.

If the baseline mortality rate is too low, the excess death toll will be too high.

The experts who reviewed the IRC's DRC research for the HNTS have all expressed skepticism about the choice of the sub-Saharan African average as an appropriate baseline mortality rate. Harvard University's Kenneth Hill, for example, notes, "the IRC counterfactual is not appropriate. [The] DRC almost certainly has had above average mortality by SSA [sub-Saharan African] standards for decades."[85]

Later in this chapter we argue that 2.0 deaths per 1,000 per month is a more plausible baseline mortality rate for the DRC and show how using this rate sharply reduces the estimated excess death toll attributable to the war throughout the entire period, with the decreases being greatest for the three most recent surveys.

The 2000 Survey: Survey Locations Inappropriately Selected

The most serious problem with the IRC's first survey is that the survey locations were inappropriately selected for the purpose of estimating excess mortality in the war-affected eastern region of the country. (This was also the case with the second survey.) In addition, too few areas were surveyed to allow much confidence in the results even if the locations had been selected appropriately.

The IRC's May 2000 report on the first survey notes: "While the 1.2 million people within the sampling universe of the five IRC studies *are not representative of the approximately 20 million people in eastern DRC*, these surveys probably represent the best broad-based data available."[86]

While the latter part of the above statement is very likely true, the fact remains that extrapolating from a small convenience sample of five nonrandomly selected populations

WHY THE NUMBERS MATTER

Since no one doubts that mortality levels in the Democratic Republic of the Congo (DRC) are tragically high, does getting it wrong about excess death toll estimates really matter? The country remains trapped in a major humanitarian crisis, and preventing further deaths and alleviating suffering remains a critically important task whatever the excess death toll.

And even if the International Rescue Committee's (IRC's) estimates are too high, they have drawn the world's attention to the previously ignored plight of the Congolese and have helped successfully pressure the international community into providing more humanitarian assistance and increasing the number of peacekeeping forces. This has made a real difference to the lives of millions.

All of this is true. But getting it wrong about excess mortality tolls, nevertheless, matters a great deal.

Take the case of Darfur. In the fall of 2006, the high-profile Save Darfur Coalition, a US-based advocacy group, claimed that since the fighting in Darfur had started some three years earlier, "400,000 innocent men, women and children have been killed."[87]

This figure was at least double that of most expert estimates at the time and the reference to innocents being "killed" was wholly misleading. The overwhelming majority of deaths in Darfur in this period were not the result of a government-instigated "slaughter"—as Save Darfur had claimed—but of disease and malnutrition, which were already major killers before the war. Determining what percentage of these deaths could be attributed to the impact of wartime violence rather than pre-existing conditions of abject poverty and malnutrition is extraordinarily difficult, if not impossible.

Getting mortality estimates wrong can have real-world consequences, and the Save Darfur campaign's claims have been sharply criticized by humanitarian groups and area specialists. As one critic noted, "Exaggerated death tolls… make it difficult for relief organizations to deliver their services. Khartoum considers the inflated numbers to be evidence that all groups that deliver aid to Darfur are actually adjuncts of the activist groups that the regime considers its enemies, and thus finds justification for delaying visas, refusing to allow shipments of supplies and otherwise putting obstacles in the way of aid delivery."[88]

Humanitarian agencies and NGOs (nongovernmental organizations), as well as human rights advocacy groups, actively publicize the plight of the war-affected populations they seek to assist—and often use excess mortality tolls to make a case for more aid. There are compelling reasons for

doing this, as the IRC's Rick Brennan and Anna Husarska pointed out in an article in *The Washington Post* on July 16, 2006: "When there is media coverage, aid increases. Large donors may be more inclined to press for a greater presence of international peacekeeping forces to protect civilians and humanitarian assistance teams. And the presence of peacekeepers makes it easier for the media to report."[89]

If these factors come together, they accomplish the goal of every humanitarian response: saving lives.

Saving lives is, of course, the raison d'être of humanitarian organizations.

However, a potential conflict of interest arises here because the institutional survival of humanitarian NGOs is dependent on donor funding. But the level of funding they receive is directly related to assessments of humanitarian need—assessments they themselves are usually responsible for generating.

Some critics believe that individual NGOs deliberately exaggerate death tolls in order to secure more funding, while others argue that lack of experience in survey design and implementation is the problem.[90]

There is also disagreement within the expert community about how to estimate excess war deaths. In Iraq, for example, a series of nationwide mortality surveys—two undertaken for United Nations agencies and two by independent researchers (whose findings were published in the UK medical journal *The Lancet*)—have produced sharply divergent excess death estimates over the same time periods. The difference between the estimates is being driven primarily by the widely divergent estimates of the violent death toll. There is no consensus as to the causes of the differences.[91]

The challenges to the IRC's findings in the DRC noted in this report and others will almost certainly generate more controversy about the value of using retrospective mortality surveys to measure excess deaths.[92]

This is cause for concern because whatever the reason for the controversies, the effect has been the same—mutual suspicion between donors, NGOs, and humanitarian agencies, and an increased risk that survey methods as a whole—which remain critically important in this field—will be discredited.

to the region's entire population is a serious violation of basic statistical principles. Furthermore, there are no indications of any attempt to implement alternative selection criteria for the survey sites that would have ensured that, even if not randomly chosen, they were nevertheless representative of the population of the eastern DRC.

It is theoretically possible that the nonrandomly chosen survey areas could by chance have been representative of the population as a whole, but the IRC's selection procedure minimized this possibility.

Three of the five areas the IRC selected were those in which it was operating—or intended to operate—humanitarian assistance missions. Since there would be little point in setting up humanitarian operations in areas where the war had had little or no impact, the IRC's selection of Kisangani, Kabare, and Katana as areas to be surveyed meant that parts of the eastern DRC that had low mortality rates had little chance of being chosen. Had the selection of locations been random, low-mortality areas could well have been selected, in which case the surveys would have revealed a lower excess death toll.

It is not clear what criteria were used to select the other two areas out of the five surveyed. But whatever the reason for the choice, both areas had extremely high mortality rates.

The information obtained from the raw survey data may well have been useful for humanitarian purposes, and it certainly indicated that parts of the eastern region of the DRC were suffering dramatically high levels of mortality, but the statistically inappropriate selection of the survey areas means that the findings should never have been used to generate excess death estimates for the eastern region as a whole.

The 2000 Survey: Estimation Methods Challenged

Even if the inappropriate selection procedure is ignored, the IRC's methodology remains highly problematic. In the first survey, the IRC's researchers use three separate estimation methods to determine the excess death toll. Each of these methods is different, but all three produce similarly large death tolls—ranging from 1.6 million to 1.8 million. The IRC takes the fact that very different estimation methods all produce comparably high death tolls as evidence for the robustness of their findings. It turns out, however, that each of the estimation methods is based on questionable methodology and/or assumptions.

The first estimation method takes the arithmetic mean of the mortality rates of the five individual areas surveyed and assumes this figure is the average mortality rate for the entire population of the conflict-afflicted eastern region of the country.

The average regional mortality rate thus estimated is 5.2 deaths per 1,000 per month. The IRC's baseline mortality rate of 1.5 per 1,000 per month is then subtracted from this figure to arrive at the excess mortality rate of 3.7 deaths per 1,000 per month for the five areas surveyed. This rate, in turn, is applied to the estimated population of some 20 million in the eastern region of the DRC for the period covered by the surveys—22 months. This estimation method yields an excess death toll of some 1.6 million.

The problem with this approach is that it biases the total estimate upwards by giving too much weight to high death rates in survey areas with small populations. Because the population sizes, as well as the death rates, of the surveyed areas are very different, the appropriate procedure would have been to take a population-weighted average of the mortality estimates.

These findings should never have been used to generate excess death estimates.

This is easy to calculate and the weighted average turns out to be 3.55 deaths per 1,000 per month, not the 5.2 rate produced by the IRC's calculations. If the weighted average mortality rate is used to determine the excess death toll, the excess death rate shrinks from 3.7 to 2.05 and the IRC's estimate of 1.6 million excess deaths is almost halved—to 897,500.

But this revised estimate uses the baseline mortality figure that we have argued is too low. Recalculating the excess death toll using the corrected crude mortality rate (CMR) estimate of 3.55 deaths per 1,000 per month for the five areas surveyed, and the more appropriate baseline mortality rate of 2.0 deaths per 1,000 per month, reduces the total excess mortality toll by some 60 percent—down from the IRC's original figure of 1.6 million to 678,600.

The second and third estimation methods the IRC uses to calculate excess deaths for the survey in 2000 are also problematic. In the survey carried out in Moba in Katanga province, the average mortality rate was 11.4 per 1,000 per month—the highest recorded in any of the IRC's DRC surveys from the earliest to the most recent. In its second and third estimation methods, the IRC extrapolates the Moba death rate to the entire population of Katanga.[93]

What is happening here is that a single survey area with an extremely high death toll and a relatively small population is being treated as typical of an entire province. Since Moba's death rate is so high, and since Katanga province has the largest population of those in which the five surveys were carried out, the impact of this single survey location on the excess death rate for the entire region is very large.

In the second estimation method, Katanga accounts for 1.4 of the estimated 1.8 million deaths (or 77 percent) for the region as a whole; in the third "conservative" estimate, it accounts for 0.9 out of 1.7 million deaths (or 54 percent). In other words, the death toll from the single Moba survey—which we have no compelling reason to assume is representative of Katanga as a whole—is driving most of the death toll estimate for the entire eastern region.

The IRC provides no argument to support its assumption that it is appropriate to extrapolate the Moba mortality rate to Katanga as a whole. In fact, it is highly improbable that the Moba rate—or indeed any other rate from a single survey in Katanga—would be equal to the Katangan provincial average. This is because, as subsequent surveys have demonstrated, there is a high degree of intraprovincial variation in death rates throughout the country, including the eastern provinces.

There are, in other words, no good reasons to accept the excess mortality estimates that derive from the IRC's second and third estimation methods. But the biases generated by the IRC's procedures are then compounded by the decision to sum the provincial totals in order to provide an excess death estimate for the eastern region as a whole. The more statistically appropriate way to provide a region-wide estimate would have been to use all five surveys together—as was done (though without the appropriate population-weighting) in the first estimation method.

To reiterate, the methodological problems with the IRC's first survey are that:

- The five areas surveyed were not chosen randomly and were in any case too few to obtain reliable projections.
- The excess mortality estimation methods:
  i) failed to weight the mortality rates from the five surveyed areas by population (in the first estimation method); or
  ii) inappropriately generalized from a single survey to a province, and then—equally inappropriately—summed the excess death tolls calculated for each province to arrive at a regional total for the eastern part of the country (in the second and third estimation methods).

All three estimation approaches applied an inappropriately low baseline mortality rate. However, the error generated by the use of the inappropriately low baseline had a much greater impact on mortality estimates in the final three surveys than in the first two.

The 2001 Survey: Survey Locations Inappropriately Selected

The second survey, whose results were published in 2001, surveyed five additional areas, but again without random sampling and using the same inappropriately low baseline mortality estimate. However, the significant bias generated by the excessive reliance on the death toll in Moba in the first survey was not an issue in the second survey. In the 2001 report, the IRC used the results of all five surveys taken in 2000, plus the five taken in 2001, as well as a single survey taken in 1999, when estimating the cumulative death toll.[94]

Although the second survey is not as problematic as the first, we believe the inappropriate selection of the areas to be surveyed means the IRC's excess death toll estimates for the eastern region of the DRC, as derived from the second survey, should also be rejected.

The Impact of the IRC's Flawed Methodology

According to the IRC's data, the nationwide U5MR in the DRC increased at an unprecedented rate between the outbreak of the war in August 1998 and 2001. The radical nature of the IRC's claim becomes evident when we compare the IRC's estimate with the under-five mortality trend data for the DRC from 1970 to 2005 provided by the Inter-Agency Child Mortality Estimation Group (IACMEG) dataset.[95]

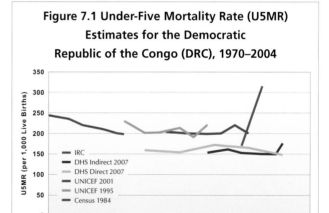

Figure 7.1 Under-Five Mortality Rate (U5MR) Estimates for the Democratic Republic of the Congo (DRC), 1970–2004

Data Sources: IACMEG; IRC.[96]

Census data and data from DHS and UNICEF surveys show that child mortality rates in the DRC, while very high, have been trending downwards for more than 30 years. By contrast, the International Rescue Committee's estimate of the U5MR in the DRC for the period 1998–2001 shows a very dramatic increase.

The under-five mortality trend data shown in Figure 7.1 track projections from the 1984 census, two UNICEF surveys, and a DHS survey that provided both "direct" and "indirect" estimates of under-five mortality and covered the same period as the IRC's survey.[97] According to these data, U5MRs, while very high, have been trending downwards in the DRC for more than 30 years—in wartime as well as peacetime.

The anomalous red line in Figure 7.1 is from the IRC survey data. It reveals a dramatic increase in mortality over a relatively short period of time—a change that is greater than any other credible increase in the child mortality rate in wartime in any country, since 1970, in the IACMEG child mortality dataset.

The DHS mortality data, which cover the same period as data from the IRC's first two surveys, show no real increase. Unless the DHS data are hugely wrong—which no one has suggested—it is inconceivable that a jump in mortality as sudden and dramatic as that recorded by the IRC could have gone undetected in the DHS survey.

It is, of course, theoretically possible the IRC's data are correct and those of the DHS are wrong. But the DHS data were collected using standard survey methodology; the IRC's data were not—as the IRC has admitted. Therefore, we conclude it is highly unlikely the huge increase in mortality that the IRC records ever took place—a conclusion shared by other critics.

As Jon Pedersen of Norway's FAFO Institute notes in his review of the IRC's methodology for the HNTS, "the use of the sub-Saharan baseline CDR [crude death rate] for estimating excess deaths is problematic, as is the implicit assumption of a very rapid increase at the outbreak of the war."[98]

Pierre Salignon, project director of the HNTS, makes essentially the same point when he notes, "It is unlikely that the war led to a sudden increase [in the mortality rate]."[99]

Unless the trend in the DHS child mortality data and the conclusions of the two reviewers of the IRC's methodology are completely wrong, it follows that the true death toll in the DRC for the period of the first two surveys is far lower than the 2.5 million deaths claimed by the IRC.

The 2002, 2004, and 2007 Surveys: The Impact of the Inappropriate Baseline Mortality Rate

This section demonstrates how the IRC's inappropriately low baseline mortality rate generates unwarrantedly high excess death estimates.

The methodology the IRC relied on in the three nation-wide surveys (i.e., the 2002, 2004, and 2007 surveys) does not suffer from the same flaws as the first two. The areas to be surveyed were selected appropriately, and the mortality rate for the country as a whole was based on a large number of surveyed areas, which increases confidence in the accuracy of the estimates. The mortality estimates are, however, subject to a number of sources of uncertainty. These include:

- Very wide confidence intervals for some mortality estimates, particularly in the case of the first of the three nationwide surveys, which was carried out in 2002.
- Uncertainties arising from design effects—especially with the survey in 2002. In 2002 the design effect was huge, which increased the magnitude of the standard errors, in turn, increasing the range of uncertainty of the excess death toll estimates.
- Lack of reliable data on population size and growth rates—which can impact excess mortality estimates.
- Absence of survey-based mortality data for the between-survey periods in 2001 and 2004 to 2005.[100]

An Alternative Baseline Mortality Estimate

The IRC's best estimate of the excess death toll calculated from the 2002, 2004, and 2007 surveys is 2.83 million. However, this does not mean the IRC believes that figure is necessarily the correct one. In fact, the very wide confidence intervals associated with the 2.83 million fatality estimate indicate the IRC's researchers are 95 percent confident that the cumulative death toll for the most recent three surveys lies somewhere between 1.34 and 4.54 million. The 2.83 million figure is simply the one that has the highest probability of being correct.[101]

It is highly unlikely the huge increase
in mortality ever took place.

But the high level of uncertainty surrounding the 2.83 million death toll estimate is not our reason for rejecting it. The problem lies with the baseline mortality rate.

We have argued that the IRC's estimated baseline mortality rate of 1.5 deaths per 1,000 per month is too low and have suggested that a more plausible baseline mortality rate is 2.0 deaths per 1,000 per month. The rationale for this claim is based on a number of logical inferences from the IRC's own data.

The survey-derived overall mortality rate recorded by the IRC in what it describes as the "nonconflict" western region of the DRC in its third survey was 2.0 deaths per 1,000 per month. During this period, the IRC recorded neither violent deaths nor any other excess deaths for this region.

The IRC's data also suggest there were no excess deaths in the west of the country for the period of the first two surveys. We can infer this from the following:

- First, the IRC recorded zero excess deaths in the west for the period of the first two surveys in the chart on page 13 of its final report.[102]
- Second, the IRC's estimate of 5.4 million excess deaths in the DRC between 1998 and 2007 is obtained by adding the 2.5 million estimated excess deaths for the eastern region during the first two surveys to the nationwide estimate for the periods covered by the final three surveys. Given that this nationwide excess death toll estimate does not include an estimate for excess deaths in the west of the country during the period of the first two surveys, we conclude the IRC assumes there were no excess deaths in the west during those periods.

We have no idea whether the IRC's assumptions about excess mortality in the west during the period of the first two surveys are correct, but they are not implausible. They are consistent with what we know about the patterns of violence in the DRC and the lack of connectedness between the east and the west of the country. From the start of the war in August 1998, the violence was concentrated in the eastern region. Much of the western region, which was controlled by the government, is half a continent away from the war-stricken east. Communication between east and west is minimal and livelihoods throughout the region are based mostly on subsistence agriculture. As such, they are less likely to be disrupted by distant armed violence—with the attendant risk of increased mortality—than would have been the case in a more economically interdependent country.

Given that, according to the IRC's findings, there were no excess deaths in the west during the periods of the first, second, or third surveys, then, other things being equal, we can infer that the average mortality rate for the region during the period of the first two surveys should be the same as that recorded in the third survey—i.e., 2.0 deaths per 1,000 per month.

Finally, other things again being equal, the mortality rate for the whole of the DRC immediately prior to the war should be the same as for the west of the country which was not affected by conflict during the period of the first two surveys. It follows that the 2.0 deaths per 1,000 per month is a plausible pre-war mortality rate for the DRC.

Like all baseline mortality estimates for the DRC, this figure is open to challenge, but HSRP is not alone in believing the 2.0 deaths per 1,000 per month is appropriate. WHO's

Francesco Checchi notes in his review of the IRC's research for the HNTS that his approach to the baseline issue would be "to use the east to west CMR [crude mortality rate] rate ratio, which in practice (though not in theory) means adopting the CMR in the west as the baseline for the entire country."[103]

We also note that in its sensitivity analysis for its report on the third survey, the IRC uses the 2.0 deaths per 1,000 per month rate to demonstrate the effect of changing the baseline mortality rate. From this we assume that, while the IRC's preferred baseline rate is 1.5, it believes the 2.0 rate is not implausible.

Recalculating the Excess Death Estimate

When the IRC's excess death figures for the period of May 2001 to April 2007 are recalculated using the revised baseline rate, the result is startling. There is a massive reduction in the excess death toll. As Table 7.1 illustrates, the best estimate of the excess death toll shrinks to less than one-third of the IRC's original figure—from 2.83 million to 0.86 million.[104]

The point of this exercise was not to produce a "correct" estimate—indeed, we do not believe the data are reliable enough to permit this. Rather, it was to show how a modest, but plausible, increase in a highly questionable baseline mortality rate can lead to a radically lower excess death toll.

To make the point even clearer, we asked a hypothetical question: What would the excess death toll be in 2017, under several different, but equally plausible, conditions?

- First, assume the average mortality rate in the DRC for the period 2007 to 2017 is the same as it was for the 2006 to 2007 period (i.e., 2.2 deaths per 1,000 per month). Using a baseline mortality rate of 1.4 deaths per 1,000 per month—which is the rate the IRC used in its final survey—there would be an additional 6.6 million excess deaths by 2017.
- Second, assume the average mortality rate for the period 2007 to 2017 declined to 2.0 per 1,000 per month, which is plausible given the mortality rate in the DRC had been trending downwards since 2002.[105] Assume also that the baseline mortality rate remained at 1.4 per 1,000 per month. There would now be an additional 5.0 million excess war deaths by 2017.
- Third, assume an average mortality rate for the period 2007 to 2017 is 2.2 deaths per 1,000 per month, and the baseline mortality rate is 2.0 per 1,000 per month—the rate suggested by HSRP and Francesco Checchi. There would be an additional 1.7 million excess deaths by 2017.
- Finally, assume the average mortality rate for the period 2007 to 2017 declined to 2.0 deaths per 1,000 per month.

Table 7.1 Excess Deaths in the Democratic Republic of the Congo (DRC), 2001–2007: International Rescue Committee (IRC) and Human Security Report Project (HSRP) Estimates

Period	IRC (Best)	HSRP (Best)	IRC (Low)	HSRP (Low)	IRC (High)	HSRP (High)
May 2001–December 2001	418,400	209,200	180,800	29,800	654,500	402,300
January 2002–December 2002	343,200	257,400	120,100	34,300	583,400	497,600
January 2003–April 2004	607,000	101,200	101,200	-404,700	1,112,900	607,000
May 2004–December 2005	735,000	136,600	419,300	-179,700	1,138,100	539,100
January 2006–April 2007	727,000	158,600	522,000	-31,800	1,050,000	371,300
May 2001–April 2007	2,830,600	863,000	1,343,400	-552,100	4,538,900	2,417,300

Data Sources: IRC and HSRP.[106]

The IRC's "best estimate" of excess deaths in the DRC for the period May 2001 to April 2007 is 2.83 million. Using the IRC's survey data, but a more realistic baseline mortality rate, HSRP's "best estimate" of the excess death toll for this period is 0.86 million. In both cases the margin of probable error is large, as indicated by the wide confidence intervals.

With a baseline mortality rate of 2.0 deaths per 1,000 per month, there would now be zero excess deaths over the 10-year period.

Again, the point of this exercise is not to determine a correct excess death toll, but rather to show how modest, but plausible, changes in the average mortality rate and/or the baseline mortality rate produce radically different excess death estimates.

Conclusion

In this analysis, we argued the IRC's inappropriate selection procedures for the areas surveyed in 2000 and 2001 mean that for this period the organization's excess death estimates are statistically invalid. The survey data leave no doubt that mortality levels in much of the eastern part of the DRC are very high. But, because the IRC failed to choose the areas it surveyed in a way that ensured they were representative of the population of the eastern region as a whole, they should not have been used to generate excess death estimates. In addition, we noted that even if this problem was ignored, other methodological errors had the effect of increasing the excess death toll estimate significantly and unwarrantedly. For these reasons, we argued the findings of both the 2000 and 2001 surveys should be rejected.

We also demonstrated how, for the May 2001 to April 2007 period, the inappropriately low baseline mortality rate

used by the IRC grossly inflated the excess death toll. Using a more appropriate baseline derived from the IRC's own data, the "best estimate" of the excess death toll for this period declines from the IRC's 2.83 million figure to just over 0.86 million.

Our revision of the IRC's estimates reduces the excess death toll dramatically, but the revised data still show a large number of excess deaths (direct as well as indirect), which, given the deadliness of the conflict measured in terms of battle deaths, is not surprising.

The accuracy of our revised estimate, which still relies on the IRC's survey data for overall mortality rates, is, however, impossible to determine.

The primary reason for concern is that the IRC's estimate of the U5MR following the onset of the war in 1998 shows an unprecedented increase, while the DHS data covering the same period show no increase at all. The IRC's U5MR for the 2006 to 2007 period is almost twice that of the 2007 DHS for the same period.

In the next chapter, we discuss a major, but generally overlooked, source of potential error that arises when retrospective mortality surveys are used to estimate excess death tolls. We demonstrate that this source of error is rarely possible to correct and, as a consequence, we argue that the goal of accurately estimating excess death tolls using surveys is effectively unachievable, except in very short wars.

Martin Adler / Panos Pictures. SRI LANKA.

CHAPTER 8

Can Retrospective Mortality Surveys Be Used to Determine Excess Death Tolls?

We now turn to a problem that has been ignored in the literature on conflict epidemiology but challenges the very idea that surveys are useful instruments for estimating excess death tolls.

We demonstrate why retrospective mortality surveys that use point estimates of the pre-war mortality as a baseline, and assume they do not change over time, will tend to produce erroneous excess death estimates, except in the case of very short wars. The longer the war lasts, the greater will be the extent of the error.

We also argue that, since war deaths are not the only factor that determine overall mortality, attributing increases (or decreases) in mortality to wartime violence may sometimes be highly inaccurate.

Finally, we point out that retrospective mortality surveys are simply too crude an instrument to detect the impact of most wars on nationwide mortality rates.

The discussion that follows is in no sense intended as a critique of nationwide retrospective mortality surveys. On the contrary, as we argue elsewhere in this chapter, such surveys are critically important sources of data for war-affected countries where there are rarely any reliable governmental statistics.

Nor do we question the utility of the local health surveys that humanitarian organizations carry out in internally displaced person and refugee camps that provide vital needs-assessment information for humanitarian missions. Our focus is rather on the use of retrospective mortality surveys for the particular purpose of measuring nationwide *excess* war death tolls.

The nationwide population health surveys undertaken by Demographic and Health Surveys (DHS), UNICEF (United Nations Children's Fund), and WHO (World Health Organization)[107] are not used by these organizations to produce such estimates—we believe with good reason.

We further argue that not only is it rarely possible to calculate accurate estimates of excess war deaths but that such estimates are of little practical utility for humanitarian policy on the ground. Excess death estimates may well be useful for advocacy purposes, and are of obvious interest to historians and conflict researchers, but their utility even for these latter purposes is very limited given their accuracy is so dubious.

The Elusive Quest for Baseline Mortality Data

In Chapter 5 we described how nationwide surveys can be used to estimate the overall mortality rate for a war-affected population. We noted that, provided the pre-war mortality rate is known, researchers can easily determine the excess mortality rate—the difference between the wartime rate and the pre-war rate—and thence, the excess death toll.[108]

The first part of this process—using survey-derived data to estimate the overall mortality rate—is subject to many sources of uncertainty and possible error—such as sampling error, reporting bias, response bias, recall bias, and survival bias. But, these challenges, which are all well described in the literature, can be taken into account and are not the focus of this discussion.

The more problematic, and much less analyzed, step involves the estimation of the baseline mortality rate. This is critically important. Without reliable baseline data, it is impossible to determine the excess mortality rate or the excess death toll. Moreover, as we saw in Chapter 7, an inappropriate choice of the baseline mortality rate can have a dramatic impact on the excess death toll estimate.

When there are no reliable official data to permit the baseline mortality to be determined directly—as there almost never are in war-affected poor countries—researchers have a number of different ways to obtain the data they need. All are error-prone.

The options include the following:

- Using the mortality rate for a neighbouring country that has similar characteristics to the country being surveyed, but which is at peace. Here, the problem is the neighbour's mortality rate can be quite different from that of the war-affected country—even where the characteristics of the two countries appear similar.
- Using the regional average mortality rate, as the International Rescue Committee (IRC) did for its surveys in the Democratic Republic of the Congo (DRC). Since all regions encompass countries with very different peace-time mortality rates, the probability that any one country in a region will have the same mortality rate as the regional average is low.
- Relying on the survey data. Here, there are two choices:
  i) Respondents can be asked if anyone died, and if so, from what causes, for a period before the war started. A major challenge with this method is recall bias—the probability that respondents will make mistakes in recalling past events.[109]
  ii) The survey-derived wartime mortality rate for the part of the country that has not been impacted by wartime violence can be used as the baseline. The assumption here is the mortality rate in an area that has not been affected by the fighting should be the same as the peacetime mortality rate for the whole country in the immediate pre-war period.[110] This is the approach that was adopted in Chapter 7 to re-estimate excess war deaths in the DRC.

The Real Challenge: Determining What Would Have Happened Had There Been No War

The challenges involved in determining pre-war mortality rates are daunting. But, even if the difficulties involved in obtaining an accurate estimate of the mortality rate immediately prior to the start of a conflict can be overcome, a more challenging problem remains to be addressed.

To determine the excess death rate, researchers must try and imagine what would have happened to mortality rates in the absence of war. In practice, they usually do this by making a simplifying assumption that is rarely correct, namely that the mortality rate immediately before the war would have stayed the same had there been no war.[111]

In the following section, we demonstrate how using a single point estimate of the pre-war mortality rate can lead to either an under- or overestimation of the excess death toll.

Calculating Excess Mortality with a Constant Pre-War Mortality Rate

Figure 8.1 depicts a situation in which the pre-war mortality rate does in fact remain constant. In this case, the excess death rate is measured correctly.

In the graph, the red-dashed line represents the average nationwide mortality rate for the war period that is derived from the survey. This rate takes into account the excess war deaths (direct as well as indirect), in addition to deaths from all other causes. The baseline mortality is represented by the black-dashed line.

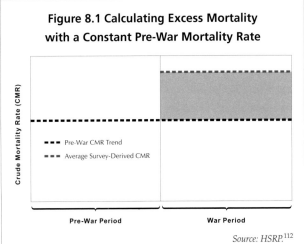

Figure 8.1 Calculating Excess Mortality with a Constant Pre-War Mortality Rate

Crude Mortality Rate (CMR)

- - - Pre-War CMR Trend
- - - Average Survey-Derived CMR

Pre-War Period   War Period

Source: HSRP.[112]

If the baseline mortality rate is constant, and could be assumed to have remained constant absent the onset of war, the light-grey area will represent a measure of the total number of excess deaths.

The excess mortality rate is determined by subtracting the baseline mortality rate from the survey-derived mortality rate. The grey-shaded area, which is a function of the time period over which the war has been waged, as well as the average excess death rate, thus becomes a measure of the extent of excess deaths.[113]

Calculating Excess Mortality with a Declining Pre-War Mortality Rate

We now turn to a situation that represents the norm in the developing world, namely one in which mortality rates are declining in peacetime and could reasonably be expected to have continued to decline had there been no war. We can immediately see from Figure 8.2 that the excess mortality rate, which is measured from the slope—i.e., the vertical distance between the black- and red-dashed lines—increases over time.

The light- and dark-grey areas taken together constitute a measure of the extent of excess mortality.

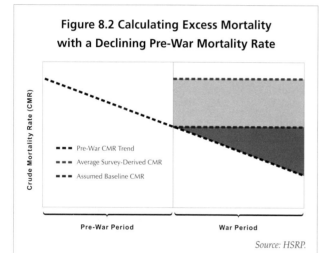

Figure 8.2 Calculating Excess Mortality with a Declining Pre-War Mortality Rate

- - - Pre-War CMR Trend
- - - Average Survey-Derived CMR
- - - Assumed Baseline CMR

Pre-War Period   War Period

Source: HSRP.

If the mortality rate had been declining in the pre-war period, and could be assumed to have continued to decline absent the onset of war, the light-grey and dark-grey areas taken together will represent a measure of the total number of excess deaths. If the mortality rate immediately preceding the onset of the war is assumed to have remained constant, the measure of excess deaths will be underestimated to the extent shown by the dark-grey area.

It is clear from Figure 8.2 that the excess death toll will be underestimated if researchers fail to take into account the declining pre-war mortality trend and instead assume the mortality rate immediately before the war will remain unchanged. The longer the period of war, the greater will be the underestimation.

Figure 8.2 represents a purely hypothetical situation. But, we can get some idea of how a declining pre-war mortality rate might impact excess mortality estimates in the real world by revisiting the IRC's excess death estimates in the DRC for the period covered by the surveys that were carried out between 2001 and 2007.

This is not a simple exercise, and it is far from precise. But the evidence from the DHS on under-five mortality and the WHO data on adult mortality suggest that the overall mortality rate in the DRC in the pre-war period was declining at a rate of approximately 1.76 percent a year. If we assume that in the absence of the war this decline would have continued through to 2007 (the last year for which there are data), and if we take this into account when calculating the excess death toll, then our previous estimate of the excess death toll of 0.86 million rises to 1.50 million—an increase of 74 percent.[114] This is approximately half the IRC's best estimate of 2.83 million excess deaths.

> ## Taking pre-war mortality trends into account can have a significant impact on estimates of excess death tolls.

Without taking the decline in pre-war mortality into account, our original estimate indicated the IRC's excess death toll for its final three surveys was too high by a factor of three. When the declining pre-war mortality rate is taken into account, it appears the IRC's estimate was too high by a factor of two.

Because of the many uncertainties, no confidence should be placed in the actual estimates noted above. But this exercise nevertheless demonstrates that taking pre-war mortality trends into account can have a significant impact on the magnitude of estimates of excess death tolls.

Calculating Excess Mortality with an Increasing Pre-War Mortality Rate

Assuming that mortality rates would have remained unchanged had there been no war usually results in an underestimation of excess death tolls, but it can also result in an overestimation on occasion. A small number of southern African countries have seen overall mortality rates increase as a consequence of the HIV/AIDS death toll.

In Figure 8.2 the assumption that the mortality rate at the beginning of the war did not change results in an underestimation of the excess death toll. In Figure 8.3, however, the same assumption results in the excess death toll being overestimated.

The extent of the overestimation is represented by the dark-grey area. When the appropriate procedure of measuring from the slope is followed, the light-grey area provides a measure of the extent of excess mortality. As Figure 8.3 shows, this declines over the period of the conflict.

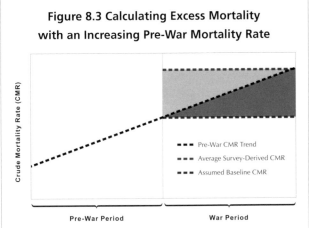

Figure 8.3 Calculating Excess Mortality with an Increasing Pre-War Mortality Rate

Source: HSRP.

If the mortality rate had been increasing in the pre-war period, and could be assumed to have continued to increase absent the onset of war, the light-grey area will represent a measure of the total number of excess deaths. If the mortality rate immediately preceding the onset of the war is assumed to remain constant, the measure of excess deaths will be overestimated to the extent shown by the dark-grey area.

Additional Methodological Challenges

In the highly schematic graphics in Figures 8.2 and 8.3, excess mortality can be determined by measuring from a changing baseline mortality rate. In the real world, things are not so simple and this is rarely possible.

Getting an accurate point estimate for the baseline mortality rate at the start of wars is, as we have already noted, extremely challenging, particularly in poor countries engulfed in, or emerging from, violent conflict. Getting accurate pre-war trend data on national mortality rates is even more difficult. But there are additional problems that are equally if not more challenging.

First, determining the cause of increased mortality during periods of conflict is difficult, if not impossible. Mortality rates can go up during peacetime. In our review of under-five mortality rates (U5MRs) discussed in Chapter 7, we found that 25 percent of countries that were conflict-free between 1970 and 2008 experienced increases in the U5MR.[115] So, clearly, as mentioned previously, political violence is not the only cause of changing mortality rates during periods of conflict.

Mortality surveys in conflict-afflicted countries measure the effect not just of war but of all factors that impact mortality rates. Some nonwar factors—a major drought taking place during a period of fighting, for example—also push mortality rates upwards; others may cause them to decline. The problem is the mortality data cannot be disaggregated to determine the impact of these different factors. In fact, there is no way of determining the extent to which changes in wartime mortality rates revealed by surveys are caused by war or other exogenous factors.

> Getting accurate pre-war trend data on national mortality rates is extremely difficult.

Second, survey-derived mortality rates often have quite wide confidence intervals. For example, the IRC's "best estimate" of the nationwide mortality rate in the DRC for the 2003 to 2004 period was 2.1 deaths per 1,000 per month. But the IRC's researchers could not be certain that this was the correct figure. Their methodology indicated they were 95 percent confident the actual rate lay between 1.6 and 2.6 deaths per 1,000 per month.

Any measurement of baseline mortality is likely to have a wider confidence interval than the survey-derived mortality rate for the war period—in part because pre-war trend data are often made up of widely divergent survey and census data.

What this means in practice is that excess death tolls from low-intensity conflicts may well be undetectable. If the real excess death toll is less than the uncertainties in wartime and pre-war mortality trend data, then the impact of war deaths may be hidden by the imprecision of the very instruments that are being used to try and detect them.

The clear implication of this analysis is that retrospective mortality surveys are rarely appropriate instruments for measuring excess death tolls in wars in poor countries, except in relatively rare circumstances—namely, very short wars.[116]

WHY NATIONWIDE POPULATION SURVEYS ARE NEEDED IN WAR-AFFECTED COUNTRIES

The evidence presented in this chapter suggests that nationwide mortality surveys are of little utility for the specific task of estimating excess war death tolls. The problem, we have argued, lies with the near-insurmountable challenges associated with establishing reliable baseline mortality trend data in the poor countries where most wars take place.

However, none of the criticisms presented in this chapter, or in Chapter 7, should be taken as suggesting nationwide population surveys are of little value for humanitarian and post-conflict peacebuilding programs. On the contrary, in the absence of reliable government statistics, such surveys could play a valuable role—for beneficiaries as well as donors—in creating a broad evidence base, both for humanitarian policies and post-conflict peacebuilding programs.

Currently, national governments, donors, international agencies, and nongovernmental organizations that confront the multiple challenges posed by complex emergencies rarely have the data needed to measure progress—or the lack thereof.

The challenges of creating a reliable evidence base for policy planning and impact evaluation for humanitarian and peacebuilding programs would be addressed in large part if the UN (United Nations) Security Council were to include in the mandate of each new peace operation a requirement to undertake a nationwide population survey of immediate post-war health, socio-economic, and security conditions. Similar surveys could be carried out in post-conflict countries where non-UN peace and stability operations were being implemented.

The widely respected Demographic and Health Surveys (DHS) offer one possible model for such an initiative. DHS surveys collect considerably more information than do mortality surveys of the type the International Rescue Committee carried out in the Democratic Republic of the Congo. They have a strong focus on maternal and child health, but they also collect data on income, livelihoods, and education.

National governments have a major responsibility for the actual implementation of the DHS, and this official buy-in has avoided the sort of public controversies encountered by other major population health surveys in Iraq and elsewhere.

Technical assistance in carrying out DHS surveys is provided at all stages by Macro International, a US corporation that has worked for many years with USAID (United States Agency for International Development) on issues related to survey design and implementation. Macro International is also responsible for collating and analyzing the data collected in the surveys.

Since Macro International is a private corporation and already contracts with UN agencies, there would be no reason in principle why it should not work with the UN and post-conflict governments to create what is a much-needed instrument to evaluate the impact of relief, recovery, and peacebuilding programs.

Unlike other approaches to impact evaluation, such surveys would provide information for national governments, not just donors and international agencies—a further advantage of official buy-in and ownership.

DHS-type surveys would not replace the surveys that humanitarian organizations carry out in and around conflict zones for needs-assessment and monitoring purposes. However, they would provide data that would not only be nationwide but would also cover a far greater range of issues relevant to relief and recovery.

DHS surveys cost up to USD 2 million each, and if the primary purpose of a Security Council-mandated survey was to provide an evidence base to evaluate the broad impact of humanitarian and post-conflict reconstruction/peacebuilding programs, follow-up surveys would obviously be required—perhaps every two years. However, relative to the USD 8 billion a year currently being spent on UN peace operations alone, these costs are minimal.

A commitment by the Security Council to conduct a DHS-type nationwide survey at the outset of every new peace operation, with follow-up surveys to measure progress, would provide national governments and donors with a unique source of data to evaluate the impact of humanitarian and post-conflict peacebuilding policies. Currently, no such evidence base exists.

Conclusion

Given that the practice of estimating excess death tolls via retrospective mortality surveys is so prone to errors, and given that some of these errors become greater the longer the war lasts, a strong case can be made for choosing an alternative approach to measuring the human costs of war.

There are, moreover, more appropriate ways for advocates to communicate the deadliness of warfare than publicizing the nationwide excess death toll—a measure that, even when accurate, takes no account of population size.[117]

The issue of reliability aside, excess death toll estimates are of little practical utility to humanitarians working on the ground. The data humanitarian workers require come from the surveys that are routinely carried out at the local level in conflict-affected areas by humanitarian agencies and nongovernmental organizations. These surveys typically estimate local mortality rates (not excess mortality rates) and provide information on the proximate causes of death.

Mortality rates are the metric most used by humanitarians. But, for nonexperts, the fact that there were, for example, 15 deaths per 1,000 of war-affected population per month—actually a very high death rate—will be largely meaningless and therefore of little use for advocacy purposes.

Perhaps the best approach—one that conveys the deadliness of wars in a way that is both meaningful and accessible to nonexperts—is to compare the mortality rate in war zones with that of the regional average. Saying that the death rate in the war-affected eastern DRC is now 10 times the sub-African average will make far more sense to nonexperts than the (equally true) statement to the effect that the crude mortality rate in the eastern DRC is 15 deaths per 1,000 of the population per month.

Finally, we reiterate a point already made in this and earlier chapters; namely, that if the controversies associated with survey-based estimates of excess deaths continue, they threaten to discredit the entire survey approach—one that remains critically important to the creation of evidence-based humanitarian and peacebuilding policies.

In Chapter 9 the focus shifts from humanitarian policy and the measurement of war deaths to the broader debate about the nexus between health and security, and in particular the program WHO calls Health as a Bridge for Peace.

Giacomo Pirozzi / Panos Pictures. SUDAN.

CHAPTER 9

Armed Conflict and Health Policy

The discussion thus far has focused on the indirect impact of armed conflict on population health. In the past three decades health professionals, particularly those in the humanitarian community, have played a key role in seeking more effective ways to reduce the death toll from war-exacerbated disease and malnutrition.

But for some health professionals, the idea that the medical profession should focus primarily on reducing the human costs of wars has not been enough. Proponents of Health as a Bridge for Peace (HBP) argue that health professionals also have a role to play in conflict prevention via education, in seeking to stop ongoing wars—"peacemaking" in UN-speak—and in post-conflict peacebuilding, where the key security goal is to prevent wars that have stopped from starting again.[118]

The WHO's (World Health Organization's) HBP program started in August 1997 and was accepted by the 51st World Health Assembly in May 1998. The various initiatives associated with the program are predicated on the assumption that health policy can help to create a more secure world in a number of different, but complementary, ways.

Three policy approaches associated with the HBP concept are discussed here. They are often pursued by NGOs (nongovernmental organizations) rather than international agencies like WHO and UNICEF (United Nations Children's Fund), and some predate WHO's HBP program.

First are the advocacy and education programs that seek to inform publics and governments about the true human costs of war. Enhancing public knowledge about warfare is seen as contributing to conflict prevention.

Second is the idea that trust generated by negotiating health interventions in conflict zones—typically to immunize children—can create enough confidence among enemies to jump-start negotiations that can eventually lead to peace settlements. From this perspective, interventions by health professionals can become stepping stones to peace.

Third is the belief that where government policy improves the health outcomes of ordinary citizens in post-conflict settings, it will enhance the legitimacy of the governments concerned and thus decrease the risks of wars restarting. Here, health policy is seen as contributing to post-conflict peace-building—although this, as we will see, is a controversial issue.

Health Education and Conflict Prevention

Advocacy programs designed to educate publics about the true costs of war are based on the assumption that if publics, and indeed governments, understand that the true costs of conflict are far greater than commonly believed, the incentive for going to war will be reduced, while the incentives for conflict prevention, peacemaking, and effective post-conflict peacebuilding will be increased.

In the 1980s, physicians' organizations, including the Nobel Prize-winning International Physicians to Prevent Nuclear War, waged a high-profile public campaign to persuade publics and policy-makers that the true costs of nuclear war, which included the possibility of a consequent "nuclear winter," were far more devastating than generally realized. Some analysts have argued that such campaigns helped create a "nuclear taboo" and that, as a consequence, nuclear war has become literally "unthinkable"—and thus less likely.[119]

The advocacy programs pursued by the International Rescue Committee in the Democratic Republic of the Congo (DRC), and those of literally hundreds of NGOs in other conflicts, are other cases in point. Advocacy is focused primarily on generating pressure to provide more resources to reduce the human costs of war via the provision of humanitarian assistance. But, few health professionals believe humanitarian assistance is enough—many support the broader security goals of conflict prevention, peacemaking, and post-conflict peacebuilding.

Focusing international attention on the human costs of war could, in principle, help further these latter goals. Indeed, there is little doubt that efforts by NGOs and international agencies to publicize the huge death tolls from war-exacerbated disease and malnutrition in the DRC, Darfur, and elsewhere have made donors and attentive publics far more aware of the hidden costs of war. Nor is there any doubt that for more than a decade, donors and international organizations have been committing far more resources to humanitarian assistance, conflict prevention, peacemaking, and post-conflict peacebuilding. Humanitarian advocacy campaigns have surely been one of the factors driving these changes.

Health Interventions and Peacemaking

In a paper prepared for the 1995 World Summit for Social Development, WHO argued:

> Health is valued by everyone. It provides a basis for bringing people together to analyze, to discuss and to arrive at a consensus acceptable to all. The potential for using health as a mechanism for dialogue, and even peace, has been demonstrated in situations of conflict.[120]

HBP advocates believe that because health, particularly children's health, is valued by all parties, and because medical professionals who have a humanitarian mandate are traditionally seen as neutral, it may be possible for them to facilitate dialogue between the warring parties where other attempts have failed. The dialogue will initially be technical with a completely apolitical goal—to gain access to children in war zones in order to deliver very basic life-saving health

interventions. But, health advocates believe the degree of trust generated by negotiating humanitarian access can be built on and used to build a process of conflict mediation and, ultimately, resolution.

As Paula Gutlove puts it, health professionals "can create a bridge of peace between conflicting communities, whereby delivery of health care can become a common objective and a binding commitment for continued cooperation."[121]

Humanitarian ceasefires, often called Days of Tranquility, have been implemented in many conflict zones and are held up as examples of the utility of the HBP approach in practice. Here, a temporary truce is negotiated between the government and rebels that permits health workers to enter conflict zones in order to immunize children against a variety of infectious diseases, or deliver food or other humanitarian assistance. As mentioned previously, humanitarian ceasefires of this type have been implemented in many conflict situations in, for example, Afghanistan, Cambodia, El Salvador, Lebanon, the Philippines, Sudan, and Uganda.[122]

Sometimes the truce can be extended for considerable periods of time. In 1994, for example:

> WHO-Afghanistan and the Afghan Ministry of Public Health brokered a cease-fire… during which children throughout the country could be immunized. The two weeks of tranquility became a two-month cease-fire during which an intensive "Mass Immunization Campaign" was carried out.[123]

These health interventions, which are most frequently referred to as HBP initiatives in the literature, have undoubtedly saved lives, but there is little evidence they have contributed in any major way to bringing wars to an end.

The claimed causal relationships in the literature between humanitarian health interventions and peace are problematic in a number of ways.[124] First, they are asserted rather than demonstrated—and they invariably ignore the possibility that Days of Tranquility initiatives might be an effect of improved relations, rather than their cause.

Second, the HBP literature is almost certainly subject to publication bias—that is, there is a higher probability that articles on successful, rather than unsuccessful, initiatives will get published in academic journals. The fact that many individuals writing in this field are advocates, who may have little interest in publicizing unsuccessful cases, does nothing to reduce the risk of bias.

Third, even where there is a clear association between HBP initiatives and peace settlements, it does not necessarily indicate any causal relationship. Many of the conflicts that have witnessed Days of Tranquility have indeed ended, but it is far from clear whether the health interventions played even a minor role in bringing them to an end.

Successes in what the UN calls "peacemaking" and "post-conflict peacebuilding" have many causes. An editorial in the *British Medical Journal* may have been overstating things when it noted in 2001 that there were few examples of successful peace through health initiatives, adding, "it is ideology that is driving the movement at present."[125] Yet, some eight years later, there has still been no systematic evaluation of the effectiveness of humanitarian interventions in driving subsequent peace negotiations.

Moreover, there is little recognition in the literature of the risks that HBP initiatives may involve. The assumption that cooperation is possible because people on both sides of a conflict value good health does not mean that rebel groups will in fact choose to cooperate. Rebel leaders may perceive state-supported initiatives to deliver humanitarian assistance into war zones as tactics intended to generate support for the government, and reject them for precisely this reason.

Humanitarian organizations are aware that aid can have perverse effects.

Moreover, humanitarian assistance, as is now widely recognized, can have profoundly negative consequences in certain circumstances. As Mary Anderson demonstrated more than a decade ago, the food and medicine provided by international agencies and NGOs can have the perverse effect of fuelling the very wars whose human costs they seek to reduce.[126] Rebels often steal aid shipments, or impose a "tax" on their delivery and use the resources thus acquired to support their war effort. Rebel groups can also use Days of Tranquility to redeploy their forces to greater strategic advantage without fear of attack.

Humanitarian organizations today are well aware that aid can have perverse effects, however, and most now seek—though not always successfully—to ensure their operations "do no harm."

Finally, while health professionals may aspire to leverage the trust generated in negotiating access to war zones to promote peace negotiations, few have the depth of knowledge of the political issues at stake, or the necessary experience mediating in such situations, to facilitate a negotiated settlement.

Health Policy and Peacebuilding

In post-conflict situations, governments that gain legitimacy in the eyes of their citizens are less likely to succumb to renewed rebel violence. As one review of the HBP literature noted:

> Through the provision of health and other public services to their populations, governments have the opportunity to (re)establish their legitimacy, reduce alienation from society and, crucially, to visibly demonstrate that they are upholding their side of the social contract.[127]

An important source of what is sometimes called "performance legitimacy" is a government's ability to provide goods and services that are desired by its citizens. And, the reliable provision of accessible health care is a critical determinant of performance legitimacy, even in poor countries where health services are often minimal. In 2007, for example, a survey of 18 African nations by Afrobarometer found that respondents' satisfaction with their government was associated with their satisfaction with the delivery of social services such as health and education, as well as its political and economic performance.[128] Factors influencing satisfaction with health care were, in order of importance: perceived ease of access, the respondent's level of poverty, perceived absence of corruption, and affordable fees for medical treatment.[129]

However, if, as is often the case, it is NGOs, rather than the government, that are providing most of the health care in post-conflict situations, the government is less likely to gain legitimacy than if its own health workers were providing the services.

As Margaret Kruk has noted, effective and equitable delivery of health care can influence citizens' perceptions of the legitimacy of oppositions, as well as governments.[130] In southern Lebanon, where the national government has long underinvested in health care services, the militant Hezbollah organization has provided generous health insurance and efficient, accessible, and reliable health services to the local Shia population. In 2005, for example, some 50 hospitals in the country were being run by the organization, which also provides life and disability insurance, as well as other social services.[131] In the wake of the August 2006 war with Israel, Hezbollah's rapid provision of health care and reconstruction aid appears to have only strengthened its legitimacy in the south.[132]

A major multi-country study by the RAND Corporation published in 2006 provided considerable support for the thesis that effective delivery of health services can enhance the legitimacy of governments in post-conflict settings.[133] In evaluating the impact of the provision of health services in rebuilding Germany and Japan after World War II, and in Somalia, Haiti, Kosovo, Iraq, and Afghanistan, the authors concluded that "health can have an important independent impact on nation-building and… on security by helping to 'win hearts and minds.'"[134]

Humanitarian Assistance and Counterinsurgency

But while the provision of health services in post-conflict settings does not sound controversial, it can pose real risks for humanitarian health professionals in those situations where armed resistance remains. The "win hearts and minds" approach that the RAND Corporation report refers to is, of course, a critically important element in contemporary counterinsurgency strategy. And it is perceived as such by forces opposed to governments in Afghanistan and elsewhere. For example, the Taliban attacks health facilities in the Afghan countryside because it has a direct interest in preventing the government in Kabul from winning hearts and minds, and thus gaining legitimacy.

Some humanitarian organizations, most notably the International Committee of the Red Cross (ICRC) and Médecins Sans Frontières (MSF), strongly repudiate any association between humanitarian actors and military campaigns in part for this reason. As the head of MSF's Afghanistan mission noted in 2004:

> The deliberate linking of humanitarian aid with military objectives destroys the meaning of humanitarianism. It will result, in the end, in the neediest Afghans not getting badly needed aid—and those providing aid being targeted.[135]

The ICRC and MSF have also refused to join the UN's integrated missions initiative, which is intended to improve the effectiveness of post-conflict reconstruction efforts via a greater degree of coordination and integration between the organizations that undertake different mission responsibilities. Integrated missions are problematic for the ICRC and MSF because in post-conflict situations, where there is still considerable armed resistance directed against a government, humanitarian organizations that join an integrated mission cease to be neutral and impartial. They become, according to Jacques Forster, ICRC vice-president, part of "a political and military strategy to defeat the enemy. In other words, the subordination of humanitarian activities to political goals, using aid as a tool for local or foreign policy."[136]

Where humanitarian assistance is no longer perceived as being neutral, health workers and clinics may be targeted by rebel movements for precisely this reason. This, in turn, will have a negative impact on population health in the areas affected.

The risk is real. Attacks against aid workers worldwide in 2008 were the highest in 12 years and have increased appreciably since 2006. They have also become increasingly politically motivated, "reflecting a broad targeting of the aid enterprise as a whole."[137]

If threats to aid workers mean service provision is reduced, then health outcomes will not improve, and any legitimacy gains that governments seek to achieve from enhancing health outcomes will not be realized.

However, while there is no doubt the incidence of violent assaults against aid workers has increased worldwide, the violence has not been uniformly distributed. Indeed, some 60 percent of these violent assaults in 2008 took place in just three countries—Afghanistan, Sudan (Darfur), and Somalia.[138] All three countries were experiencing ongoing conflicts, and both Afghanistan and Somalia have Islamist movements strongly opposed to what they see as Western political agendas. The risks to aid workers are minimal in countries where there are major peacebuilding missions underway and no active rebel movements.

Conclusion

WHO's HBP program is less actively promoted today than even five years ago. The HBP page is still active on WHO's website, but the links are now very dated. A recent UK review of the program suggests the declining interest may be in part because the effectiveness of HBP policies has been more asserted than demonstrated. The review, by Colin McInnes and colleagues, noted that:

> Critically, the evidentiary base appears slim and overly reliant on anecdotal evidence rather than rigorous and systematic empirical work. Moreover, there has been little conceptual work done on key questions including: what works and why? What conditions are susceptible to such an approach? What level and form of health investment is required? When might it backfire and allow a conflict to continue? Can it be used to assist in ending conflicts, or just in post-conflict reconstruction? And can it be used to prevent conflict?[139]

None of this means HBP initiatives—like the Days of Tranquility immunization programs for children in conflict zones—are not worthwhile from a health perspective. Rather, it simply means their security benefits have yet to be compellingly demonstrated.

PART II

ENDNOTES

INTRODUCTION

1. The release of the first draft of Part II, The Shrinking Costs of War, generated considerable controversy. The resulting debate is reviewed on HSRP's website. See the 14 April 2010 posting on the Latest News section of HSRP's website, http://www.hsrgroup.org/press-room/latest-news/latest-news-view.aspx (accessed 6 December 2010).

CHAPTER 5

2. The terms *indirect* and *excess* deaths are sometimes—incorrectly—used interchangeably. They are not the same: indirect deaths are those resulting from war-exacerbated disease and malnutrition, while excess deaths include all deaths—direct and indirect—that would not have occurred in the absence of war.

3. Christopher Murray et al., "Armed Conflict as a Public Health Problem," *British Medical Journal* 324 (2002), http://gking.harvard.edu/files/armedph.pdf (accessed 19 November 2009).

4. Cited in Hugo Slim, *Killing Civilians: Method, Madness, and Morality in War* (New York: Columbia University Press, 2008), 91.

5. See Geneva Declaration Secretariat, *Global Burden of Armed Violence*, 2008, http://www.genevadeclaration.org/fileadmin/docs/Global-Burden-of-Armed-Violence-full-report.pdf (accessed 19 November 2009).

6. See Figure 4.1 in the *Human Security Report 2005*. Human Security Centre, *Human Security Report 2005: War and Peace in the 21st Century* (New York: Oxford University Press, 2005).

7. See Human Security Centre, *Human Security Report 2005*, 129–130.

8. Some may be able to avoid the worst consequences of displacement by finding refuge with friends and relatives in more secure parts of the country.

9. Malnutrition was responsible for almost as many deaths as diarrheal disease, while almost 30 percent of deaths were attributed to "other causes." Loretxu Pinoges and Evelyn Depoortere, "Analysis of Excess Mortality in Recent Crises" (Paris: Epicentre, 2004).

10. Goma Epidemiology Group, "Public Health Impact of Rwandan Refugee Crisis: What Happened in Goma, Zaire, in July 1994?" *The Lancet* 345, no. 8946 (11 February 1995): 341.

11. Peter Salama et al., "Lessons Learned from Complex Emergencies over Past Decade," *The Lancet* 364, no. 9447 (13 November 2004): 1804.

12. WHO (World Health Organization) Global Task Force on Cholera Control, "First Steps for Managing an Outbreak of Acute Diarrhoea," 2004, http://www.who.int/topics/cholera/publications/en/first_steps.pdf (accessed 5 November 2009).

13. United Nations Children's Fund, *The State of the World's Children 2008: Women and Children—Child Survival*, 2007, http://www.unicef.org/publications/files/The_State_of_the_Worlds_Children_2008.pdf (accessed 5 November 2009).

14. WHO, "Fact Sheet No. 211: Influenza," April 2009, http://www.who.int/mediacentre/factsheets/fs211/en/ (accessed 5 November 2009).

15. Salama et al., "Lessons Learned," 1809.

16. M. Biot, D. Chandramohan, and J. D. H. Porter, "Tuberculosis Treatment in Complex Emergencies," *Tropical Medicine & International Health* 8, no. 3 (March 2003): 212.

17. Centers for Disease Control and Prevention, "Mortality During a Famine—Gode District, Ethiopia, July 2000," *MMWR Morbidity and Mortality Weekly Report* 50, no. 15 (20 April 2001), http://www.cdc.gov/mmwr/preview/mmwrhtml/mm5015a2.htm (accessed 5 November 2009).

18. Peter Salama, Jeff McFarland, and Kim Mulholland, "Reaching the Unreached with Measles Vaccination," *The Lancet* 366, no. 9488 (3 September 2005): 787.

19. WHO, "Ten Facts on Immunization," October 2009, http://www.who.int/features/factfiles/immunization/en/index.html (accessed 5 November 2009).

20. *Recall bias* arises when respondents forget events or get the dates wrong. This can have the effect of either increasing or decreasing the mortality rate. *Survivor bias* arises when whole families get wiped out, so that no family member is available to report deaths to interviewers. This form of bias has the effect of reducing the excess mortality rate.

CHAPTER 6

21. These estimates are for armed conflicts in which a state is one of the warring parties. Conflicts between non-state armed groups and the deliberate killing of defenseless civilians are not included because there are no data on these forms of violence for the full period covered. However, since these forms of violence mostly kill fewer people than "state-based" violence, their exclusion is unlikely to affect the findings.

22. Moreover, child mortality rates are often used as proxies for adult mortality rates, which are far less commonly measured. Indeed, in Africa, the UN Population Division and WHO use child mortality rates in their estimates of adult mortality and life expectancy in the countries of the region. See Debbie Bradshaw and Ian M. Timaeus, "Levels and Trends of Adult Mortality," in *Disease and Mortality in Sub-Saharan Africa*, 2nd ed., ed. Dean T. Jamison et al. (Washington, DC: World Bank, 2006), http://www.ncbi.nlm.nih.gov/bookshelf/br.fcgi?book=dmssa&part=A206 (accessed 24 November 2009).

23. The DHS is sometimes criticized for underestimating child mortality rates—in part, it is claimed, because, unlike humanitarian NGOs (nongovernmental organizations) and agencies, they do not conduct surveys in areas affected by conflict. In fact, the DHS does survey conflict-affected areas, but they do so retrospectively. Moreover, the child mortality trend data available online at http://www.childmortality.org do not indicate that DHS mortality estimates are consistently lower than those of UNICEF or other survey data—or indeed census data where available.

24. Under-five mortality rates declined in some 90 percent of country-years in war. In the remaining 5 percent of cases, under-five mortality rates remained constant.

25. Center for the Study of Civil War, International Peace Research Institute, Oslo, (PRIO), Battle Deaths Dataset 3.0, http://www.prio.no/CSCW/Datasets/Armed-Conflict/Battle-Deaths/The-Battle-Deaths-Dataset-version-30/ (accessed 17 February 2010), updated from Bethany Lacina and Nils Petter Gleditsch, "Monitoring Trends in Global Combat: A New Dataset of Battle Deaths," *European Journal of Population* 21, no. 2–3 (2005): 145–166; Uppsala Conflict Data Program (UCDP)/Human Security Report Project (HSRP); Inter-Agency Child Mortality Estimation Group (IACMEG), "Child Mortality Estimates Info," 20 November 2009, http://www.childmortality.org (accessed 17 February 2010).

The UCDP and PRIO datasets code battle deaths by conflict rather than by country. In the absence of additional information on the location of battle deaths, HSRP divided annual death tolls in interstate conflicts by the number of parties involved.

Five countries were excluded from the analysis due to data limitations: The IACMEG had no data for Kosovo; Montenegro is not counted as a separate country because the IACMEG had data entries for Montenegro, as well as Serbia and Montenegro, and HSRP could not determine whether the data overlap. East Timor, Eritrea, and Namibia were excluded because all three fought successful wars of independence during the period under review and it was unclear whether the IACMEG data for these three countries overlap with the entries for the "parent countries."

Because the battle deaths from the wars of independence in East Timor, Eritrea, and Namibia took place in the territories that later became independent countries, the tolls were subtracted from the tolls of Indonesia, Ethiopia, and South Africa, respectively.

Battle deaths from the conflict over the Golan Heights were excluded from the analysis as it is unclear whether the IACMEG includes the disputed area in Israel or Syria.

26. Kosovo, Montenegro, East Timor, Eritrea, and Namibia were excluded from the analysis for the same reasons they were excluded from Table 6.1.

   An additional five countries were excluded from the analysis in Table 6.2: Angola, Cambodia, Chad, Cyprus, and Guinea-Bissau. The five were excluded because the IACMEG did not have under-five mortality rate (U5MR) data for all the periods of war experienced by these countries. Assuming that all five excluded countries experienced an increase in the U5MR during the periods of war for which U5MR data are not available, the percentage of countries that experienced an increase in the U5MR during war would be 25 percent (as opposed to 15). This hypothetical scenario still strongly supports the finding that the vast majority of countries saw no increase in the nationwide U5MR during war.

27. PRIO's best estimate of the number of battle deaths in Rwanda in 1994 falls below the 1,000 threshold. However, for the purposes of Figure 6.1, HSRP has coded 1994 as a year in conflict because of the extraordinarily high number of deaths from one-sided violence.

28. In some countries, the survey data that go into making up the best fit trend line will cluster very close to the line; in others there may be quite large differences in the survey results. The IACMEG's website, http://www.childmortality.org, reveals the degree of uncertainty associated with different estimates via a shaded band on either side of the best fit trend line.

29. Siyan Chen, Norman V. Loayza, and Marta Reynal-Querol, "The Aftermath of Civil War," *World Bank Economic Review* 22, no. 1 (2008): 63–85.

30. Ibid., 73.

31. Julie Knoll Rajaratnam et al., "Worldwide Mortality in Men and Women Aged 15–59 Years from 1970 to 2010: A Systematic Analysis," 30 April 2010, http://www.thelancet.com (accessed 22 July 2010).

32. Ruth Levine, *Case Studies in Global Health: Millions Saved* (Sudbury, MA: Jones and Bartlett, 2007), http://www.jbpub.com/catalog/0763746207, xxviii (accessed 25 November 2009).

33. Chen, Loayza, and Reynal-Querol, "The Aftermath of Civil War," 82.

34. UNICEF, "Immunization Fact Sheet," http://www.unicef.org/media/media_46851.html (accessed 25 November 2009).

35. UNICEF, "The 1980s: Campaign for Child Survival," in *The State of the World's Children 1996—Children in War*, 1995, http://www.unicef.org/sowc96/1980s.htm (accessed 1 December 2009).

36. Ibid.

37. UNICEF, *The State of the World's Children 2008: Women and Children—Child Survival*, 2007, http://www.unicef.org/sowc08/docs/sowc08.pdf (accessed 1 December 2009).

38. See David Oot, "Coalition Launches the Second Child Survival Revolution," *International Health* (Spring 2005), http://www.apha.org/membergroups/newsletters/sectionnewsletters/interna/spring05/1670.htm (accessed 21 December 2009); and Kofi A. Annan, *We the Children: Meeting the Promises of the World Summit for Children*, 2001, http://www.unicef.org/specialsession/about/sgreport-pdf/sgreport_adapted_eng.pdf (accessed 9 December 2009).

39. UNICEF India, "Global Data Sheet: SOWC—Key Statistics," 2008, http://www.unicef.org/india/media_3896.htm (accessed 1 December 2009).

40. UNICEF, *The State of the World's Children 2008* (accessed 12 January 2009).

41. Robert E. Black, Saul S. Morris, and Jennifer Bryce, "Where and Why Are 10 Million Children Dying Every Year?" *The Lancet* 361, no. 9376 (28 June 2003): 2226.

42. Gareth Jones et al., "How Many Child Deaths Can We Prevent this Year?" *The Lancet* 362, no. 9377 (5 July 2003): 65.

43. UNICEF, "Statistics by Area/Child Survival and Health," http://www.childinfo.org/mortality.html (accessed 16 November 2009).

44. Ibid.

45. Kenneth Hill, "Adult Mortality in the Developing World; What We Know and How We Know It" (paper presented at the UN Population Division Training Workshop on HIV/AIDS and Adult Mortality in Developing Countries, New York City, 8-13 September 2003), 13, http://www.un.org/esa/population/publications/adultmort/HILL_Paper1.pdf, 13 (accessed 9 December 2009).

46. UNICEF, "Nutrition Indicators: Exclusive Breastfeeding," *Progress for Children*, May 2006, http://www.unicef.org/progressforchildren/2006n4/index_breastfeeding.html (accessed 25 November 2009).

47. UNICEF, "Infant and Young Child Feeding," *Nutrition*, http://www.unicef.org/nutrition/index_breastfeeding.html (accessed 25 November 2009). See also, Stanley Ip et al., "Breastfeeding and Maternal and Infant Health Outcomes in Developed Countries," *Evidence Report/Technology Assessment*, no. 153 (April 2007), http://www.ahrq.gov/downloads/pub/evidence/pdf/brfout/brfout.pdf (accessed 25 November 2009).

48. WHO: Western Pacific Region, "Key Strategies for Promotion of Breastfeeding," http://www.unicef.org/eapro/factsheet.pdf (accessed 25 November 2009).

49. WHO Statistical Information System, Geneva, Switzerland, http://apps.who.int/whosis/data/Search.jsp (accessed 7 October 2009).

   "Period of violence" refers to medium- to high-intensity state-based armed conflict, non-state armed conflict, and one-sided violence.

   DTP3 immunization coverage is the percentage of one-year-olds who have received three doses of the combined diphtheria, tetanus toxoid, and pertussis vaccination in a year.

   MCV is measles-containing vaccine.

50. See WHO Statistical Information System, http://apps.who.int/whosis/data/Search.jsp (accessed 25 November 2009).

51. WHO, "Health as a Bridge for Peace—Humanitarian Cease-Fires, Project (HCFP)," May 2001 http://www.who.int/hac/techguidance/hbp/cease_fires/en/index.html (accessed 25 November 2009).

52. The campaign also offered health assistance to women of child-bearing age, including "breastfeeding promotion; and tetanus toxoid vaccination of girls and women aged 15–49." See UNICEF, "Largest Ever, Life Saving Campaign to Reach 1.5 Million Somali Children," 29 December 2008, http://www.unicef.org/infobycountry/media_46968.html (accessed 25 November 2009).

53. The latest update of the childmortality.org website now shows the "best fit" line for Somalia running parallel to the horizontal axis for the entire period, essentially ignoring the survey data that show a clear decline. Previously, using the same data, the best fit line showed a decline. The straight line is not in fact a best fit line. Rather, it represents an unexplained lack of agreement among experts about what conclusions to draw from the data. The data from the most recent individual surveys for Somalia continue to show a decline, however, and there would have to be massive error in these survey data for some decline not to have taken place.

54. Data from various sources collated by Phil Orchard, University of British Columbia, 2007; Global Humanitarian Assistance, http://www.globalhumanitarianassistance.org/data-space/excel-data/total-humanitarian-assistance-0 (accessed 28 September 2009).

   The data exclude United Nations Relief and Works Agency-mandated refugees.

55. Peter Salama et al., "Lessons Learned from Complex Emergencies Over Past Decade," *The Lancet* 364, no. 9447 (13 November 2004): 1801–1813.

56. Charles B. Keely, Holly E. Reed, and Ronald J. Waldman point out that while there is considerable variation, usually caused by political factors, "the general pattern is one of elevated mortality, followed by rapid declines with the arrival of assistance and a modicum of stable and safe living conditions." See Keely, Reed, and Waldman, "Understanding Mortality Patterns in Complex Humanitarian Emergencies," in *Forced Migration and Mortality*, eds. Holly E. Reed and Charles B. Keely (Washington, DC: National Academies Press, 2001), 12, http://books.nap.edu/openbook.php?record_id=10086&page=12 (accessed 25 November 2009).

57. Dominique Legros, Christophe Paquet, and Pierre Nabeth, "The Evolution of Mortality Among Rwandan Refugees in Zaire between 1994 and 1997," in *Forced Migration and Mortality*, eds. Holly E. Reed and Charles B. Keely (Washington, DC: National Academies Press, 2001), 61, http://books.nap.edu/openbook.php?record_id=10086&page=61 (accessed 25 November 2009).

58. Hazem Adam Ghobarah, Paul Huth, and Bruce Russett, "Civil Wars Kill and Maim People—Long after the Shooting Stops," *American Political Science Review* 97, no. 2 (2003): 189–202.

59. Hazem Adam Ghobarah, Paul Huth, and Bruce Russett, "The Post-War Public Health Effects of Civil Conflict," *Social Science & Medicine* 59 (2004): 881. The authors also calculated the impact of civil wars on neighbouring countries—estimating that these added another 3 million healthy years of life lost worldwide in 1999.

60. See Quan Li and Wen Ming, "Immediate and Lingering Effects of Armed Conflict on Adult Mortality: A Time Series Cross-National Analysis," *Journal of Peace Research* 42, no. 4 (2005): 487. See also, Zaryab Iqbal, "Health and Human Security: The Public Health Impact of Violent Conflict," *International Studies Quarterly* 50, no. 3 (2006): 631–649.

61. Matthew Hoddie and Jason Mathew Smith, "Forms of Civil War Violence and Their Consequences for Future Public Health," *International Studies Quarterly* 53, no. 1 (March 2009): 175–202.

62. Ibid., 185. The authors, however, also show that the distinction between warfare and the more exceptional genocidal events is important when studying the health consequences of organized violence—a finding mirrored in the under-five mortality data in sub-Saharan Africa reviewed elsewhere in this section.

63. In Rwanda 500,000 to 800,000 people were killed in a matter of months with the most basic weapons.

64. Personal communication from Clionadh Raleigh of ACLED to HSRP director, Andrew Mack, 2 March 2009.

65. The data include battle deaths from state-based armed conflict only.

66. United Nations Population Division, "World Population Prospects: The 2008 Revision, Population Database," 11 March 2009, http://esa.un.org/unpp (accessed 20 October 2009).

    The data include battle deaths from state-based armed conflict only.

67. The lower estimate for deaths in the DRC is derived from the PRIO dataset and is just under half the estimate derived from the International Rescue Committee's (IRC's) figures. Population data for Korea and the DRC are from the UN Population Division (2009).

68. Bethany Lacina, Nils Petter Gleditsch, and Bruce Russett, "The Declining Risk of Death in Battle," *International Studies Quarterly* 50 (2006): 675.

69. See Benjamin Coghlan et al., *Mortality in the Democratic Republic of Congo: An Ongoing Crisis* (New York: IRC, 2007), 16, http://www.theirc.org/resources/2007/2006-7_congomortalitysurvey.pdf (accessed 20 December 2009). The IRC's data indicate that, on average, well under 10 percent of the deaths were due to violence.

70. See Benjamin Coghlan et al., *Mortality in the Democratic Republic of Congo: An Ongoing Crisis* (New York: IRC, 2007), http://www.theirc.org/resources/2007/2006-7_congomortalitysurvey.pdf (accessed 20 December 2009). A single survey was also carried out by the IRC in the eastern Congo in 1998–1999.

71. Benjamin Coghlan et al., "Mortality in the Democratic Republic of Congo: A Nationwide Survey," *The Lancet* 367, no. 9504 (13 January 2006): 44–51.

72. Richard Brennann et al., "Mortality Surveys in the Democratic Republic of Congo: Humanitarian Impact and Lessons Learned," *Humanitarian Exchange Magazine* 35, November 2006, http://www.odihpn.org/report.asp?id=2838 (accessed 10 January 2010).

73. UN, "Democratic Republic of the Congo—MONUC—Facts and Figures," MONUC Fact Sheet, http://www.un.org/Depts/dpko/missions/monuc/facts.html (accessed 6 January 2010). Figure on total uniformed personnel as at 30 November 2009.

74. André Lambert and Louis Lohlé-Tart, "La Surmortalité au Congo (RDC) Durant les Troubles de 1998–2004: Une Estimation des Décès en Surnombre, Scientifiquement Fondée à Partir des Méthodes de la Démographie," ADRASS, October 2008, http://www.obsac.com/E20090105172451/index.html (accessed 22 December 2009). Both authors had been invited by the European Commission to assess the voter registration process in 2005 and 2006.

75. Ibid.

76. The Human Security Report Project (HSRP) also commissioned Yale University's Dr. Beth Daponte to review the Belgian demographers' findings. Her findings, which are critical, are available on request.

77. The review done for the Health and Nutrition Tracking Service (HNTS) was released into the public domain after this section of the *Report* was completed. See HNTS, "Peer Review Report: Re-examining mortality from the conflict in the Democratic Republic of Congo, 1998–2006," Geneva, 15 May 2009, http://www1.icn.ch/HNTS_peer_review.pdf (accessed 22 December 2009).

78. Macro International Inc., "Democratic Republic of the Congo: Demographic and Health Survey 2007 Key Findings," August 2008, http://www.measuredhs.com/pubs/pdf/SR141/SR141.pdf (accessed 20 December 2009). While the main DHS report was published in French, its key statistics were also published in English. Interestingly, the DHS report does not mention the very different IRC findings, let alone challenge them, though it does cite other survey research on the DRC.

79. The IRC does not publish nationwide under-five mortality estimates. However, a nationwide figure can be derived from the under-five mortality rates the IRC reports for its survey areas by making the same assumptions that the IRC employed for its own estimate procedure for excess deaths. A detailed explanation of how HSRP calculated the IRC's nationwide under-five mortality rate for the period of the first two surveys can be obtained from HSRP by e-mailing a request to hsrp@sfu.ca.

80. Macro International Inc., "Democratic Republic of the Congo," 16 (accessed 20 December 2009).

81. The IRC and DHS calculate child mortality differently. The IRC, like most humanitarian organizations, is interested in determining short-term mortality levels, so it measures child mortality in deaths per 1,000 per month. The DHS focuses its analyses on long-term trends, and its mortality estimates are measured in deaths per 1,000 live births over a five-year period. The different approaches to measuring child mortality are not comparable in some cases—when comparing, for example, countries with markedly different underlying demographic structures. But since there is little difference in the IRC's child mortality estimates between 2003 and 2007, the two rates are in fact reasonably comparable in this case. Jon Pedersen, in his review of the IRC's research for the HNTS, notes that the IRC's estimate of child mortality would translate into 350 to 400 deaths per 1,000 live births over five years. This is well in excess of double the DHS estimate of circa 150 deaths per 1,000 live births over five years in 2006. Pedersen notes, "It is difficult to see how the DHS 2007 could be that wrong without glaring data quality problems." See HNTS, "Peer Review Report," 19 (accessed 22 December 2009).

82. The recall period of the first survey only went back to January 1999. The researchers extrapolated backwards in order to cover the first five months of the fighting.

83. More detailed discussion of this issue appears later in the chapter.

84. During the fifth survey, the sub-Saharan average mortality rate was revised downwards, so for part of the period covered by this survey—January 2006 through April 2007—the IRC used the new baseline mortality rate of 1.4 deaths per 1,000 per month. This change had the somewhat bizarre consequence of increasing the IRC's excess death toll estimate for the DRC, regardless of whether or not a single additional Congolese person actually died.

85. Kenneth Hill, "Comments on IRC Estimates of Mortality in the DRC and on Estimates by Lambert and Lohlé-Tart" (undated, unpublished review of IRC research on mortality in the DRC undertaken for the WHO-affiliated HNTS). WHO's Francesco Checchi notes, "It is plausible to assume a higher CMR [crude mortality rate] for DRC than for the rest of Sub-Saharan Africa, even in the absence of a war." And Jon Pedersen from Norway's FAFO writes, "The average Sub-Saharan rate for comparison is also problematic . . . [the] DRC in 1998 was a country that had for many years undergone a profound crisis of governance, which may well have affected mortality patterns." For Checchi's and Pedersen's comments, respectively, see HNTS, "Peer Review Report," 8–9, 30 (accessed 22 December 2009). Note the Checchi paper comes after the paper by Jon Pedersen in this file.

    These are not the only grounds for skepticism about the IRC's choice of baseline. The IRC stresses the sub-Saharan African average mortality rate of 1.5 deaths per 1,000 per month is "conservative" because it is higher than UNICEF-reported rates of 1.2 deaths per 1,000 per month in 1996 and 1.25 in 1998. These lower figures are intended to lend credibility to the use of the 1.5 sub-Saharan African figure as a baseline for the DRC at the beginning of the war. But are the figures reported by UNICEF credible? There are certainly reasonable grounds to challenge them. First, they both indicate that the DRC's pre-war mortality rate is *lower* than the sub-Saharan African average rate. This is despite the fact that all reviewers believe the sub-Saharan African average is too low to be used as the baseline rate for the DRC. Second, with reference to these UNICEF-reported rates, the IRC acknowledges the "limitations of such data, including reservations concerning its validity and ability to capture regional differences in a country as vast as DR Congo." See Coghlan et al., "Mortality in the Democratic Republic of Congo: An Ongoing Crisis" (accessed 14 January 2010). This is presumably why the IRC chose not to use either of these figures as its baseline. Third, both of these rates are given as single figures. In fact, there is no way that a mortality rate that is derived from a survey can be determined with the degree of precision that a single figure suggests. The usual way of indicating the extent of uncertainty is with confidence intervals; in this case they would likely have been large. Whether or not a confidence interval was reported in the original data, there would necessarily have been uncertainty around that figure. But the IRC gives no indication that this figure would necessarily have been subject to considerable uncertainty.

86. IRC, *Mortality in Eastern DRC: Results from Five Mortality Surveys* (New York: IRC, May 2000), 12. Emphasis added.

87. Cited in Sam Dealey, "An Atrocity that Needs No Exaggeration," *New York Times*, 12 August 2007, http://www.nytimes.com/2007/08/12/opinion/12iht-eddealy.1.7088161.html (accessed 8 December 2009).

88. Ibid.

89. Richard Brennan and Anna Husarska, "Inside Congo, An Unspeakable Toll," *The Washington Post*, 16 July 2006, http://www.washingtonpost.com/wp-dyn/content/article/2006/07/14/AR2006071401389.html (accessed 8 December 2009).

90. See Ian Smillie and Larry Minear, *The Charity of Nations: Humanitarian Action in a Calculating World* (Bloomfield, CT: Kumarian Press, 2004) for a detailed discussion on inflated claims by NGOs seeking humanitarian funding.

91. See, for example, J. Bohannon, "Iraqi Death Estimates Called Too High; Methods Faulted," *Science* 314 (20 October 2006): 396–397; J. Bohannon, "Calculating Iraq's Death Toll: WHO Study Backs Lower Estimate," *Science* 319 (18 January 2008): 273; B. O. Daponte, "Wartime Estimates of Iraqi Civilian Casualties," *International Review of the Red Cross* 89, no. 868 (2007): 943–957; J. Giles, "Death Toll in Iraq: Survey Team Takes on Its Critics," Nature 446, no. 7131 (2007): 6–7; D. Guha-Sapir and O. Degomme, "Estimating Mortality in Civil Conflicts: Lessons from Iraq: Triangulating Different Types of Mortality Data in Iraq," CRED working paper (June 2007), http://www1.cedat.be/Documents/Working_Papers/CREDWPIraqMortalityJune2007.pdf (accessed 8 December 2009).

92. One way to address this challenge would be to make assessments of the health consequences of armed conflicts *independent* of the organizations responsible for on-the-ground implementation of humanitarian assistance. This idea, canvassed by Paul Spiegel of the UNHCR (United Nations High Commissioner for Refugee) among others, would improve the often uneven quality of data from the field, while addressing donor concerns that NGOs may inflate the seriousness of crises to secure more assistance. NGOs, on the other hand, would be able to point to independent assessments when making the case that more assistance is needed.

93. The IRC's third, preferred, estimation method is simply a variation on the second. Here, the IRC assumes in addition that "one-third of the population has escaped Katanga and is somewhere else, having never experienced excess mortality from this war." No reason is given for this latter assumption, which is dropped in the survey that follows. See Les Roberts et al., *Mortality in Eastern DRC: Results from Five Mortality Surveys* (New York: IRC, 2000), 13.

94. See Les Roberts et al., *Mortality in Eastern Democratic Republic of Congo: Results from Eleven Mortality Surveys* (New York: IRC, 2001).

95. See endnote 82.

96. IACMEG, "Child Mortality Estimates Info," 20 November 2009, http://www.childmortality.org (accessed 26 February 2010). The IACMEG website includes the UNICEF and the DHS data. The UNICEF data referred to here are from its Multiple Indicator Cluster Surveys (MICS); Roberts et al., *Mortality in Eastern DRC*; Roberts et al., *Mortality in Eastern Democratic Republic of Congo*.

There are two different methods for estimating the under-five mortality rate: direct and indirect. "Direct methods of calculation use data on the date of birth of children, their survival status, and the dates of death or ages at death of deceased children. Indirect methods use information on survival status of children to specific age cohorts of mothers." For more information on direct and indirect estimation methods, see http://www.measuredhs.com/help/Datasets/Methodology_of_DHS_Mortality_Rates_Estimation.htm (accessed 22 April 2010).

97. The modest fluctuations in the mortality data in the individual surveys are not unusual and do not mean very much. They are likely the result of sampling and other errors. What matters are not the short-term variations—that may not reflect real changes in mortality—but rather the long-term trend.

98. HNTS, "Peer Review Report," 9 (accessed 22 December 2009).

99. Ibid., 4.

100. Such uncertainty has many other possible causes, including sampling error, reporting bias, response bias, recall bias, and survival bias.

101. When presenting survey results, standard statistical practice is to provide not only the single best estimate but also some measure that indicates the degree of certainty about its accuracy. The conventional approach is to provide "95 percent confidence intervals" for the point estimate. What does this mean? Put simply, it means if one were to sample the same population repeatedly, then the range within which 95 percent of the samples fall would constitute the confidence interval.

102. Benjamin Coghlan et al., *Mortality in the Democratic Republic of Congo: Results from a Nationwide Survey* (New York: IRC, 2004); Benjamin Coghlan et al., "Mortality in the Democratic Republic of Congo: A Nationwide Survey," *The Lancet* 367, no. 9504 (13 January 2006): 44–51; Benjamin Coghlan et al., "*Mortality in the Democratic Republic of Congo: An Ongoing Crisis*" (New York: IRC, 2007), http://www.theirc.org/sites/default/files/migrated/resources/2007/2006-7_congomortalitysurvey.pdf (accessed 14 January 2010); Les Roberts et al., *Mortality in Eastern DRC: Results from Five Mortality Surveys* (New York: IRC, 2000); Les Roberts et al., *Mortality in Eastern Democratic Republic of Congo: Results from Eleven Mortality Surveys* (New York: IRC, 2001); *Les Roberts et al., Mortality in the Democratic Republic of Congo: Results from a Nationwide Survey* (New York: IRC, 2003).

The figures in Table 7.1 have been rounded to the nearest hundred.

103. Coghlan et al., *Mortality in the Democratic Republic of Congo: An Ongoing Crisis* (accessed 14 January 2010).

104. HNTS, "Peer Review Report," 7, 39 (accessed 22 December 2009). Note the Checchi paper comes after the paper by Jon Pedersen in this file.

105. In the following chapter, we challenge the standard assumption that baseline rates remain constant—mostly, they do not.

106. What is the case for assuming an average mortality rate of 2.0 deaths per 1,000 per month for the 10 years following the IRC's last survey in 2007? The nationwide mortality rate has been declining steadily throughout the new millennium, so it is not at all unreasonable to assume that for the 10 years after 2007, the nationwide death rate could continue to decline from 2.2 deaths per 1,000 per month—which is the survey-measured nationwide crude mortality rate in the DRC as of 2007 (Coghlan et al., *Mortality in the Democratic Republic of Congo: An Ongoing Crisis*, ii (accessed 14 January 2010)—to an average of 2.0. Note it is not being argued this figure is correct, simply that it is plausible.

CHAPTER 8

107. See WHO's relatively new World Health Surveys, WHO, Health Statistics and Health Information Systems, World Health Survey, http://www.who.int/healthinfo/survey/en/index.html (accessed 22 July 2010).

108. Such a calculation would obviously require information on the size of the population and the population growth rate.

109. This source of potential error is of sufficient concern among epidemiologists for the Standardized Monitoring and Assessment of Relief and Transitions (SMART) guidelines on survey methodology to state categorically that "recall periods longer than one year should not be used." (See Standardized Monitoring and Assessment of Relief and Transitions (SMART), "Measuring Mortality, Nutritional Status, and Food Security in Crisis Situations: SMART Methodology," 31, http://www.smartindicators.org/SMART_Methodology_08-07-2006.pdf (accessed 15 January 2010). The longer the war, the greater the risk that mistakes will be made in remembering the years in which deaths occurred. This risk is growing because wars are getting longer. In the early 1990s, less than 25 percent of conflicts had been active for 20 years or more, but by 2007 this figure had risen to roughly 50 percent.

110. This assumes the mortality rate for part of the country is an appropriate proxy measure for the whole country. It may not be.

111. The IRC changed its baseline mortality rate during the last survey period when the sub-Saharan African rate changed. However, as we have argued, this rate was not the appropriate one to have used in the first place.

112. Human Security Report Project (HSRP).

113. To calculate the excess death toll, the average excess mortality rate in deaths per 1,000 of the population per month (a common way of measuring mortality in retrospective mortality surveys) is multiplied by the number of months the conflict lasts and then by the war-affected population. The resulting figure is then divided by 1,000.

114. In calculating its estimate, HSRP used the annual rate of decline in the child mortality rate from the DHS data at childmortality.org and the annual rate of decline in the adult mortality rate from the WHO data. See WHO, WHO Statistical Information System, http://apps.who.int/whosis/data/Search.jsp?countries=%5bLocation%5d.Members (accessed 30 December 2009), and childmortality.org, "COD_Demographic and Health Survey_Direct (5 year)_2007," http://www.childmortality.org (accessed 11 January 2010). Further information on the methodology and data used in these calculations is available on request from hsrp@sfu.ca.

115. We define "conflict-free" countries as those that experienced fewer than 25 battle deaths in a given year. Of the 22 conflict-free countries that experienced increases in the under-five mortality rate between 1970 and 2008, 11 were in Europe (Luxembourg, Norway, Denmark, Iceland, Finland, and Ireland were among the 11). We know that developed countries generally have under-five mortality rates that are both lower and more constant than those in the developing world. This means that relatively slight changes can be enough to result in increases at the national level. However, this finding also suggests that increases in the under-five mortality rate may be more easily detected in developed countries than in developing countries.

116. In very short wars—those that last a year or less—the errors introduced by failing to take into account pre-war mortality trends will be minimal.

117. For example, 100,000 deaths is a more significant toll in a country with a population of 10 million than it is in one with a population of 100 million.

CHAPTER 9

118. This chapter draws on an unpublished background paper on "Health as a Bridge for Peace" prepared by Dr. Margaret Kruk for the Human Security Report Project (HSRP).

119. See, for example, Nina Tannenwald, *The Nuclear Taboo: The United States and the Non-Use of Nuclear Weapons Since 1945* (Cambridge: Cambridge University Press, 2007), http://www.cambridge.org/catalogue/catalogue.asp?ISBN=9780521524285 (accessed 5 November 2009).

120. WHO Task Force on Health in Development, "Health in Social Development" (WHO position paper prepared for the World Summit for Social Development, Copenhagen, Denmark, March 1995), 19. Cited in Paula Gutlove, "Health as a Bridge for Peace: Briefing Manual," Institute for Resource and Security Studies, May 2000, http://www.irss-usa.org/pages/documents/HBPbriefmanual.pdf (accessed 5 November 2009).

121. Gutlove, "Health as a Bridge for Peace," 2 (accessed 5 November 2009).

122. A major review of the literature in this field reported the process of negotiating such ceasefires "can have spill-over effects in terms of building trust among conflicting parties"; R. Rodriquez-Garcia, M. Schlesser, and R. Bernstein, "How Can Health Serve as a Bridge for Peace?" *CERTI Crisis and Transition Tool Kit* Policy Brief, May 2001, 9, http://www.certi.org/publications/policy/gwc-12a-brief.PDF (accessed 5 November 2009).

123. Gutlove, "Health as a Bridge for Peace," 3 (accessed 5 November 2009).

124. A. Ciro, C. A. de Quadros, and Daniel Epstein, "Health as a Bridge for Peace: PAHO's Experience," *The Lancet* 360, Supplement (2002): 360; (Supplement 1): s25-s26.

125. Alex Vass, "Peace through Health," *British Medical Journal* 323, no. 7320 (3 November 2001): 1020.

126. See, for example, Anderson's "Humanitarian NGOs in Conflict Intervention," in *Managing Global Chaos*, eds. Chester Crocker, Fen Hampson, and Pamela Aall (Washington, DC: United States Institute of Peace Press, 1996), 343–354.

127. Simon Rushton, "Health and Peacebuilding: Resuscitating the Failed State in Sierra Leone," *International Relations* 19, no. 4 (December 2005): 442.

128. Michael Bratton, "Are You Being Served? Popular Satisfaction with Health and Education Services in Africa" (Afrobarometer Working Paper 65, Michigan State University, January 2007), http://www.afrobarometer.org/papers/AfropaperNo65.pdf (accessed 22 December 2009).

129. Ibid.

130. Taken from Kruk's background paper on "Health as a Bridge for Peace," prepared for HSRP.

131. Matthew A. Levitt. "Hezbollah: Financing Terror through Criminal Enterprise" (testimony given to the Committee on Homeland Security and Governmental Affairs, Washington, DC, 25 May 2005), http://www.washingtoninstitute.org/html/pdf/hezbollah-testimony-05252005.pdf (accessed 21 December 2009); Sabrina Tavernise, "Charity Wins Deep Loyalty for Hezbollah," *New York Times*, 6 August 2006, http://www.nytimes.com/2006/08/06/world/middleeast/06tyre.html (accessed 15 January 2010).

132. Richard J. Brennan and Egbert Sondorp, "Humanitarian Aid: Some Political Realities," *British Medical Journal* 333, no. 7573 (21 October 2006), 817–818.

133. Seth G. Jones et al., "Securing Health: Lessons from National Building Missions," Santa Monica, CA: RAND Center for Domestic and International Health Security, 2006, http://www.rand.org/pubs/monographs/2006/RAND_MG321.pdf (accessed 5 November 2009).

134. Ibid., 281.

135. Kenny Gluk, "Coalition Forces Endanger Humanitarian Action in Afghanistan," MSF, 6 May 2004, http://www.msf.org/msfinternational/invoke.cfm?objectid=409F102D-A77A-4C94-89E0A47D7213B4D5&component=toolkit.article&method=full_html&CFID=7677556&CFTOKEN=44236300 (accessed 5 November 2009).

136. Jacques Forster, "An ICRC Perspective on Integrated Missions" (speech presented at an event hosted by the Norwegian Ministry of Foreign Affairs and the Norwegian Institute of International Affairs, Oslo, Norway, 31 May 2005), http://www.icrc.org/Web/eng/siteeng0.nsf/html/6DCGRN (accessed 5 November 2009).

137. Abby Stoddard, Adele Harmer, and Victoria DiDomenico, "Providing Aid in Insecure Environments: 2009 Update," ODI HPG Policy Brief 34, London, UK, April 2009, 1, http://www.cic.nyu.edu/internationalsecurity/docs/HPG%20Briefing%2034crc.pdf (accessed 5 November 2009).

138. Ibid.

139. Colin J. McInnes, Kelley Lee, and Egbert Sundorp, "Health, Security and Foreign Policy," *Review of International Studies* 32, no. 1 (January 2006): 18.

Martin Adler / Panos Pictures. ETHIOPIA.

PART III

TRENDS IN HUMAN INSECURITY

Part III describes and analyzes the post-World War II global trends in the number of state-based armed conflicts, non-state armed conflicts, campaigns of one-sided violence, and their associated death tolls.

TRENDS IN HUMAN INSECURITY

Introduction

There has been a moderate increase in the number of minor state-based armed conflicts since 2003. It is, however, too early to tell whether this signals a permanent reversal of the major decline in conflict numbers that followed the end of the Cold War.

Non-state armed conflicts—those that do not involve a government—are much less deadly and shorter-lived than state-based armed conflicts. Non-state conflicts are also concentrated within particular regions, and particular countries within those regions.

The trends in the number of campaigns of one-sided violence and the resulting death tolls do not support the frequently cited claim that civilians are being increasingly targeted by both governments and rebel groups.

INTRODUCTION

Trends in Human Insecurity reviews the global and regional trends in state-based armed conflicts—those involving a government as one of the warring parties—and non-state armed conflicts—those fought between non-state groups. It also looks at the trends in one-sided violence, or deadly assault against civilians by governments and non-state armed groups.

From 1992 until 2003, the number of state-based armed conflicts around the world declined by more than 40 percent. As discussed in Chapter 10, that decline has since been partially reversed—the data show a modest but consistent increase in the number of state-based armed conflicts between 2005 and 2008.

While the total number of active conflicts increased, it is equally clear that the long-term decline in the deadliness of state-based conflicts has not been reversed. The number of high-intensity conflicts has seen an uneven but sharp decline over the last two decades. In the new millennium, the average state-based conflict resulted in 90 percent less battle deaths per year than did the average state-based conflict in the 1950s. Battle-death tolls have seen only a small increase over the past few years, mostly due to the conflict in Iraq. Wars, or high-intensity conflicts that result in 1,000 or more battle deaths per year, are still rare, the numbers having dropped by 79 percent from 1984 to 2008.

Chapter 10 also attempts to grapple with the question of which countries have been the most conflict-prone. We look at four different measures that produce quite different results. However, it is clear that France, the United Kingdom, the US, and Russia/USSR are among the countries that have been involved in the greatest number of conflicts, while India, Russia/USSR, and Burma are the most prone to civil wars.

Our discussion of state-based conflict concludes with an analysis of how conflicts end. Peace agreements negotiated since the late 1990s appear to be more stable than those concluded in earlier periods. Only 14 percent of conflicts that terminated in a peace agreement between 2000 and 2003 restarted in under five years. This compares with 46 percent in the previous decade. However, conflict terminations have become less stable overall. In the 1950s less than 20 percent of all terminated conflicts restarted in under five years; at the beginning of the new millennium, that figure was nearly 60 percent. This would at first appear to support claims that conflicts are becoming more intractable. However, the data indicate otherwise—the percentage of conflicts starting each decade and lasting for more than 10 years has in fact decreased since the 1970s.

Chapter 11 focuses on non-state conflicts, which more than doubled in number between 2007 and 2008. Most of the increase was associated with fighting that erupted in just two countries, Kenya and Pakistan, but that together made up some 40 percent of the global total in 2008. The increase in conflict numbers was accompanied by a much less dramatic increase in battle deaths, making 2008 only the fourth-deadliest year covered by the dataset.

It is important to note that non-state conflicts are quite different from conflicts that involve states. Non-state conflicts are concentrated in a small number of countries—just seven countries account for more than 70 percent of all non-state armed conflicts between 2002 and 2008. They also tend to be very short-lived, with some 80 percent of the recorded conflicts having been active for only a single year between 2002 and 2008. Finally, non-state armed conflicts are much less deadly than state-based armed conflicts. Indeed, the non-state battle-death toll in 2008 was about one-tenth of the state-based death toll.

Chapter 12 focuses on trends in one-sided violence. Despite claims that civilians are increasingly being targeted, the data suggest that civilians face no greater threat today than they have over the last 20 years. Indeed, in 2008 the number of deaths from one-sided violence was the lowest ever recorded.

What has changed over the past two decades is the identity of the perpetrators of one-sided violence. In 1989 governments were responsible for most deaths from one-sided violence—today non-state armed groups are the major killers. This shift can be partly explained by the increase in the number of people killed in terrorist attacks relative to the number of people killed by other forms of one-sided violence.

Sub-Saharan Africa is home to the majority of the worst perpetrators of one-sided violence, including the government of Rwanda, the government of Sudan, and the Lord's Resistance Army. This is not surprising given that sub-Saharan Africa has experienced both more campaigns of one-sided violence and more deaths from one-sided violence than any other region in the world. The overwhelming majority (nine out of 10) of the worst perpetrators were also involved in state-based conflicts, demonstrating a close association between deadly assaults against civilians and armed conflict.

CHAPTER 10

State-Based Armed Conflict

The *Human Security Report 2005* challenged the commonly held assumption that armed conflict around the world had become more widespread and more violent. It showed that the number of *state-based armed conflicts*—those in which a government is one of the warring parties—had declined sharply since the end of the Cold War, and that they had become dramatically less deadly since the end of World War II.

That decline stopped in 2003, and in 2004 conflict numbers started to increase; by 2008 they had gone up by nearly 25 percent.[1] This trend can be explained in part by an increase in conflicts associated with Islamist political violence and the so-called War on Terror. There are too few years of data to determine whether we are seeing a sustained reversal of the dramatic downward trend since the end of the Cold War, but this is quite possible.

The increase in the number of conflicts primarily reflects an increase in minor armed conflicts. The number of high-intensity conflicts or wars—i.e., those that cause 1,000 or more battle deaths per year—has declined steeply, but unevenly, since the end of the Cold War.[2] The pronounced, though uneven, downward trend in the number of battle deaths has continued.

In this chapter, in addition to presenting the latest figures on state-based armed conflicts and battle deaths, we rank countries in terms of the number of conflicts they have experienced. We find that the United Kingdom (UK), France, Russia/USSR, and the US have been involved in the greatest number of conflicts of all types. When it comes to the number of intra-state (i.e., civil) conflicts, India takes the lead, while Burma has experienced the greatest number of conflict years.

Finally, we also examine trends in the way that conflicts end. While conflict terminations on the whole are generally becoming less stable—i.e., conflicts are more likely to restart—it would appear that peace agreements negotiated in the late 1990s and into the new millennium are more stable, i.e., less likely to break down, than those concluded in earlier periods.

The fact that conflict terminations are becoming more likely to break down might seem to support claims that conflicts are becoming more intractable. However, our research shows that conflicts that started in the 1980s and 1990s are far less likely to last for 10 or more years than those that started in the 1960s or 1970s—that is, conflicts are becoming *less* intractable.

Global Trends in State-Based Armed Conflict

The Uppsala Conflict Data Program (UCDP), on whose data The Human Security Report Project (HSRP) relies, defines *state-based armed conflicts* as those in which at least one of the warring parties is the government of a state, and that result in 25 or more reported codable battle deaths in a given calendar year. State-based conflicts include fighting between:

- Two or more states (*interstate conflicts*).
- The government of a state and one or more non-state armed groups (*intrastate or civil conflicts*).
- The government of a state and one or more non-state armed groups with the armed forces of another state

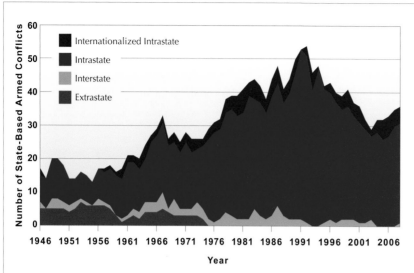

Figure 10.1 Trends in State-Based Armed Conflicts by Type, 1946–2008

Extrastate conflicts (anticolonial struggles) were over by the mid-1970s. Interstate conflicts, which were never very numerous, have become even rarer in the past two decades, while intrastate conflicts declined dramatically from 1992, but have increased modestly since 2003.

Data Source: UCDP/PRIO.[3]

Note: Figure 10.1 is a "stacked graph," meaning that the number of conflicts in each category is indicated by the depth of the band of colour. The top line shows the total number of conflicts of all types in each year.

supporting one of the warring parties *(internationalized intrastate conflict)*.

- A state and an armed group outside the state's own territory *(extrastate conflicts)*. The conflicts that fall into this category are mostly colonial wars of independence.

Not only has the number of state-based conflicts around the world changed over the last several decades but, as Figure 10.1 reveals, the prevalence of different types of conflict has also changed.

By the mid-1970s, the wars of colonial liberation that spread rapidly through the developing world following the end of World War II had ended. But they were often replaced by violent struggles over who should control the post-colonial state. The end of colonialism did not lead to a net decline in conflict numbers in part for this reason, and in part because the geopolitical tensions of the Cold War were also driving conflicts in the developing world.

The overwhelming majority of armed conflicts are now fought *within* states. These intrastate conflicts have relatively low annual battle-death tolls on average and have made up an increasing proportion of all conflicts since the end of World War II. In the late 1940s, they made up little over half of all conflicts; by the early 1990s, their share was closer to 90 percent.

Internationalized intrastate conflicts have never been very numerous. There were only two conflicts of this type between 1946 (the first year covered by the conflict data) and the mid-1950s. In addition, as Figure 10.1 makes clear, they have only ever made up a small percentage of conflicts since then. But—not surprisingly given the involvement of foreign

troops—their death tolls are higher on average than those from intrastate conflicts in which there is no intervention. An example of an ongoing internationalized intrastate conflict is the conflict in Afghanistan, where the US and other external powers are fighting with the government against the Taliban and other domestic insurgent groups.

Conflicts between states, which have been by far the deadliest form of conflict in the post-World II period, have become extremely rare. From 2004 to 2007, there were no interstate conflicts. There was a small border conflict between Eritrea and Djibouti in 2008.[4]

Explaining the Recent Increase in Armed Conflicts

The most recent data indicate that over 25 percent (nine out of 34) of conflicts that started or restarted in the period from 2004 to 2008 were associated with Islamist political violence. The most deadly of these conflicts—in Pakistan and Somalia—were clearly also associated with international and local efforts to crush the Islamist violence.[5] Since the beginning of 2004, there have also been new or reignited Islamist struggles on a much smaller scale in southern Russia, India, Israel (Lebanon), Uzbekistan, and Nigeria. The major conflicts in Iraq and Afghanistan restarted before 2004 but were active during the entire period under investigation and therefore impact the count of the total number of active conflicts.

The rise of Islamist political violence has many causes, but there is little doubt that the US-led international campaign against it—the so-called War on Terror—has increased the level of anti-Americanism throughout the Muslim world, where the "war" has been widely viewed as a war against Islam.[6] In a recent *Foreign Policy* article, Robert Pape argues that US policies are an important reason for the increase in support by some, but by no means all, Muslims for the radical Islamist cause:

> In the decade since 9/11, the United States has conquered and occupied two large Muslim countries (Afghanistan and Iraq), compelled a huge Muslim army to root out a terrorist sanctuary (Pakistan), deployed thousands of Special Forces troops to numerous Muslim countries (Yemen, Somalia, Sudan, etc.), imprisoned hundreds of Muslims without recourse, and waged a massive war of ideas involving Muslim clerics to denounce violence and new institutions to bring Western norms to Muslim countries.[7]

Polling data in Muslim countries support Pape's contention. In November 2009 the president of the US-based polling organization Terror Free Tomorrow, which specializes in tracking attitudes towards Islamist terrorism in the Muslim world, testified to the US House Committee on Foreign Affairs that Muslims who support al-Qaeda and Osama bin Laden "are principally motivated by their perception of Western hostility to Islam."[8]

Levels of Islamist political violence have remained very high in Afghanistan and Iraq and since 2003 have increased in Pakistan and Somalia. However, other conflicts in the Muslim world associated with Islamist political violence, for example those in Algeria and Indonesia, have become much less deadly in recent years.

It is important to point out here that the existence of new or reignited armed conflicts associated with Islamist political violence is not a reflection of increasing popular support for violent Islamist extremism in the Muslim world as a whole. Indeed, polls conducted by the Pew Research Centre show that support for al-Qaeda/Osama bin Laden has declined markedly in almost all Muslim countries over the past five years.[9] The growing popular rejection of the Islamists' indiscriminate violence—most of which is directed against fellow Muslims—is a reaction to their extremist ideology and their harshly repressive policies. As Terror Free Tomorrow's president points out, levels of support for al-Qaeda in the Muslim world have been "consistently declining over time. These changing attitudes are largely the result not of America's actions, but al-Qaeda's: citizens in Pakistan and other countries are becoming increasingly disgusted with the group's barbaric violence."[10]

Of the 34 conflicts that started or restarted between 2004 and 2008, 25 had no common characteristics beyond the fact that they occurred in poor countries. What makes the nine Islamist conflicts that started during this period significant is the commitment of the insurgents to extreme Islamist radicalism.

The conflicts that pit Islamist radicals against the governments of Iraq, Afghanistan, and Pakistan, and their US allies, are among the deadliest in the world, so any increase in conflicts associated with Islamist violence is bound to be a cause for concern.

There is, however, little evidence to suggest that the recent increase in Islamist conflict numbers indicates growing support for al-Qaeda and other extremist groups. Indeed, the reverse is true. As noted above, the harsh and repressive ideology that the Islamists seek to impose on their coreligionists, and the savagely brutal tactics they employ, has progressively shrunk their support base across the Muslim world. This suggests that a truly global Islamist jihad is highly unlikely.

High-Intensity Conflicts

The increase in the total number of state-based armed conflicts has been due to an increase in the number of relatively minor armed conflicts—i.e., those with annual battle-death tolls that are more than 25 but less than 1,000. As Figure 10.2 shows, the number of *wars*—those conflicts with 1,000 or more battle deaths per year—declined steeply, but unevenly, from the mid-1980s until 2007.

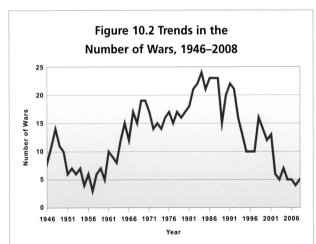

Figure 10.2 Trends in the Number of Wars, 1946–2008

Data Sources: PRIO; UCDP/HSRP Dataset.[11]

The decline in the number of *wars*—defined as armed conflicts that cause 1,000 or more battle deaths per year—is more pronounced than the decline in overall conflict numbers.

FIGURE 10.3

Regional Trends in State-Based Armed Conflicts, 1946–2008

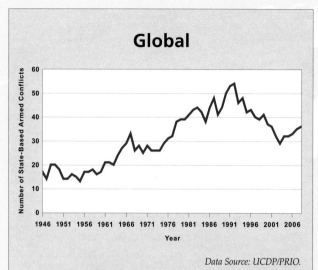

Global

Data Source: UCDP/PRIO.

Worldwide, the number of armed conflicts rose quite steadily from the late 1950s until 1992 and then declined sharply. There has been a modest increase since 2003.

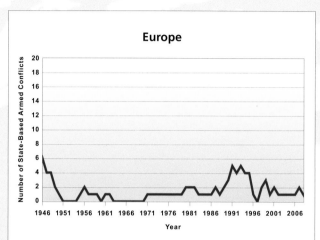

Europe

Europe has been the most peaceful region in the world for the past 60 years. The minor peaks in the 1990s correspond to the conflicts in the Balkans following the breakup of Yugoslavia.

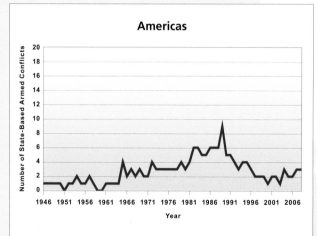

Americas

The end of the Cold War led to a dramatic decline in the number of armed conflicts in the Americas, many of which had been exacerbated by the East/West tensions.

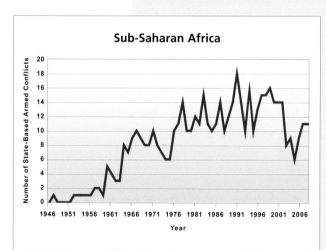

Sub-Saharan Africa

Sub-Saharan Africa has been one of the most conflict-prone regions since 1946. It has endured anticolonial conflicts, struggles over the control of post-colonial states, and Cold War proxy wars.[12]

Middle East and North Africa

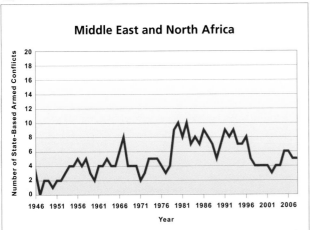

Notwithstanding the much-publicized invasion of Lebanon by Israel in 2006, and the ongoing war in Iraq, conflict numbers have declined unevenly in the Middle East and North Africa since the early 1980s.[13]

East and Southeast Asia and Oceania

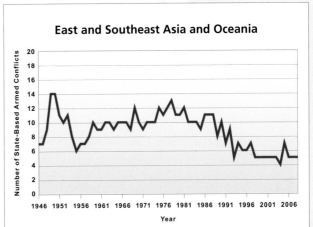

The decline in conflicts in East and Southeast Asia and Oceania started in 1979. Democratization, rising prosperity, and the ending of foreign intervention have all played a role in reducing the number and deadliness of conflicts in the region.

Central and South Asia

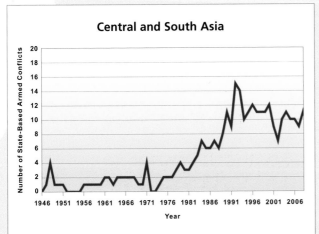

The breakup of the Soviet Union in 1991 triggered a number of new conflicts in Central Asia. However, India accounts for almost half of the conflicts in Central and South Asia since the 1980s.

These graphs show the total number of state-based armed conflicts per year, i.e., those conflicts in which at least one of the warring parties was the government of a state, and which resulted in at least 25 reported codable battle deaths per year. These include interstate conflicts, extrastate conflicts (anticolonial conflicts), intrastate conflicts, and internationalized intrastate conflicts. They do not include conflicts in which neither of the parties was a state; nor do they include cases of deadly attacks against civilians.

In 2007 there were just four wars being fought around the world—in Iraq, Afghanistan, Sri Lanka, and Somalia—the lowest total since 1957. Each of these wars continued in 2008, and the conflict in Pakistan escalated and crossed the 1,000-battle-death threshold to bring the total for 2008 to five. Despite this minor increase, the number of wars was still 79 percent lower in 2008 than in 1984, the peak year.

Not only has the world seen fewer and fewer wars in recent years but the average number of people that these high-intensity conflicts kill has also declined. In the 1950s, the average war killed more than 20,000 people per year on the battlefield; in the new millennium, the figure has been less than 4,000.[14]

Europe has been the most peaceful of the world's six regions since World War II.

High-intensity conflicts have become less deadly in large part because extensive involvement by the major powers in civil wars has become less frequent. In many of the proxy wars of the Cold War period, major power interventions brought large numbers of heavy conventional weapons and sometimes combat troops to the battlefield, pushing battle-death tolls dramatically higher.

Today major power interventions—in Iraq, Afghanistan, and Pakistan, for example—are mostly associated with attempts to crush radical Islamist movements.

Regional Trends in State-Based Armed Conflicts

Figure 10.3 shows global and regional trends in conflict numbers. At the global level, the number of state-based conflicts increased steadily from the late 1950s until 1992. Conflicts then declined by 46 percent between 1992 and 2003. Since 2003 conflict numbers have risen by almost 25 percent, going from 29 to 36 in 2008.

In East and Southeast Asia and Oceania, the number of state-based conflicts dropped by more than 60 percent between 1978 and 1993 and has remained relatively stable. In 2008 there was a conflict in southern Thailand, and the Philippines and Burma each had two active conflicts.

In the Middle East and North Africa, conflict numbers peaked in 1980 and then declined unevenly until 2002. The number of conflicts doubled between 2002 and 2005—going from three to six. The increase was a result of Israel's invasion

of Lebanon, and the resurgence of previously active conflicts in Iraq, Iran, and Turkey. In 2007 the number of conflicts in the region declined slightly, and remained at the same number in 2008.

Central and South Asia experienced relatively few conflicts until the 1980s. Between 1981 and 1992, the number of conflicts in the region increased significantly, then dropped by almost half between 1992 and 2002. New or resurgent conflicts in Afghanistan, Pakistan, and Sri Lanka, as well as in India and Georgia, have largely been responsible for the increase in conflict numbers since 2002. The region has not been devoid of positive developments in recent years, however: the decade-long civil war in Nepal ended in 2006 and has not restarted, despite the troubled transition to democracy.

Conflict numbers in sub-Saharan Africa increased unevenly from the mid-1950s until the early 1990s, reflecting wars of independence from colonial rule, struggles over control of the post-colonial state, and proxy wars associated with the Cold War.[15] There was no clear trend in the 1990s, but between 1999 and 2005, the number of conflicts declined by almost two-thirds. Conflict numbers increased again in recent years as a result of conflicts starting or recurring in Angola, the Central African Republic, the Democratic Republic of Congo (DRC), Somalia, Mali, and Niger. However, a number of the deadliest conflicts in the region that terminated early in the new millennium—including those in Sierra Leone, Liberia, Angola, and Côte d'Ivoire—have not restarted.

The number of armed conflicts in the Americas has never been very high, though it declined markedly following the end of the Cold War. Since 2001 this region has seen either two or three state-based armed conflicts per year, with the exception of 2003 in which only one conflict—that in Colombia—was active. The Colombian conflict has been active every year since 1964. In 2007 and 2008, the Americas saw a resurgence of a conflict that had been inactive since 1999—that between the government of Peru and the Shining Path rebel group.

Europe has been the most peaceful of the world's six regions since the end of World War II. In recent years, the only active armed conflicts in the region have been those over Chechnya and the Caucasus Emirate.

Which Countries Have Experienced the Most Conflicts since the End of World War II?

HSRP is sometimes asked which countries have been involved in the most armed conflicts. There are a number of ways of answering this question—and they produce somewhat different results.

International Conflicts and External Intervention in Civil Wars

Historians have celebrated the post-World War II decades as the longest period without major-power warfare in centuries. However, although the "Long Peace," as John Lewis Gaddis dubbed it,[16] might accurately describe relations between the countries in the industrialized world during this period, it does not extend to the developing world. While industrialized countries did not fight each other, they repeatedly went to war in the poor nations of the world. Indeed, the overwhelming majority of conflicts involving industrialized nations between 1946 and 2008 have been waged against the governments or peoples of poor countries.

India experienced more intrastate conflicts from 1946 to 2008 than any other country.

With respect to international conflicts and external intervention in civil wars,[17] France (with 24 conflicts) and the UK (with 21) occupy the top two spots because they were the two major colonial powers. The US (17 conflicts) and Russia/USSR (nine conflicts) are in second and third place because they were the Cold War superpowers. The Netherlands (eight conflicts), Portugal (eight conflicts), and Spain (seven conflicts) follow by virtue of their role as colonial powers. Australia (with eight conflicts) is also on this list primarily because it has fought in so many of Washington's wars—in Korea, Vietnam, the Gulf War, the Iraq War, and Afghanistan. There are no developing countries in the top eight spots, in part because few of them have the capacity to sustain cross-border or overseas military campaigns.

Intrastate Conflicts

One of the few robust findings to emerge from the quantitative literature on conflict research is, as we noted in Chapter 2, that country and population size are correlated with the risk of war.

India, a country with a population comparable to that of sub-Saharan Africa, has experienced 13 intrastate conflicts during the 1946 to 2008 period—this is more than any other country in the world. India is followed by Russia/USSR, which has experienced 10 conflicts and is the only industrialized country in the top nine. Then come Burma (eight conflicts), Ethiopia (six conflicts), Indonesia (five conflicts), and the DRC (Zaire), Iran, Nigeria, and Yemen (each with four conflicts).

With the exception of Yemen, all of these countries have a population of at least 50 million—some have populations several times this figure.[18]

The Combined List: All Types of State-Based Armed Conflict

Table 10.1 ranks countries according to their involvement in all types of state-based armed conflicts. It is clear that the countries that have been involved in the most international conflicts and as external powers in civil wars—France, the UK, the US, and Russia/USSR—have also experienced the greatest number of conflicts of all types. However, four developing countries also make it into the top eight because they have experienced high numbers of intrastate conflicts.

Table 10.1 Countries Involved in the Greatest Number of State-Based Armed Conflicts, 1946–2008

Country	Number of Conflicts
France	25
United Kingdom	22
Russia/USSR	19
United States of America	17
India	14
Ethiopia	10
Burma	10
China	9

Data Source: UCDP/PRIO.

The two major colonial powers and the two superpowers of the Cold War have been involved in more state-based armed conflicts than any other country.

Conflict Years

Because the duration of conflicts varies so greatly, considering the number of conflict years a country has experienced—as opposed to the number of conflicts—provides a different perspective on conflict's societal impact.

To calculate *conflict years*, we count the number of state-based conflicts a country has experienced, and then add the number of years each conflict was active. For example, if a country experienced one conflict that lasted 20 years, and another that lasted one year, the country would have experienced 21 conflict years. The result is the same regardless of whether the conflicts occurred in the same or different years.

Using this calculation, it is clear from Table 10.2 that one country—Burma—has experienced by far the most conflict years. Although Burma has not been involved in as many conflicts as a number of other countries, the conflicts it has been involved in have been very long-running.

Table 10.2 Countries with the Greatest Number of Conflict Years, 1946–2008

Country	Conflict Years
Burma	246
India	180
Ethiopia	113
Philippines	100
United Kingdom	91
France	89
Israel	79
Vietnam	71

Data Source: UCDP/PRIO.

Burma has, on average, experienced four conflicts in each of the 61 years since its independence in 1948 until 2008.[19]

Burma has experienced an average of some four years of conflict for each of the 61 calendar years between 1948 and 2008. That makes for an extraordinary 246 conflict years. India and Ethiopia occupy the second and third spots, respectively, in Table 10.2. Both countries have also been involved in a high number of long-running conflicts. The UK and France, which have been involved in the highest number of international conflicts and interventions in civil conflicts, are among the top eight. However, they are in the fifth and sixth positions, respectively. Israel comes in at number seven because it has been involved in at least one conflict for every year of its existence.

None of these ranking methods is more "correct" than the other: together they provide a more comprehensive overview of the patterns of conflict around the world.

Trends in Battle Deaths from State-Based Armed Conflict

The core message that emerges from more than six decades of battle-death data is that warfare has become progressively less deadly since the end of World War II. Even though conflict

numbers have increased since 2003, the striking, though very uneven, long-term decline in the deadliness of state-based conflict has not been reversed.

The average state-based armed conflict in the 1950s killed almost 10,000 people per year on the battlefield, while in the new millennium, the number has dropped to less than 1,000. As explained in Chapter 3, and Part II: The Shrinking Costs of War, this remarkable decline has been due in large part to profound changes in the nature of warfare during this period.

Battle deaths—which include not just combatant deaths but also "collateral damage"—i.e., civilians "caught in the crossfire"—are the most basic and universal indicator of conflict intensity.

The battle-death tolls discussed in this chapter are estimated by collating all credible reports about violent deaths attributable to conflict. The data are reviewed, reconciled, and used to produce a *best estimate* of the annual battle-death toll for each conflict. For reasons explained later in the chapter, battle-death data are inherently less accurate than the data on conflict numbers.

Figure 10.4 shows the total number of reported codable battle deaths from state-based armed conflict between 1946 and 2008.[20] The graph shows not only the total number of battle deaths but also the share of deaths accruing to each of the world's regions.

The highest annual battle-death toll since the end of World War II was in 1950, with the fatalities driven primarily by the slaughter in the Korean War, the Chinese Civil War, and Vietnam's war of independence. East and Southeast Asia and Oceania remained the world's greatest killing ground until the mid-1970s when the Vietnam War ended; since then it has been one of the least violent regions.[21]

By the mid-1980s, battle-death numbers in East and Southeast Asia and Oceania had shrunk dramatically. The global death toll was now being driven by conflicts in the Middle East and North Africa—where the long Iran-Iraq war was the major killer—sub-Saharan Africa, and Central and South Asia.

Battle deaths declined worldwide from the late 1980s until the late 1990s when there was another sharp spike in deaths caused by a series of deadly conflicts in sub-Saharan Africa—in Angola, the Great Lakes region, and between Ethiopia and Eritrea. Fatalities in sub-Saharan Africa accounted for more than two-thirds of the global battle-death toll in 1999.

After 1999 battle deaths again dropped steeply, and despite the increase in 2008, they are less than one-fifth of the toll in 1999. Since 2005 most battle deaths have occurred

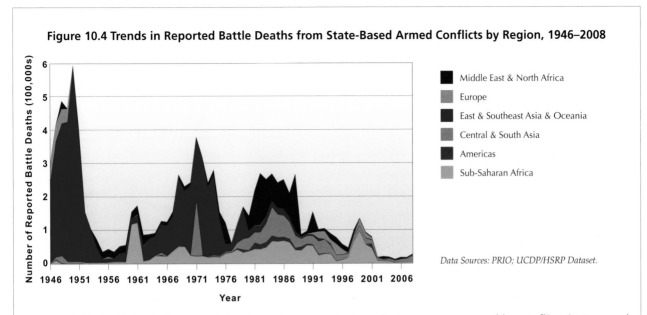

Figure 10.4 Trends in Reported Battle Deaths from State-Based Armed Conflicts by Region, 1946–2008

Legend:
- Middle East & North Africa
- Europe
- East & Southeast Asia & Oceania
- Central & South Asia
- Americas
- Sub-Saharan Africa

Data Sources: PRIO; UCDP/HSRP Dataset.

The peaks in the late 1940s to early 1950s, and late 1960s to early 1970s, were caused by conflicts in East and Southeast Asia and Oceania. From the mid-1970s until the early 1990s, the locus of battle deaths shifted to the Middle East and North Africa, Central and South Asia, and sub-Saharan Africa. In the late 1990s, more people were being killed in the conflicts in sub-Saharan Africa than in the rest of the world combined.[22]

Note: Figure 10.4 is a "stacked graph," meaning that the number of battle deaths in each region is indicated by the depth of the band of colour. The top line shows the global total number of battle deaths in each year.

in Central and South Asia and have been driven by the wars in Sri Lanka, Afghanistan, and Pakistan. In 2008 the war in Sri Lanka was the world's deadliest.

Can We Trust the Conflict and Battle-Death Trend Data?

We can be confident about the broad trends in conflict numbers presented in this *Report* because estimating conflict numbers is a relatively straightforward process. Researchers must verify that there have been at least 25 reported codable battle deaths in a calendar year to determine whether a state-based conflict was active.[23]

A further reason for confidence in the reliability of UCDP/ International Peace Research Institute, Oslo (PRIO) conflict data is that they are very similar trends to those produced by data from two independent groups: Hamburg University's Working Group for Research into the Causes of War (AKUF), and the Center for Systemic Peace (CSP) in Maryland. The CSP dataset focuses on medium to high-intensity armed conflicts, and both CSP and AKUF use different definitions of "conflict" to that used in the UCDP/PRIO dataset. As a consequence, neither AKUF nor CSP show the increase in conflict numbers visible in the UCDP/PRIO data since 2003.

Despite the different definitions, as Figure 10.5 demonstrates, the trend line produced by the AKUF data, like that produced by the UDCP/PRIO data (see Figure 10.1), shows a strong increase in conflict numbers starting in the 1950s and continuing into the early 1990s. This change was followed by a steep decline.

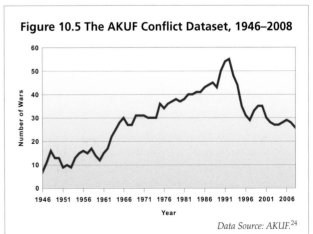

Figure 10.5 The AKUF Conflict Dataset, 1946–2008

Data Source: AKUF.[24]

Researchers at AKUF use different definitions of conflict to those used by UCDP/PRIO; however, the two datasets show similar trends.

The much-cited trend data in Figure 10.6 were collated by CSP. The decline in conflict *magnitude scores* in the 1990s and beyond is steeper than UCDP/PRIO's decline in conflict numbers, but it follows roughly the same trend. Unlike UCDP/PRIO, CSP produces annual estimates not of conflict numbers but of the total *societal impact* of all armed conflicts worldwide. This is achieved by calculating *magnitude scores* for individual conflict-affected countries based on an evaluation of the annual impact of the conflict on the society as a whole.

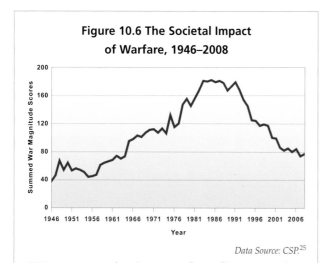

Figure 10.6 The Societal Impact of Warfare, 1946–2008

Data Source: CSP.[25]

CSP measures the impact of conflict on society rather than simply counting conflict numbers, but the overall trend is similar to both AKUF and UCDP/PRIO data.

Magnitude scores take into account the "number of combatants and casualties, affected area, dislocated population, and damage to infrastructure."[26] The scores are on a scale of one to 10, with one representing minimal societal impact and 10 representing total destruction. Because the difference between each level on the scale is assumed to be the same, the impact-of-war scores for all individual countries can be added to arrive at an annual global impact score. This "expert estimation" method is very similar to those used by Transparency International's Corruption Perception Index to estimate the degree of societal corruption, and to various World Bank measures of governance.

The Battle-Death Trend Data
Estimating battle-death numbers is not only far more challenging than determining conflict numbers, it can also be an exercise fraught with controversy as the intense debates over death tolls in Iraq remind us. UCDP and PRIO use estima-

tion methods that involve collating data from a wide range of independent sources—NGOs (nongovernmental organizations), governments, international agencies, and the media. Getting precise estimates is impossible because some deaths will always go unreported, even though access to fatality data has improved dramatically since the advent of the Internet, powerful search engines, and news databases like Factiva.

> Estimating battle-death numbers is far more challenging than determining conflict numbers.

UCDP and PRIO datasets are sometimes criticized for providing battle-death estimates that are too low. The reasons undercounting may occur are obvious enough. Governments may forbid the reporting of war deaths—particularly of their own forces. Journalists and other observers are sometimes banned from war zones, or stay away because they are simply too dangerous. And in wars with high daily death tolls—such as Iraq during the peak years of violence—individual deaths may well go unreported.

Researchers at UCDP and PRIO are well aware of these challenges and address them by relying on as many different independent sources of fatality data as possible. Coders critically evaluate the source material and constantly update past estimates as new data become available. To demonstrate the uncertainty that characterizes the data, UCDP and PRIO use "low" and "high" battle-death estimates, and provide a best estimate that is based on their evaluation of the sources' credibility.[27] The best-estimate figures, which tend to be conservative, are the ones used in this *Report*. In many cases, it is likely that more people were killed on the battlefield than the best estimates would suggest. This is certainly the case with respect to Iraq.[28] For the analysis of trends, however, conservative and consistent coding practices are the highest priority.

There are other well-established methods of estimating violent deaths during war (a category that is broader than UCDP and PRIO's battle-death measures). The US-based Human Rights Data Analysis Group (HRDAG) uses a multiple systems estimation methodology in painstaking investigations of gross human rights abuses—some perpetrated in wartime. These investigations produce highly detailed fatality estimates and other data on human rights violations for truth and reconciliation commissions, criminal tribunals, and other clients.[29]

Other researchers use nationwide retrospective mortality surveys to estimate national war death tolls, non-violent as well as violent.[30] Demographers produce estimates of war death tolls from national census data.[31]

Given the range of different ways of collecting data, why do conflict researchers seeking to understand the causes, duration, and deadliness of conflicts rely increasingly on the battle-death data produced by organizations like PRIO and UCDP? The short answer is that notwithstanding their utility for the purposes for which they were intended, none of the other estimation methods can be used to provide annual global and regional battle-death trend data in a timely manner.

HRDAG investigations, while far more detailed than those of UCDP and PRIO, are usually one-off efforts and can sometimes take years to complete, plus they only cover a relatively small percentage of war-affected countries. This means that their data cannot be used to create annual data to track global war death trends each year.

Nationwide retrospective mortality surveys confront particular technical challenges in estimating violent deaths because such deaths are *relatively* few in number compared with other types of deaths, and the surveys are not repeated frequently enough to produce annual data at the national, let alone global, level.

Census data have many advantages, but in war-affected countries censuses may be decades apart and as such cannot be used to produce timely annual trend data. Nor can they differentiate between the different kinds of deaths (e.g., between battle deaths and war deaths more generally).

While the accuracy of estimates of battle deaths from armed conflicts in particular countries in particular years can be contested, the estimates are sufficiently accurate to permit researchers to map broader trends in national, regional, and global battle-death tolls. For example, the data demonstrate that the average battle-death toll per conflict in the 1950s was almost 10,000, while the equivalent figure for the new millennium has been less than 1,000. These estimates leave no doubt that there has been a huge decline in the deadliness of warfare since the 1950s. The uncertainty around annual death tolls in individual conflicts is not great enough to put the broad trend in question. This finding is important and contradicts recent research based on retrospective mortality surveys that shows that war deaths have increased over time.[32]

How Conflicts End

In order to make sense of global trends in armed conflicts, we need to understand not only why conflicts start but also why they end. The conflict terminations dataset compiled by UCDP for HSRP provides rich insights into the way in which state-based armed conflicts have ended since 1946.

UCDP considers a conflict to have terminated when fighting has either stopped completely, or the battle-death toll has dropped below the 25-deaths-per-year threshold.[33] Because UCDP's coding rules require a full year of inactivity before a conflict is considered terminated, the most recent data on conflict terminations always lag one year behind the conflict data. This means that the most recent terminations in the dataset are for 2007, even though the conflict data extend to 2008.

Whether overall conflict numbers increase or decrease in a year is a function of two things—the number of conflicts starting and the number ending. If two conflicts start in a year while three others end, the graph of the number of conflicts will show one less conflict.[34]

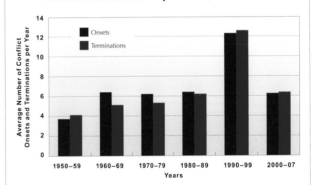

Figure 10.7 Number of Conflict Onsets versus Conflict Terminations per Year, 1950–2007

Data Source: UCDP/HSRP Dataset.

The average number of conflict onsets and terminations per year in the chaotic 1990s was double that of the 1980s. But the 1990s was also the first decade since the 1950s in which more conflicts ended than started.

Figure 10.7 shows the average number of conflict onsets and terminations each year by decade. We can see that in the 1960s, 1970s, and 1980s the average number of onsets each year exceeded the number of terminations. This is what drove the progressive increase in overall conflict numbers in this period.

In the 1990s, the instability associated with the ending of the Cold War brought about a remarkable change: the average number of conflict onsets per year was twice what it was in the 1980s. Those analysts who believed the 1990s represented a

Table 10.3 State-Based Armed Conflict Terminations, 1950–2003

Years	PEACE AGREEMENTS			CEASEFIRES			VICTORIES			OTHER			TOTAL TERMINATIONS		
	Total No.	No. Restarted in under 5 Years	% Restarted in under 5 Years	Total No.	No. Restarted in under 5 Years	% Restarted in under 5 Years	Total No.	No. Restarted in under 5 Years	% Restarted in under 5 Years	Total No.	No. Restarted in under 5 Years	% Restarted in under 5 Years	Total No.	No. Restarted in under 5 Years	% Restarted in under 5 Years
1950–59	7	0	0.0	2	0	0.0	18	3	16.7	14	5	35.7	41	8	19.5
1960–69	5	1	20.0	7	0	0.0	21	2	9.5	18	4	22.2	51	7	13.7
1970–79	9	1	11.1	8	1	12.5	23	7	30.4	13	3	23.1	53	12	22.6
1980–89	3	1	33.3	6	0	0.0	22	4	18.2	31	21	67.7	62	26	41.9
1990–99	22	10	45.5	22	9	40.9	23	2	8.7	59	35	59.3	126	56	44.4
2000–03	7	1	14.3	4	2	50.0	3	2	66.7	15	12	80.0	29	17	58.6
Total 1950–2003	53	14	26.4	49	12	24.5	110	20	18.2	150	80	53.3	362	126	34.8

Data Source: UCDP/HSRP Dataset.

Peace agreements are the only form of conflict termination that has become more stable in the new millennium. Victories, the most stable type of termination for the entire 1950–2003 period, appear to have become significantly less stable.

period in which conflict numbers increased dramatically were correct. But the number of terminations in this decade was even greater—exceeding for the first time, since the 1950s, the number of onsets. The net effect of this was a decline in overall conflict numbers.

As a result, the unprecedented increase in conflict onsets in the 1990s was followed by the biggest—though much less noticed—net decline in conflict numbers since the end of World War II.

Overall, the situation with respect to onsets and terminations in the new millennium is very similar to that in the 1980s, although conflict numbers were higher then than they are today. The other difference is that in the 1980s there were more onsets than terminations per year on average, whereas in the new millennium there have been more terminations than onsets—between 2000 and 2003, there were 29 terminations versus only 19 onsets. Since 2003, however, there have been more onsets than terminations.

Patterns of Conflict Termination

Figure 10.7 tells us about the average number of state-based conflicts terminating per year by decade, but it does not tell us how those conflicts were terminating. Nor does it tell us anything about the stability of the different types of termination—i.e., the probability that conflicts that stop will start up again within a specific period. To determine the stability of conflict terminations, HSRP tests whether the conflicts restart within five years. The five-year threshold means that Table 10.3 only includes data on conflicts that terminated before 2004.

In the conflict terminations dataset, conflicts can terminate in one of four ways: with a peace agreement, a ceasefire, a victory, or by "other" means. "Other" is a catch-all category for situations where the fighting simply dies down and the number of recorded battle deaths drops below 25 per year, or when a conflict ends in a manner that does not fit within any of the other three categories listed above.

Since 2003, there have been more conflict onsets than terminations.

It is clear from Table 10.3 that the pattern of conflict terminations has changed over time. There have been changes both in the way in which conflicts end and in the stability of terminations.

In the 1950s, 1960s, and 1970s, more conflicts ended each decade with victories than with peace agreements, ceasefires, or by simply petering out—the "other" category. In each decade since then, however, the "other" category has accounted for the greatest number of terminations and these conflicts have been highly prone to restart. Indeed, from 1990 to 2003, "other" terminations had a 64 percent probability of restarting in under five years.

The share of conflicts terminating with a peace agreement or ceasefire has fluctuated but has always been relatively small. Peace agreements have never accounted for more than 24 percent of conflict terminations in any decade; ceasefires have never accounted for more than 20 percent.

As Table 10.3 demonstrates, conflict terminations have become progressively less stable—i.e., more likely to restart within five years. In the 1950s, less than 20 percent of all terminated conflicts restarted in under five years. By the 1990s, that figure had risen to 44 percent.

Peace agreements in the early to mid-1990s were prone to breakdown; those negotiated later have been more stable.

In the new millennium, almost six out of every 10 terminated conflicts (i.e., some 60 percent) restarted in under five years. While both victories and ceasefires have become less stable, it is the increase in the number of "other" terminations that restart, combined with the fact that they constitute an increased share of all terminations, that has driven up the number of conflicts that recur.

The reason that relatively fewer conflicts are ending in peace agreements or victories is likely related to the fact that modern warfare has become less deadly. Very low intensity conflicts present neither threats to international peace and security nor the prospect of large death tolls. Given this, they are unlikely to be the subject of international mediation efforts, which in turn means there will be less pressure on the warring parties to pursue negotiated settlements. And as Chapter 3 pointed out, governments confronted by low-intensity insurgencies that pose no threat to their security, and are difficult to defeat, have few incentives to push for either military victories or negotiated settlements.

The overwhelming majority of "other" terminations in the dataset are the result of low-intensity conflicts either stopping completely or slipping below the 25-battle-deaths-per-year threshold.

The fact that these low-intensity conflicts have quite a high probability of restarting is clearly a source of concern. However, the conflicts that restart are likely to continue to be low-intensity affairs—and as such, do not pose a major threat to human security. Indeed, the annual death toll from most

of these conflicts will typically be far below the state's annual death toll from traffic accidents or homicides.

The Increasing Stability of Peace Agreements

Peace agreements are the only form of conflict termination that appear to have become more stable in the new millennium—though we stress the need for caution in interpreting these results since the number of cases remains small and there are few years of data.

The failure rate of peace agreements was at its highest in the chaotic 1990s. More peace agreements were signed in this decade than ever before, but many were poorly designed and inadequately supported. Almost half failed within five years.

Of the seven conflicts that terminated with a peace agreement between 2000 and 2003, only one restarted in less than five years.[35] By contrast, two out of three victories—the most stable type of termination for the entire 1950 to 2003 period—failed during the same period.

Figure 10.8 Percentage of Failed Peace Agreements, Three-Year Moving Average, 1990–2002

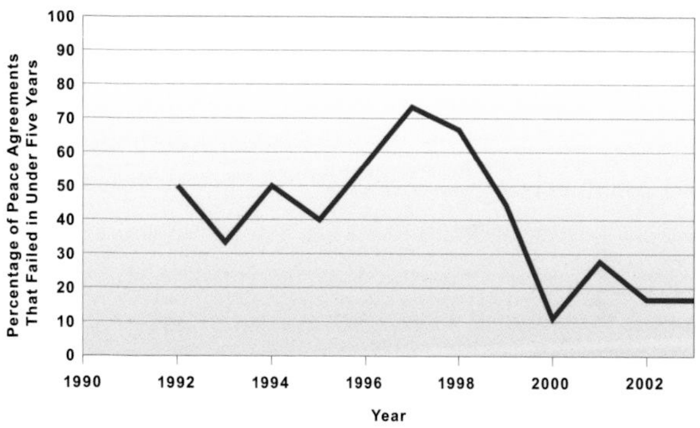

Data Source: UCDP/HSRP Dataset.

Peace agreements signed since 1998 have been less likely to breakdown than those of the early 1990s.

Note: The trend line is a three-year moving average that smoothes the year-on-year fluctuations and makes the short-term trend more discernible.

The improved durability of peace agreements is also apparent in Figure 10.8, which shows the percentage of peace agreements that were followed by a resumption of conflict within five years.[36] It is apparent that the peace agreements of the early to mid-1990s were highly prone to breakdown; those negotiated towards the end of the decade have been much more stable. The trend in the increased stability of peace agreements has continued, albeit somewhat unevenly, into the early years of the new millennium.

We cannot be sure what has caused the increased stability of terminations that end in peace agreements over the last decade, but it is likely linked, in part at least, to the fact that they are better crafted, better implemented, and better supported than they were in the 1990s.

Are Conflicts Becoming More Intractable?

In 2005 a major collaborative study directed by Chester Crocker, Fen Olser Hampson, and Pamela Aall at the United States Institute of Peace (USIP) argued that conflicts were becoming increasingly "intractable," meaning they were both persistent and "refused to yield to efforts… to arrive at a political settlement."[37]

The study also suggested that even though conflict numbers had been declining since the end of the Cold War, the prospects for future declines were limited by the fact that "the low-hanging fruit" had already been picked—i.e., the conflicts that had been brought to an end were those that were most amenable to resolution. James Fearon, writing in 2004, noted that civil wars are lasting longer on average.[38] This might suggest that they are becoming more intractable—as would the data showing that conflict terminations are becoming more likely to break down. If this is indeed the case, this is not an encouraging prognosis for future efforts at conflict resolution. However, the average duration of active conflicts is *not* a good measure of trends in intractability because it is biased by the long duration of some conflicts.

We can get some idea of whether conflicts are becoming more intractable by looking at the percentage of conflict onsets per decade that is followed by 10 years or more of continuous fighting. We took a 10-year continuous conflict duration as a reasonable indicator of intractability, given that the majority of conflicts last less than three years in total. If a greater percentage of new conflicts is lasting for 10 or more years in each successive decade, this would support claims that conflicts are becoming more intractable. However, this is not what the data show.

We can see immediately from Figure 10.9 that since the 1970s, a decreasing percentage of conflict onsets has been followed by 10 or more consecutive years of fighting.

Between 1990 and 1998, less than 10 percent of the conflicts that started lasted for 10 years or more, compared to some 25 percent of conflicts in the 1970s. The trend holds true even when we consider 10 cumulative years of fighting as opposed to 10 consecutive years of fighting (i.e., cases where there was a break but then fighting resumed). This suggests that, notwithstanding the handful of very long duration conflicts, the trend is towards fewer, not more, intractable conflicts.

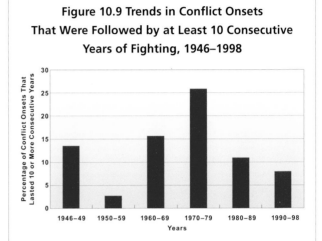

Figure 10.9 Trends in Conflict Onsets That Were Followed by at Least 10 Consecutive Years of Fighting, 1946–1998

Data Source: UCDP/HSRP Dataset.

In the 1970s, more than 25 percent of conflicts that started lasted for 10 or more years; in the 1990s, just 10 percent of new conflicts lasted for 10 years or more.[39]

Ironically, the USIP study itself provides supportive evidence for this supposition. Of the 18 examples of post-World War II intrastate conflicts that Crocker and his colleagues identified as "intractable," five (Angola, East Timor/Timor Leste, Liberia, Sierra Leone, and Northern Ireland), as the authors indicate, had already stopped by 2005.[40] And since the study was published, more of the USIP's "intractable" conflicts have ended—including the conflicts in Nepal and Aceh.

There are, in other words, few compelling reasons to believe that conflicts are becoming more intractable and therefore resistant to peacemaking initiatives.

CHAPTER 11

Non-State Armed Conflict

Conflict research has traditionally focused on armed conflicts that involve a government as one of the warring parties. As a consequence, conflicts between non-state armed groups—warlords, clans, or rebel groups for example—are missing from most conflict datasets. This has been a serious omission since these so-called non-state conflicts make up a significant proportion of the total number of conflicts. Indeed, in 2008 there were as many non-state conflicts as there were conflicts involving a government.

To address this gap in the knowledge about security trends, the Human Security Report Project (HSRP) commissioned the Uppsala Conflict Data Program (UCDP) to start collecting data on non-state armed conflicts in 2003.

Non-state armed conflicts are defined as conflicts that involve "the use of armed force between two organized groups—neither of which is the government of a state—which results in at least 25 battle deaths in a year."[41]

There are two broad categories of cases captured by the non-state armed conflict dataset. The first includes fighting between different rebel groups, or factions of rebel groups, that are involved in state-based armed conflicts. An example is the conflict between the Palestinian groups Hamas and Fatah that broke out in 2006.

The second category includes clashes between ethnic, religious, or other groups that are usually not involved in a state-based armed conflict.[42] The violence that erupted in 2008 between the Luo, Kikuyu, and other groups in Kenya is an example of such a conflict.

Non-state armed conflicts differ from state-based armed conflicts in that they tend to be very short in duration—most last only a year. Non-state conflicts are also much less deadly—the battle-death toll of the average non-state conflict is almost 80 percent lower than that of the average state-based conflict.

The short duration of non-state armed conflicts helps explain the dramatic fluctuation in conflict numbers in recent years. The year 2007 marked a low in the number of non-state conflicts around the world. However, a significant increase in new conflicts in 2008 meant there were more non-state conflicts recorded in that year than ever before. Fortunately, the increase in the number of battle deaths from non-state conflict did not mirror the increase in the number of conflicts—2008 was only the fourth most deadly year in the dataset.

Trends in the Number of Non-State Armed Conflicts

The trend in the number of non-state conflicts over the last seven years has been uneven. Between 2002 and 2007, the number of non-state conflicts declined by 52 percent—from 34 to 16. However, the decline came to an abrupt end in 2008 when the number of non-state conflicts was higher than ever recorded. The increase was accounted for in large part by the new conflicts that erupted in just two countries—Pakistan and Kenya—which together made up some 40 percent of the global total in 2008.

Figure 11.1 Trends in Non-State Armed Conflicts by Region, 2002–2008

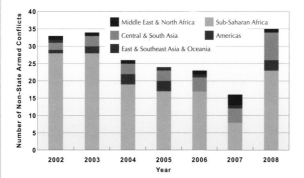

Data Source: UCDP/HSRP Dataset.[43]

Sub-Saharan Africa has experienced more non-state armed conflicts than all other regions combined. Europe was free of non-state conflict between 2002 and 2008.

As Figure 11.1 shows, a single region—sub-Saharan Africa—accounts for the vast majority of the total number of non-state conflicts that have occurred since 2002. In fact, sub-Saharan Africa accounts for more non-state conflicts than all of the other regions combined.

The number of non-state conflicts in sub-Saharan Africa declined sharply from 2002 to 2007—going from 28 to eight. However, in 2008 the number of non-state conflicts in the region increased, largely as a result of violence in Kenya. Kenya had been free of non-state conflict in 2007, but in 2008 the country recorded eight non-state conflicts—more than any other country that year. Much of the violence was sparked by the contested re-election of President Mwai Kibaki in December 2007, with many of the clashes taking place in the Rift Valley region. Other non-state conflicts in Kenya in 2008 were associated with land disputes and cattle raids. New conflicts in Ethiopia and Somalia in 2008 also contributed to the increased regional total.

Central and South Asia is the second most conflict-prone region when it comes to non-state conflicts. Like sub-Saharan Africa, Central and South Asia has experienced non-state conflict every year since 2002. In 2008, the number of non-state conflicts in Central and South Asia was double what it was in 2007. The increase was due to fighting in Pakistan where the number of conflicts went from two in 2007 to six in 2008. The increase in non-state conflicts in Pakistan coincided roughly with an increase in both state-based conflicts and campaigns of one-sided violence.

The Americas were free of non-state conflict in 2006 and 2007. In 2008, however, fighting between drug cartels in Mexico again drove the regional total up to three conflicts. The conflict between the United Self-Defense Forces of Colombia (AUC) and the Revolutionary Armed Forces of Colombia (FARC), which is one of the longest running conflicts in the dataset, has been inactive since 2005.

The Middle East and North Africa has experienced relatively few non-state armed conflicts. The region was free of non-state conflict in 2005 and with the exception of 2007, when there were three non-state conflicts, the annual total has never exceeded one. The increase in 2007 was due to developments in Iraq and Israel. In 2008 there was only one non-state conflict in the region, that in Lebanon.

East and Southeast Asia and Oceania experienced a total of three non-state conflicts during the period from 2002 to 2008. Two of these conflicts occurred in Burma between groups that are also linked to state-based armed conflicts in that country. The only other conflict in the region occurred in the Philippines; in this case, neither group was directly involved in state-based conflict. In 2008 there were no non-state conflicts recorded in East and Southeast Asia and Oceania.

Europe is the only region that has been free of non-state conflict for the entire period for which there are data.

Trends in Battle Deaths from Non-State Armed Conflicts

The trend in reported codable battle deaths from non-state armed conflicts is less discouraging than the trend in the number of conflicts. Figure 11.2 shows that although the battle-death toll in 2008 was higher than in 2007, it did not increase as much as might have been expected given that conflict numbers more than doubled. Despite the increase, the death toll for 2008 was still lower than in 2003 and 2004, and was less than half that recorded in 2002, the deadliest year.

Sub-Saharan Africa, which has consistently experienced more non-state conflicts than any other region, has also suffered more battle deaths than the other regions combined. Despite the recent increase, the annual battle-death toll in sub-Saharan Africa has declined significantly over the last seven years. This is true both in terms of the absolute numbers and in terms of sub-Saharan Africa's share of the global total. In 2002, 85 percent of the battle-death toll from non-state conflict occurred in sub-Saharan Africa. In 2007 and 2008, the region's share of the global total had dropped to some 50 percent.

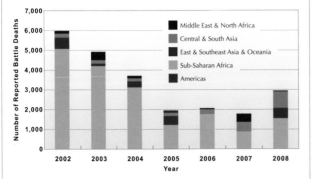

Figure 11.2 Reported Battle Deaths from Non-State Armed Conflicts by Region, 2002–2008

Data Source: UCDP/HSRP Dataset. [44]

The battle-death toll from non-state armed conflict in sub-Saharan Africa has declined significantly. Death tolls in Central and South Asia have been increasing in recent years.

Central and South Asia is the only region to have experienced a sustained increase in the number of battle deaths from non-state conflict over the period from 2002 to 2008. The sharp increase in non-state battle deaths in the last two years was entirely driven by increasing violence in Pakistan. The number of deaths in Pakistan accounted for some three-quarters of the region's non-state battle-death toll in 2007. By 2008 Pakistan's share had risen to almost 90 percent. The death toll in the rest of the region has been declining, with 2007 and 2008 being the least deadly years since 2002.

The Americas witnessed an uneven decline in non-state battle deaths from 2002 to 2007 but experienced an increase in the death toll in 2008. Until 2005 most of the non-state violence in the region took place in Colombia between left-wing and right-wing armed groups. As fighting between these groups died down, battle-death counts in the region dropped to zero in 2006 and 2007. As mentioned earlier, 2008 saw outbreaks of non-state conflict in Mexico that account for the region's entire death toll that year.

The Duration of Non-State Conflicts

The most notable characteristic of non-state armed conflicts is their short duration. As Figure 11.3 demonstrates, the vast majority—some 80 percent—of non-state conflicts recorded between 2002 and 2008 have been active for no more than a year. Only three conflicts have been active for four years, namely those between AUC and FARC in Columbia; the Dioula and the Krou in Côte d'Ivoire; and the conflict between the two factions of the National Socialist Council of Nagaland in India (the NSCN–Isaac Muivah faction and the NSCN–Khaplang faction). No non-state armed conflict has been active for more than four years.

Countries Most Affected by Non-State Armed Conflicts

Non-state conflicts are not only concentrated in particular regions, they are also concentrated in particular countries within those regions. As Figure 11.4 demonstrates, all of the non-state conflicts that occurred between 2002 and 2008 occurred in just 28 of the world's countries, most of which are developing countries.

Just seven countries—Somalia, Ethiopia, Sudan, Nigeria, Kenya, the Democratic Republic of the Congo (DRC), and Pakistan—account for more than 70 percent of all non-state armed conflicts in the dataset.

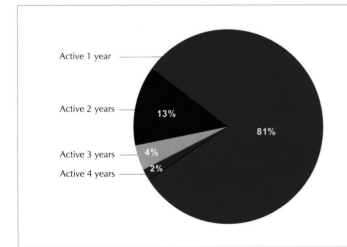

Figure 11.3 Duration of Non-State Armed Conflicts, 2002–2008

The vast majority (81 percent) of non-state conflicts have lasted only one year. None has lasted more than four years.

Data Source: UCDP/HSRP Dataset.

Not surprisingly, Somalia, Ethiopia, Sudan, and Nigeria—the countries that have experienced the greatest number of non-state conflicts since 2002—are also among the countries with the highest battle-death tolls. However, a single country—the DRC—accounted for almost one-quarter of all battle deaths from non-state conflict recorded between 2002 and 2008. Although the DRC has experienced significantly fewer conflicts than Somalia, Ethiopia, and Sudan, those that have taken place have been particularly deadly. In 2008 the highest death tolls were in Pakistan, Mexico, Nigeria, and Kenya.

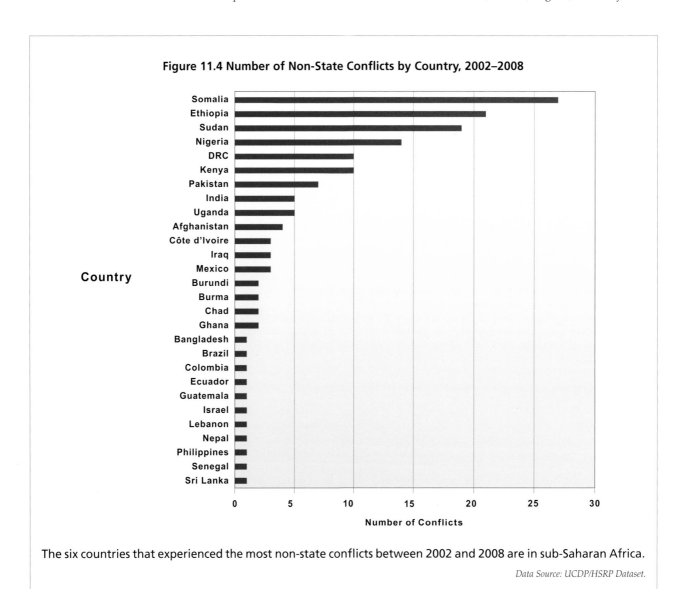

Figure 11.4 Number of Non-State Conflicts by Country, 2002–2008

The six countries that experienced the most non-state conflicts between 2002 and 2008 are in sub-Saharan Africa.

Data Source: UCDP/HSRP Dataset.

Stringer / AFP / Getty Images. PAKISTAN.

CHAPTER 12

Deadly Assaults on Civilians

Attacks on civilians are different from both state-based and non-state armed conflicts. Armed conflicts involve at least two warring parties; deadly assaults against civilians involve an armed group attacking unarmed civilians who are rarely able to fight back. It is often claimed that civilians are being deliberately targeted more than ever before. There is, however, little hard evidence to support this assertion.

This chapter presents data that the Human Security Report Project (HSRP) commissioned from the Uppsala Conflict Data Program (UCDP) on organized violence against civilians—known as *one-sided violence*. A *campaign of one-sided violence* refers to the lethal use of force against civilians by a government or an organized non-state armed group that results in 25 or more reported codable deaths in a calendar year.[45] UCDP's one-sided violence dataset has information on both the number of violent campaigns against civilians around the world and the resulting death tolls.

The data reveal that, while one-sided violence represents a significant threat to many individuals and communities around the world, the threat today is no greater than it was in the early years covered by the dataset. In fact, the death toll from one-sided violence in 2008 was the lowest recorded since 1989.

For policy-makers, one of the most important findings to emerge from the data is that the share of deaths perpetrated by governments versus the share perpetrated by non-state actors has changed significantly over the past two decades. In 1989 governments were responsible for most deaths from one-sided violence; today it is non-state armed groups that are the biggest killers.

Campaigns of One-Sided Violence

The term "one-sided violence" refers to campaigns of organized violence that are directed at unarmed civilians who cannot fight back. The term avoids the controversies associated with both the word "genocide," and with efforts to define "terrorism"—most definitions of the latter focus on violence perpetrated against civilians by non-state actors, while ignoring attacks perpetrated by governments.[46]

Although the post-Cold War period saw a dramatic decline in the number of state-based armed conflicts, there was no comparable decline in one-sided violence. Indeed, there was an uneven upward trend in deadly assaults against civilians until early in the new millennium. As Figure 12.1 shows, from 1989 to 2002, the number of campaigns of one-sided violence increased by some 70 percent. However, after peaking in 2002 and again in 2004, the number of campaigns has been declining. In 2008 UCDP recorded 26 campaigns of one-sided violence around the world—the second-lowest number recorded between 1989 and 2008.

Figure 12.1 also shows the number of campaigns of one-sided violence in each of the world's six regions. We can immediately see that sub-Saharan Africa has experienced a significant decline in the number of campaigns of one-sided

FIGURE 12.1

Regional Trends in Campaigns of One-Sided Violence, 1989–2008

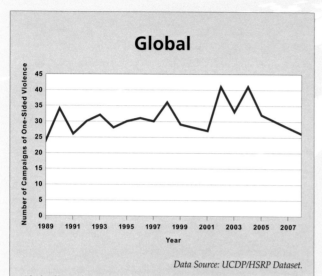

Global

Data Source: UCDP/HSRP Dataset.

Globally, there has been no clear trend in the number of campaigns of one-sided violence, although there has been a substantial decline from 2004 to 2008.

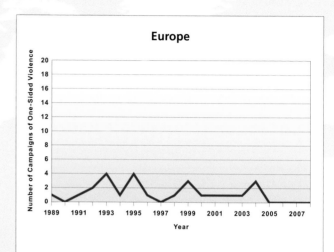

Europe

In the 1990s one-sided violence in Europe was mostly associated with the conflicts in the Balkans. Since then, it has been mostly associated with the conflict in Chechnya.

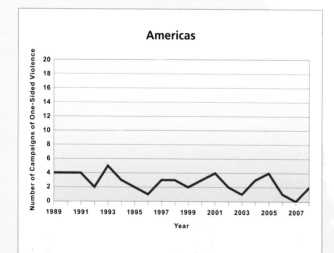

Americas

The Americas has seen an uneven decline in the number of campaigns of one-sided violence.

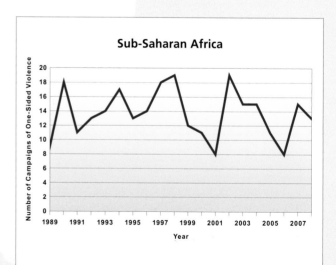

Sub-Saharan Africa

There has been no clear trend in the incidence of one-sided violence in sub-Saharan Africa.[47]

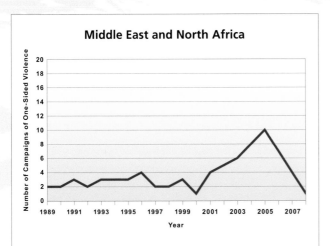

Middle East and North Africa

There were relatively few campaigns of one-sided violence in the Middle East and North Africa until the new millennium. The peak in 2005 was primarily associated with attacks in Iraq.[48]

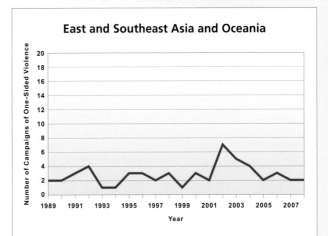

East and Southeast Asia and Oceania

Campaigns of one-sided violence in East and Southest Asia and Oceania peaked in the early years of the new millennium. They were primarily associated with violence in the Philippines and Indonesia.

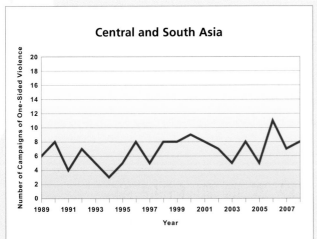

Central and South Asia

There has been an uneven upward trend in the number of campaigns of one-sided violence in Central and South Asia.

These graphs show the total number of campaigns of one-sided violence, i.e., deadly attacks against civilians by governments and non-state armed groups that resulted in 25 or more reported codable deaths per year. The deaths need not have occurred at the same time. Included in these totals are terrorist attacks against civilians and genocides, such as that which took place in Rwanda in 1994.

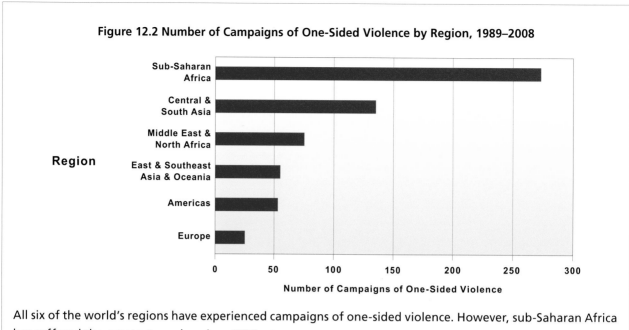

Figure 12.2 Number of Campaigns of One-Sided Violence by Region, 1989–2008

Region

Number of Campaigns of One-Sided Violence

All six of the world's regions have experienced campaigns of one-sided violence. However, sub-Saharan Africa has suffered the greatest number since 1989.

Data Source: UCDP/HSRP Dataset.[49]

violence since 2002. This has in turn driven the global total down. From 2002 to 2006, campaigns of one-sided violence in sub-Saharan Africa dropped by almost 60 percent. Numbers increased again in 2007 and remained high in 2008. In spite of the recent increase, the number of campaigns of one-sided violence in 2008 was still lower than in the peak year in 2002.

In the Americas, the number of campaigns of one-sided violence has fluctuated between one and four in almost every year for the last two decades, but the region appears to be experiencing a gradual, albeit uneven, decline in campaign numbers. This is not that surprising given that the deadliest conflicts in the Americas (in Peru and Guatemala), which were notable for the number of civilians killed, largely came to an end in the mid-1990s. Most one-sided violence in the region in recent years has been associated with the long-running conflict in Colombia.

In Central and South Asia, one-sided violence appears to be on the increase. From 1989 to 2008, there was an upward trend in the number of campaigns of violence against civilians. Some of these recent campaigns have been linked to armed conflicts that had started or escalated in the aftermath of 9/11.

In East and Southeast Asia and Oceania, most of the years covered by the dataset have seen between one and four campaigns of one-sided violence. The year with the highest number of campaigns was 2002. In Indonesia both the government

and the Acehnese rebel group Gerakan Aceh Merdeka (GAM) killed defenseless civilians, while the militant group Jemaah Islamiya carried out the bombings in Bali that killed over 200 people. In the Philippines, two of the three campaigns of one-sided violence perpetrated in 2002 were linked to the separatist conflict being waged by Muslim radicals in Mindanao. Since 2002, however, there has been a decline in the number of campaigns of one-sided violence in the region. When the conflicts in Aceh and East Timor ended, major sources of one-sided violence disappeared. The number of perpetrators of one-sided violence in the region has also dropped in recent years, from seven in 2002 to two in 2008.

Europe has experienced fewer campaigns of one-sided violence than any other region, and has been free of one-sided violence since 2005. The region was, however, the site of significant levels of one-sided violence during the early 1990s, with attacks on civilians occurring in the Balkans and, to a lesser extent, in Russia where it was linked to the conflict in Chechnya. Despite the absence of campaigns in recent years, it is entirely possible that Europe may again see organized assaults on civilians if violence increases in the volatile Caucasus region.

In 2008 the Middle East and North Africa experienced its third consecutive year of decline in the number of campaigns of one-sided violence. The region had, however, seen a large increase in the number of campaigns from 2000 to 2005—

going from one to 10. This increase was driven by heightened activity in the context of the Iraq and Israel-Palestine conflicts. The decline since 2005 was driven by decreases in these same locations.

Figure 12.2 clearly demonstrates that sub-Saharan Africa has suffered by far the greatest number of campaigns of one-sided violence between 1989 and 2008. Central and South Asia has suffered roughly half as many campaigns as sub-Saharan Africa but almost twice as many as the next most afflicted region, the Middle East and North Africa. While Europe has experienced the fewest campaigns, it is home to the actor responsible for the second-highest death toll from one-sided violence—the government of the Serbian Republic of Bosnia and Herzegovina.

Deaths from One-Sided Violence

Estimating death tolls from one-sided violence is a process fraught with challenges. In order to maintain legitimacy and avoid censure from the international community, governments and rebel groups that attack civilians often attempt to conceal their actions, and, as a result, many deaths go unreported. UCDP's stringent coding rules requiring that the perpetrator of deaths be identified also mean that many civilian fatalities cannot be included in the one-sided-violence dataset. As a consequence, while the one-sided-violence fatality data can

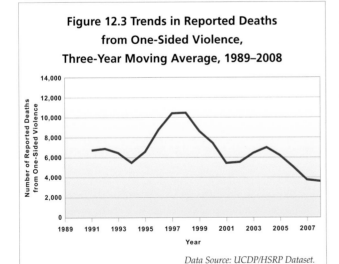

Figure 12.3 Trends in Reported Deaths from One-Sided Violence, Three-Year Moving Average, 1989–2008

Data Source: UCDP/HSRP Dataset.

Although it is impossible to give precise estimates of the number of deaths from one-sided violence, there has been a clear downward trend since 1998.

Note: Data excludes all deaths occurring in Rwanda in 1994. The trend line is a three-year moving average which smoothes the year-on-year fluctuations and makes the short-term trend more discernible.

be used to show broad global and regional trends, specific death counts must be viewed with considerable caution.

Because of the inherent unreliability of fatality data for one-sided violence, Figure 12.3, which shows the global trend in deaths for the period from 1989 to 2008, presents the data as a three-year moving average—a technique that helps to reveal underlying trends rather than specific annual totals. For the purpose of this graph, deaths occurring in Rwanda in 1994 have been excluded—the estimated 500,000 deaths would render any trend in the data invisible.[50] The exclusion of the fatalities from the Rwandan genocide does not, however, affect the direction of the trend.

Death tolls from one-sided violence have declined since the late 1990s.

At the global level, the death tolls from one-sided violence reveal a clear, though uneven, decline since the late 1990s. Indeed, in 2008 the death toll from one-sided violence was the lowest recorded since 1989—the first year in the dataset.

Sub-Saharan Africa, the region that accounts for the majority of the campaigns of one-sided violence for the period from 1989 to 2008, also accounts for the majority of deaths during this period. After 1994 the highest death tolls in sub-Saharan Africa were recorded in 1996 and 1997. Since then, they have been significantly lower. The death toll in 2007 was the lowest on record. It increased somewhat in 2008, but was still the fifth-lowest annual toll for the region.

In the Americas, the trend in deaths from one-sided violence is somewhat different from the trend in the number of campaigns. The region experienced significantly fewer campaigns of one-sided violence between 1998 and 2008 than during the preceding 10 years, but in the latter period the disproportionately high casualty count from the 9/11 attacks pushed the death toll to a new level.[51] While no one would dispute the seriousness of these attacks, the resulting death toll overshadows what are otherwise positive trends elsewhere in the region. For example, as mentioned above, the conflicts in Peru and Guatemala ended in the mid-1990s, removing a significant source of conflict-related violence against civilians. The death toll from one-sided violence related to the ongoing conflict in Colombia has been slowly declining as well. Fewer countries in the region are being affected by one-sided violence, and those countries that are affected are experiencing fewer deaths.

Central and South Asia saw a net increase in deaths from one-sided violence between 1989 and 2008. The year with the highest death toll was 1998, when the Taliban (then the government of Afghanistan) killed nearly 6,000 civilians. The death toll from Afghanistan alone in that year led to a region-wide total that was more than four times greater than for any other year during the period.

In East and Southeast Asia and Oceania, 1989 was the single deadliest year for one-sided violence in the period from 1989 to 2008. The high death toll in 1989 was due almost exclusively to the Tiananmen Square massacre. Since then, annual fatalities from one-sided violence in the region have been significantly lower, although some lesser peaks stand out. For example, 1999 saw a disproportionately high death toll that was driven by attacks against civilians in the context of East Timor's secessionist conflict. In 2006 there was a smaller spike, due primarily to deaths perpetrated by the government of Burma and Patani insurgents in Thailand. These same actors have been the most active perpetrators of one-sided violence in the region in recent years. Indeed, since 2005 they have accounted for more than 80 percent of all deaths from one-sided violence in the region.

Despite the fact that Europe has been free of one-sided violence since 2005, the total number of one-sided deaths in Europe in the 1989 to 2008 period is the third highest of the six regions—only sub-Saharan Africa, and Central and South Asia experience more deliberate killings of civilians. The death tolls in Europe were greatest in 1995 and 1992 respectively, due to attacks by Serbian armed groups against civilians in Bosnia and Herzegovina. There are two smaller subsequent peaks: one occurred during the years 1999 and 2000, mostly representing the attacks by forces loyal to the government of Yugoslavia on ethnic Albanians in Kosovo (1999) and the violence at the hands of the government of Russia against civilians in Chechnya (1999 to 2000); the second peak occurred in 2004 and corresponds to the Madrid train bombings.

The Middle East and North Africa saw a net increase in deaths from one-sided violence from 1989 to 2008. The large increase in deaths from 2000 to 2007 was followed by a sharp drop in 2008. Both the increase, and the subsequent decline, were driven to a large extent by events in the Iraq and Israel-Palestine conflicts. By far the most deaths from one-sided violence in the last five years have occurred in Iraq, followed by the attacks against civilians in the context of the conflicts between Israel and the Palestinians, as well as the Lebanese group Hezbollah. Other affected countries include Saudi Arabia, Jordan, and Algeria.

Perpetrators of One-Sided Violence

The one-sided-violence data reveal a remarkable change in the share of deaths perpetrated by governments versus non-state groups over the last two decades. The extent of the change has been remarkable.

Figure 12.4 shows the percentage of one-sided-violence deaths perpetrated by non-state actors from 1989 to 2008, and reveals a clear, though uneven, upward trend.[52] In 1989, 75 percent of deaths from one-sided violence were perpetrated by governments. By 2008 the figure was just under 20 percent. Non-state groups, responsible for 25 percent of one-sided-violence fatalities in 1989, perpetrated over 80 percent of the deaths in 2008.

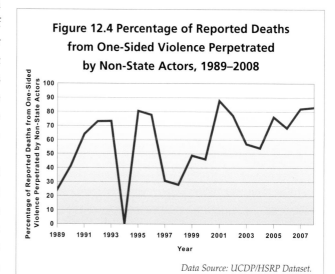

Figure 12.4 Percentage of Reported Deaths from One-Sided Violence Perpetrated by Non-State Actors, 1989–2008

Data Source: UCDP/HSRP Dataset.

In 1989 non-state actors were responsible for some 20 percent of deaths from one-sided violence. By 2008 that share had risen to more than 80 percent.

Compared with governments, non-state actors were particularly active in Central and South Asia, and the Middle East and North Africa. In 2008 all the reported deaths from one-sided violence in these regions were perpetrated by non-state actors, though in Iraq, Shiite militias, who were responsible for killing many civilians, have long been suspected of connections to political parties and state institutions.

Some of the shift from state to non-state perpetrators can be explained by the fact that while the global one-sided death toll has been declining, in recent years terrorist attacks by radical Islamist groups have been responsible for a larger share of deaths relative to other types of violence against civilians. Roughly one-third of the deaths perpetrated by non-state actors since 2001 can be attributed to radical Islamist groups.

Table 12.1 Perpetrators of the Greatest Number of Reported Deaths from One-Sided Violence, 1989–2008

Perpetrator	Global Rank
Government of Rwanda	1
Serbian Rebublic of Bosnia and Herzegovina	2
Government of Sudan	3
Alliance of Democratic Forces for the Liberation of Congo-Kinshasa (AFDL)	4
Government of Afghanistan	5
Government of the DRC	6
Lord's Resistance Army (LRA)	7
Government of Burundi	8
Janjaweed	9
Islamic State of Iraq (ISI)	10

Data Source: UCDP/HSRP Dataset.

The death toll wrought by the government of Rwanda and its militias in 1994 dwarfs that of all other perpetrators of one-sided violence for the entire 1989 to 2008 period.

Table 12.1 shows the 10 actors responsible for the greatest number of deaths from one-sided violence between 1989 and 2008. During the Rwandan genocide, the Rwandan government and affiliated Hutu militias killed an estimated 500,000 civilians in just a few months, making it by far the worst perpetrator of one-sided violence in the period.[53] The second-worst perpetrator of one-sided violence—the government of the Serbian Republic of Bosnia and Herzegovina—killed 98 percent fewer civilians than did the Rwandan government's Hutu militias. The government of Sudan comes in third.

It is clear from Table 12.1 that seven out of 10 of the worst perpetrators of one-sided violence are in sub-Saharan Africa. This is not surprising, since the region has experienced more campaigns of one-sided violence, and a higher number of deaths from one-sided violence, than any other region. Governments and non-state actors are represented in equal number in Table 12.1, while nine out of 10 of the worst perpetrators were also involved in state-based armed conflicts. Again, this is not surprising given that most one-sided violence is associated with conflict.

PART III

ENDNOTES

CHAPTER 10

1. The Uppsala Conflict Data Program (UCDP), on whose data the Human Security Report Project (HSRP) relies, not only records new data but also updates earlier findings as new material becomes available.

2. There was an increase of one war from 2007 to 2008, but the overall trend is clearly downward.

3. Uppsala Conflict Data Program (UCDP), Uppsala University, Uppsala, Sweden/Centre for the Study of Civil War, International Peace Research Institute, Oslo (PRIO), Armed Conflict Dataset v4-2009, http://www.prio.no/CSCW/ Datasets/Armed-Conflict/UCDP-PRIO/ (accessed 16 November 2010).

4. In 2003 there were two interstate conflicts: the recurring conflict between India and Pakistan, and the invasion of Iraq by the US, the UK, and Australia.

5. This is a conservative estimate. The total number of conflicts increased by seven from 2003 to 2008; conflicts associated with Islamist political violence and the war on terror increased by three, i.e., the latter accounted for almost half the increase.

6. See Pew Research Center, Pew Global Attitudes Project, "America's Image in the World: Findings from the Pew Global Attitudes Project," 14 March 2007, http://pewglobal.org/2007/03/14/americas-image-in-the-world-findings-from-the-pew-global-attitudes-project/ (accessed 12 November 2010).

7. Robert Pape, "It's the Occupation, Stupid," *Foreign Policy*, 18 October 2010, http://www.foreignpolicy.com/articles/2010/10/18/ it_s_the_occupation_stupid (accessed 16 November 2010).

8. Kenneth Ballen, Terror Free Tomorrow: The Center for Public Opinion, House Committee on Foreign Affairs, Subcommittee on Terrorism, Nonproliferation, and Trade, "Foreign Assistance, Support for Extremism and Public Opinion in Muslim Majority Countries," 18 November 2009, http://www.terrorfreetomorrow.org/upimagestft/Balllen%20Opening%20 Statement.pdf, 1 (accessed 15 November 2009).

9. Pew Research Center, Pew Global Attitudes Project, "Obama More Popular Abroad than at Home, Global Image of U.S. Continues to Benefit," 17 June 2010, http://pewglobal.org/2010/06/17/obama-more-popular-abroad-than-at-home/ (accessed 15 November 2010).

10. Ballen, "Foreign Assistance," 5 (accessed 15 November 2009).

11. Centre for the Study of Civil War, International Peace Research Institute, Oslo, (PRIO), Battle Deaths Dataset 3.0, http://www.prio.no/CSCW/Datasets/Armed-Conflict/Battle-Deaths/The-Battle-Deaths-Dataset-version-30/ (accessed 16 November 2010), updated from Bethany Lacina and Nils Petter Gleditsch, "Monitoring Trends in Global Combat: A New Dataset of Battle Deaths," *European Journal of Population* 21, no. 2–3 (2005): 145–166; UCDP/Human Security Report Project (HSRP), School for International Studies, Simon Fraser University, Vancouver, Canada.

12. Note that Sudan is now included in the sub-Saharan Africa region. In previous HSRP publications Sudan was treated as being part of the Middle East and North Africa region, and so while state-based conflicts in Sudan were closely related to other sub-Saharan African conflicts, they were not included in the sub-Saharan Africa conflict or battle-death totals. As a result of the change, the total number of state-based conflicts and battle deaths since the 1960s is greater than previously reported in sub-Saharan Africa, and lower in the Middle East and North Africa. The trends, however, remain the same.

13. See note 12.

14. These numbers compare straight averages (means). If the median death tolls per conflict per year are considered, the trend stays largely the same, though the decline is less dramatic. But the median value for the new millennium is still roughly half that of the 1950s.

15. See note 12.

16. John Lewis Gaddis, *The Long Peace: Inquiries into the History of the Cold War* (New York: Oxford University Press, 1989).

17. This includes involvement in interstate and extrastate conflict as the primary or secondary party, as well as secondary-party intervention in internationalized intrastate conflicts, i.e., deploying troops in support of a warring party in a civil war.

18. World Bank, *World dataBank: World Development Indicators (WDI) & Global Development Finance (GDF)*, http://databank.worldbank.org/ddp/home.do?Step=12&id=4&CNO=2 (accessed 12 November 2010).

19. The count of conflict years includes only countries that are independent as of 2008. For countries that gained independence from a colonial power or as a result of a war of secession, conflict years were counted for the colonial power as well as the future independent country.

20. UCDP and PRIO both have global battle-death estimates for the years 2002 to 2008. These differ considerably. PRIO's global battle-death figure for 2008, for example, is around 50,000, while UCDP's estimate for the same year is less than 30,000. The difference is due in large part to the way in which the two institutions code deaths in Iraq.

    For example, UCDP's stringent coding rules mean that where the perpetrators of violent deaths cannot be indentified the deaths will not be recorded.

    Despite the differences, the two datasets are in agreement on broad trends.

21. Chapter 3 focuses on East Asia, which is made up of Northeast and Southeast Asia. Although East Asia does not include the countries of Oceania, there were no conflicts in Oceania in the 1946 to 2008 period, save one minor conflict in Papua New Guinea. The two regional groupings (East Asia, and East and Southeast Asia and Oceania) are therefore basically equivalent for purposes of this discussion.

22. See note 12.

23. To be coded as a *state-based conflict*, the violence has to have occured between two formally organized parties, at least one of which is the government of a state, over a stated incompatibility concerning either government or territory.

24. Arbeitsgemeinschaft Kriegsursachenforschung (AKUF), University of Hamburg, Hamburg, Germany, Wars and Armed Conflict 1945-2009, http://www.sozialwiss.uni-hamburg.de/publish/Ipw/Akuf/index.htm (accessed 16 November 2010).

25. Center for Systemic Peace, Maryland, USA, http://www.systemicpeace.org/conflict.htm (accessed 16 November 2010).

26. Monty G. Marshall and Benjamin R. Cole, *Global Report 2009: Conflict, Governance, and State Fragility*, CSP, Center for Global Policy, 7 December 2009, http://www.systemicpeace.org/Global%20Report%202009.pdf (accessed 12 November 2010).

27. There are some occasions in which PRIO does not provide a best estimate, i.e., if the sources for the annual battle deaths in a given conflict are deemed to be insufficiently reliable. Researchers must decide for themselves how to address those cases; HSRP uses the arithmetic mean of the low and high estimates and checks the results against different treatments of the data.

28. See note 21.

29. HRDAG, "Core Concepts: HRDAG Notes on Data Analysis Technology and Research," http://www.hrdag.org/resources/core_concepts.shtml (accessed 12 November 2010).

30. See Part II of this *Report* for a discussion of retrospective mortality surveys.

31. See Patrick Heuveline, "Between One and Three Million: Towards the Demographic Reconstruction of a Decade of Cambodian History (1970–79)," *Population Studies* 52, no. 1 (March 1998): 49–65.

32. Ziad Obermeyer, Christopher J. L. Murray, and Emmanuela Gakidou, "Fifty Years of Violent War Deaths from Vietnam to Bosnia: Analysis of Data from the World Health Survey Programme," *British Medical Journal* 336, no. 7659 (June 2008): 1482A–1486. For a critique of this methodology, see Michael Spagat et al., "Estimating War Deaths: An Arena of Contestation," Journal of Conflict Resolution 53, no. 6 (December 2009): 934–950.

33. Note that, strictly speaking, UCDP's termination dataset records the end of conflict episodes. A conflict that was inactive for one year or more may restart at any time. See Joakim Kreutz, "How and When Armed Conflicts End: Introducing the UCDP Conflict Termination Dataset," *Journal of Peace Research* 47, no. 2 (March 2010): 243–250.

34. In other words, the change in conflict numbers in any given year is determined by the difference between the number of conflict onsets in that year and the number of conflict terminations recorded for the previous year.

35. This was the 2003 agreement in the DRC. The conflict restarted in 2006 with a rebel group—Laurent Nkunda's National Congress for the Defence of the People (CNDP)—that had not been involved in earlier episodes of the conflict.

36. To show the trend more clearly, the data are presented as a three-year moving average.

37. Chester A. Crocker, Fen Osler Hampson, and Pamela Aall, "Introduction: Mapping the Nettle Field," in *Grasping the Nettle: Analyzing Cases of Intractable Conflict*, eds. Chester A. Crocker, Fen Osler Hampson, and Pamela Aall (Washington: USIP, 2005), 5.

38. James D. Fearon, "Why Do Some Civil Wars Last So Much Longer than Others?" *Journal of Peace Research* 41, no. 3 (May 2004): 275–301.

39. For the purposes of this analysis, a previously active conflict was re-coded as a new conflict if both of the following conditions applied: a) the interim period between bouts of fighting was 10 years or more, and b) all of the original non-government parties to the conflict were no longer active. This re-coding was applied only to conflicts over government incompatibilities.

40. Crocker, Hampson, and Aall, "Introduction: Mapping the Nettle Field," 13.

CHAPTER 11

41. Ralph Sundberg, *Non-State Conflict Dataset Codebook v 2.1* (Uppsala, Sweden: Uppsala University, Department of Peace and Conflict Research, 2009), 2. Available at http://www.pcr.uu.se/digitalAssets/15/15908_UCDP_Non-state_conflict_Dataset_Codebook_v2.1.pdf (accessed 2 November 2010).

42. Ralph Sundberg, "Collective Violence 2002–2007: Global and Regional Trends," in *States in Armed Conflict 2007*, Research Report 83, ed. Lotta Harbom and Ralph Sundberg (Uppsala, Sweden: Uppsala University, Department of Peace and Conflict Research, 2008), 167.

43. Uppsala Conflict Data Program (UCDP), Uppsala University, Uppsala, Sweden/Human Security Report (HSRP), School for International Studies, Simon Fraser University, Vancouver, Canada.

    Note that Sudan is now included in the sub-Saharan Africa region. In previous HSRP publications Sudan was treated as being part of the Middle East and North Africa region. As a result of the change, the total number of non-state conflicts and battle deaths is greater than previously reported in sub-Saharan Africa, and lower in the Middle East and North Africa. The trends, however, remain the same.

44. See note 43.

45. The 25 deaths need not occur at the same time but they must occur during a single calendar year and in the same country for a campaign to be recorded.

46. Genocide is both a narrower and a broader category than one-sided violence. It requires the intention on the part of the perpetrators to destroy a group in whole or in part. But unlike one-sided violence, it can include attacks on non-civilians.

47. Ibid.

48. Ibid.

49. Uppsala Conflict Data Program (UCDP), Uppsala University, Uppsala, Sweden/Human Security Report Project (HSRP), School for International Studies, Simon Fraser University, Vancouver, Canada.

    Note that Sudan is now included in the sub-Saharan Africa region. In previous HSRP publications Sudan was treated as being part of the Middle East and North Africa region. As a result of the change, the total number of campaigns of one-sided violence and deaths from one-sided violence is greater than previously reported in sub-Saharan Africa, and lower in the Middle East and North Africa. The trends, however, remain the same.

50. This is UCDP's best estimate; its high estimate is 800,000.

51. The United States is, of course, part of the Americas.

52. The outlier in 1994 with a value near zero is a result of the fact that the Rwandan genocide, perpetrated by the Rwandan government and its militias, was so deadly that it accounted for nearly 100 percent of the deaths from one-sided violence in that year. As a result, non-state actors perpetrated an extremely small share of the one-sided violence in 1994.

53. See note 50.